Ireland Travel Guide

May the Irish hills caress you.
May her lakes and rivers bless you.
May the luck of the Irish enfold you.
May the blessings of Saint Patrick behold you.

Welcome to your guide to a Luxury Trip to Ireland on a budget!	11
Who this book is for and why anyone can enjoy luxury travel on a budget	13
Weird and wonderful facts about that most people don't know	16
What you need to know before you visit	17
Some of Ireland's Best Bargains	19
Irish Discount Passes	19
Island Stays	20
Heritage Walks	21
Boat Cruises	22
Churches	24
Performing Arts	26
Seaweed Baths	28
Free Tours	29
Secret Beaches	30
Oyster Happy Hours	32
Hidden Waterfalls	33
Private Gardens	34
Free Workshops	35
Hiking	36
Surfing or Kayaking	38
Irish Sports	39
Irish Literature	41
Stargazing	42
Film	43
Ireland Today	45
How to Enjoy ALLOCATING Money in Ireland	46
How to feel RICH in Ireland	49
How to use this book	50
The seasons in Ireland and what to pack for each	55
Booking Flights	57

How to Find Heavily Discounted Private Jet Flights to or from Ireland	57
How to Find CHEAP FIRST-CLASS Flights to Ireland	58
How to Fly Business Class to Ireland cheaply	61
How to ALWAYS Find Super Cheap Flights to Ireland	62
Accommodation	65
How to Book a Five-star Hotel consistently on the Cheap in Ireland	65
Where to stay?	66
Enjoy the Finest Five-star Hotels for a 10th of the Cost	69
Strategies to Book Five-Star Hotels for Two-Star Prices in Ireland	71
Priceline Hack to get a Luxury Hotel on the Cheap	72
Best Areas to Stay in an Airbnb in Ireland	74
Unique Accommodation in Ireland	78
Camping Sites	78
Farm Stays	80
Castles	81
Universities	83
20 cheap eats in Ireland and where to eat them	87
Irish Beer Culture	91
Irish Whiskey Culture	93
First-day Itinerary	95
The Best of Ireland in One week	96
The Best of Ireland in Two weeks	98
Snapshot: How to have a $10,000 trip to Ireland for $1,000	100
Here are our specific super cheap tips for enjoying a $10,000 trip to Ireland for just $1,000.	101
How to Find Super Cheap Flights to Ireland	101
How to Find CHEAP FIRST-CLASS Flights to Ireland	103
Getting Around	106
Driving	110
Top 20 attractions in Ireland with money saving tips	111
National Parks	114

Castles	116
Regions of Ireland	118
Irish Slang	123
Now you know some of the lingo, we are ready to delve in to the cities, towns and regions and their bargains!	124
Dublin	125
Interesting facts	128
Luxurious Yet Affordable Experiences in Dublin	131
Dublin Whiskey Tour	135
County Dublin	140
Swords	140
Blanchardstown	143
Dún Laoghaire	146
Tallaght	149
Malahide	153
Howth	155
Galway	158
Clifden	162
County Kerry	165
Killarney: The Jewel of County Kerry	169
Dingle	173
Kenmare	178
County Cork	181
County Clare	188
County Wicklow	190
Wicklow Town	194
Bray	196
Glendalough	198
Mayo	200
Westport	206
Waterford	210

Limerick	213
Kilkenny	217
County Donegal	221
Letterkenny	224
Wexford	226
Sligo	230
Northern Ireland	233
Belfast	235
Londonderry	238
Enniskillen	241
Unmissable things to do in Ireland	243
1. An Insider's Guide to Visiting Giant's Causeway	243
Shopping	248
Cheapest Onward Flights and Airlines Flying Cheap from Ireland	251
Cheapest Airport Lounges in Ireland	252
Irish Language	253
Common Complaints of Tourists Visiting Ireland with Solutions	255
Irish History	258
Saint Patrick and The Irish Patron Saints	261
The Viking Age: Raiders and Settlers	264
Key Figures in Irish History	273
Irish Superstitions	274
Top 20 Luxury experiences to have in Ireland on a Budget	276
Checklist of Top 20 Things to Do	278
Recap: how to have a $10,000 trip to Ireland for $1,000	279
The secret to saving HUGE amounts of money when travelling to Ireland is… 280	
Thank you for reading	283
DISCOVER YOUR NEXT VACATION	284
Bonus Travel Hacks	286

Common pitfalls when it comes to allocating money to your desires while traveling	287
Hack your allocations for your Ireland Trip	289
MORE TIPS TO FIND CHEAP FLIGHTS	291
What Credit Card Gives The Best Air Miles?	294
Frequent Flyer Memberships	298
How to get 70% off a Cruise	300
Relaxing at the Airport	302
How to spend money	303
How NOT to be ripped off	307
Small tweaks on the road add up to big differences in your bank balance	310
Where and How to Make Friends	312
When unpleasantries come your way…	313
Hacks for Families	319
How to Believe Something You Don't Believe	321
How I got hooked on luxury on a budget travelling	325
A final word…	326
Copyright	328

Titles also by Phil Tang

COUNTRY GUIDES

Super Cheap AUSTRALIA
Super Cheap AUSTRIA
Super Cheap BAHAMAS
Super Cheap BARBADOS
Super Cheap BERMUDA 2024
Super Cheap BRAZIL
Super Cheap CANADA
Super Cheap DENMARK
Super Cheap Dominican Republic
Super Cheap FIJI
Super Cheap FINLAND
Super Cheap FRANCE
Super Cheap GRENADA
Super Cheap GERMANY
Super Cheap GREECE
Super Cheap ICELAND
Super Cheap ITALY
Super Cheap IRELAND
Super Cheap JAMAICA
Super Cheap JAPAN
Super Cheap LUXEMBOURG
Super Cheap MALAYSIA
Super Cheap MALDIVES 2024
Super Cheap MEXICO
Super Cheap NETHERLANDS
Super Cheap NEW ZEALAND
Super Cheap NORWAY
Super Cheap Saint Martin/ Sint Maarten
Super Cheap SOUTH KOREA
Super Cheap SPAIN
Super Cheap SWITZERLAND
Super Cheap UAE
Super Cheap UNITED KINGDOM
Super Cheap UNITED STATES

CITIES / TOWNS

Super Cheap ADELAIDE 2024
Super Cheap ALASKA 2024
Super Cheap AUSTIN 2024
Super Cheap BANFF 2024
Super Cheap BANGKOK 2024
Super Cheap BARCELONA 2024
Super Cheap BELFAST 2024
Super Cheap BERMUDA 2024
Super Cheap BORA BORA 2024
Super Cheap BRITISH VIRGIN ISLANDS
Super Cheap BUDAPEST 2024
Super Cheap Great Barrier Reef 2024
Super Cheap CAMBRIDGE 2024
Super Cheap CANCUN 2024
Super Cheap CHIANG MAI 2024
Super Cheap CHICAGO 2024
Super Cheap Copenhagen 2024
Super Cheap DOHA 2024
Super Cheap DUBAI 2024
Super Cheap DUBLIN 2024
Super Cheap EDINBURGH 2024
Super Cheap GALWAY 2024
Super Cheap Guadeloupe 2024
Super Cheap HELSINKI 2024
Super Cheap LIMA 2024
Super Cheap LISBON 2024
Super Cheap MALAGA 2024
Super Cheap Martinique 2024
Super Cheap Machu Pichu 2024
Super Cheap MIAMI 2024
Super Cheap Milan 2024
Super Cheap Montpellier 2024
Super Cheap NASHVILLE 2024
Super Cheap NAPA
Super Cheap NEW ORLEANS 2024
Super Cheap NEW YORK 2024
Super Cheap PARIS 2024
Super Cheap PRAGUE 2024
Super Cheap SANTORINI
Super Cheap SEATTLE
Super Cheap St. Vincent and the Grenadines
Super Cheap SEYCHELLES 2024
Super Cheap SINGAPORE 2024
Super Cheap ST LUCIA 2024
Super Cheap TORONTO 2024
Super Cheap Turks and Caicos 2024
Super Cheap VANCOUVER
Super Cheap VENICE 2024
Super Cheap VIENNA 2024
Super Cheap YOSEMITE 2024
Super Cheap ZURICH 2024
Super Cheap ZANZIBAR 2024

Who am I?

I have been traveling for 30 years and I have been writing Luxury on a Budget travel guides full-time for seven, starting in 2017. My bestsellers include "Super Cheap Bora Bora" and "Super Cheap Norway."

Both my parents are from Ireland: my mum is from Donegal and my father from Kilkenny. As such, I have spent many summers since childhood, and now as an adult, exploring Ireland. I delve into every nook and cranny to unearth hidden gems and insider secrets.

This book is dedicated to the art of savoring the finer things in Ireland without breaking the bank. It's about leveraging resourcefulness and imagination to unlock luxury experiences without excessive spending. It's infused with love, magic and hope that you, dear reader will create unforgettable memories at a fraction of the cost.

FREE BOOK

Leave a verified purchase honest review and select any book of your choice for **free**. Simply send me a screenshot of your review along with the book you desire, and I'll promptly send it to you. My email is at the end of the guide.

The Magical Power of Bargains

Legends of leprechauns, fairies, and other mystical creatures have been passed down through Irish generations. These stories come to life in the rolling green hills, misty forests, and secluded glens that dot the Irish countryside, where it's easy to imagine mythical beings hiding just out of sight but this book is going to show you magic really lives.

Have you ever felt the rush of getting a bargain? And then found good fortune just keeps following you?

Let me give you an example. In 2009, I graduated into the worst global recession for generations. One unemployed day, I saw a suit I knew I could get a job in. The suit was £250. Money I didn't have. Imagine my shock when the next day I saw the exact same suit (in my size) in the window of a second-hand shop (thrift store) for £18! I bought the suit and after three months of interviewing, without a single call back, within a week of owning that £18 suit, I was hired on a salary far above my expectations. That's the powerful psychological effect of getting an incredible deal. It builds a sense of excitement and happiness that literally creates miracles.

I have no doubt that the natural wonders of Ireland and its warm people will uplift and inspire you but when you add the bargains from this book to your vacation, not only will you save a ton of money; you are guaranteed to enjoy a truly and completely magical trip to Ireland.

This is my favourite Irish blessing and I wish it wholeheartedly for you:

May your troubles be less
And your blessings be more,
And nothing but happiness come through your door.

Welcome to your guide to a Luxury Trip to Ireland on a budget!

This travel guide is your step-by-step manual for unlocking luxury hotels, enjoying the best culinary offerings and once-in-a-lifetime luxury experiences in Ireland at a fraction of the usual cost.

Everyone's budget is different, but luxury is typically defined by first or business class seats on the airplane, five-star hotels, chauffeurs, exclusive experiences, and delectable fine dining. Yes, all of these can be enjoyed on a budget.

Finding luxury deals in Ireland simply requires a bit of research and planning, which this book has done for you. We have packed this book with local insider tips and knowledge to save you tens of thousands.

If the mere mention of the word luxury has you thinking things like "Money doesn't grow on trees," "I don't need anything fancy," "I don't deserve nice things," or "People who take luxury trips are shallow and materialistic/environmentally harmful/lack empathy, etc.," then stop. While we all know travel increases our happiness, research on the effects of luxury travel has proven even better results:

Reduced stress: A study published in the Journal of Travel Research found that individuals who visited luxury hotels reported feeling less stressed than those who in standard hotels.[1]

Increased happiness: A study conducted by the International Journal of Tourism Research found that luxury travel experiences lead to an increase in happiness and overall life satisfaction.[2] Researchers also found that luxury travel experiences can improve individuals' mental health by providing a sense of escape from daily stressors and enhancing feelings of relaxation and rejuvenation.

Enhanced creativity: Researchers found engaging in luxury travel experiences can stimulate creativity and lead to more innovative thinking.[3]

While all of this makes perfect sense; it feels much nicer to stay in a hotel room that's cleaned daily than in an Airbnb where you're cleaning up after yourself. What you might not know is that you can have all of that increased happiness and well-being without emptying your bank account. Does it sound too good to be true? I assure you that by the

---

[1] Wöber, K. W., & Fuchs, M. (2016). The effects of hotel attributes on perceived value and satisfaction. Journal of Travel Research, 55(3), 306-318.

[2] Ladhari, R., Souiden, N., & Dufour, B. (2017). Luxury hotel customers' satisfaction and loyalty: An empirical study. International Journal of Hospitality Management, 63, 1-10.

[3] Kim, S., Kim, S. Y., & Lee, H. R. (2019). Luxury travel, inspiration, and creativity: A qualitative investigation. Tourism Management, 71, 354-366.

end of this book, you'll not only possess insider tips and tricks but also wholeheartedly believe that budget-friendly luxury travel is within everyone's reach.

Who this book is for and why anyone can enjoy luxury travel on a budget

Did you know you can fly on a private jet for $500? Yes, a fully private jet. Complete with flutes of champagne and reclinable creamy leather seats. Your average billionaire spends $20,000 on the exact same flight. You can get it for $500 when you book private jet empty leg flights. This is just one of thousands of ways you can travel luxuriously on a budget. You see there is a big difference between being cheap and frugal.

When our brain hears the word "budget" it hears deprivation, suffering, agony, even depression. But budget travel need not be synonymous with hostels and pack lunches. You can enjoy an incredible and luxurious trip to Ireland on a budget, just like you can enjoy a private jet flight for 10% of the normal cost when you know how.

Over 20 years of travel has taught me I could have a 20 cent experience that will stir my soul more than a $100 one. Of course, sometimes the reverse is true, my point is, spending money on travel is the best investment you can make but it doesn't have to be at levels set by hotels and attractions with massive ad spends and influencers who are paid small fortunes to get you to buy into something you could have for a fraction of the cost.

This book is for those who love bargains and want to have the cold hard budget busting facts to hand (which is why we've included so many one page charts, which you can use as a quick reference), but otherwise, the book provides plenty of tips to help you shape your own Ireland experience.

We have designed these travel guides to give you a unique planning tool to experience an unforgettable trip without spending the ascribed tourist budget.

This guide focuses on Ireland's unbelievable bargains. Of course, there is little value in traveling to Ireland and not experiencing everything it has to offer. Where possible, we've included super cheap workarounds or listed the experience in the Loved but Costly section.

When it comes to luxury budget travel, it's all about what you know. You can have all the feels without most of the bills. A few days spent planning can save you thousands. Luckily, we've done the planning for you, so you can distill the information in minutes not days, leaving you to focus on what matters: immersing yourself in the sights, sounds and smells of Ireland, meeting awesome new people and feeling relaxed and happy.

This book reads like a good friend has travelled the length and breadth of Ireland and brought you back incredible insider tips.

So, grab a cup of tea or coffee, put your feet up and relax; you're about to enter the world of enjoying Ireland on the Super Cheap. Oh, and don't forget a biscuit. You need energy to plan a trip of a lifetime on a budget.

Discover Ireland

Cliffs of Moher

Ireland, often referred to as the Emerald Isle for its lush green landscapes, is a place of breathtaking beauty, rich history, and vibrant culture. This island nation, with its rugged coastlines, mystical landscapes, and ancient ruins, offers a journey through time, where the past and present merge seamlessly.

The story of Ireland is a tapestry woven with the threads of ancient civilizations, Viking invasions, and the struggle for independence. Its history stretches back over 5,000 years, evident in the megalithic tombs of Newgrange, which predate the Egyptian pyramids. Ireland's turbulent history, marked by Viking raids, English rule, and the fight for sovereignty, has left a rich legacy of castles, monasteries, and historical sites. The Rock of Cashel, Dublin Castle, and the ancient city of Tara are just a few landmarks that offer a glimpse into Ireland's storied past.

Ireland is the land of saints and scholars, producing literary giants like James Joyce, W.B. Yeats, and Samuel Beckett. The traditional music sessions in cozy pubs, where the melodic tunes of the fiddle and the bodhrán create an enchanting atmosphere, are central to Irish culture. The Irish language, though less commonly spoken, adds to the mystique of the Emerald Isle, with its melodic sounds and rich literary tradition.

Ireland's reputation for being expensive stems from various economic and social factors that can impact travelers' budgets. High living costs, particularly in urban hubs like Dublin, contribute to pricey accommodations, dining, and transportation. To counter this, we have devoted 40 pages to hacking Irish accommodation.

Transportation costs, including flights, car rentals, and fuel, can add up quickly. Opting for public transportation like buses and trains, utilizing multi-day or regional transportation passes, and carpooling with other travelers can all help trim transportation expenses.

Despite its reputation, Ireland offers numerous ways for tourists to enjoy a more budget-friendly experience. With careful planning and savvy decision-making, travelers can explore the Emerald Isle without breaking the bank, ensuring a memorable and affordable journey.

The country offers a range of accommodations, from historic castles turned hotels to charming bed and breakfasts that offer comfort and luxury at reasonable prices. Many of these accommodations provide a unique window into Irish culture and hospitality, with gourmet breakfasts and the warmth of Irish welcome.

Dining out can also be an affordable luxury, with many pubs serving high-quality, locally sourced food. The farm-to-table concept is big in Ireland, offering visitors the chance to indulge in fresh seafood, artisan cheeses, and traditional Irish dishes without a hefty price tag.

Ireland's landscape is a treasure trove of natural beauty, from the Cliffs of Moher's dramatic sea cliffs to the mystical Ring of Kerry. These natural wonders can be explored freely or with guided tours that offer insight into their history and significance without a significant expense.

As you explore Ireland's storied past, from the megalithic tombs of Newgrange to the historic landmarks like the Rock of Cashel and Dublin Castle, you'll be immersed in a rich legacy of castles, monasteries, and historical sites that tell the tales of Ireland's turbulent history.

But Ireland is more than just its history. It's the land of saints and scholars, producing literary giants like James Joyce, W.B. Yeats, and Samuel Beckett. Dive into the heart of Irish culture as you join traditional music sessions in cozy pubs, where the melodic tunes of the fiddle and bodhrán create an enchanting atmosphere, and the Irish language adds to the mystique with its melodic sounds and rich literary tradition.

In essence, experiencing luxury in Ireland on a budget is about embracing the essence of Irish culture, connecting with nature, and cherishing the small moments that make your journey memorable. By adopting a mindset of appreciation, mindfulness, and gratitude, you can create a deeply fulfilling and enriching experience that leaves a lasting impression.

Weird and wonderful facts about that most people don't know

Ireland is full of fascinating quirks and hidden gems. Here are some weird and wonderful facts about Ireland that many people might not know:

- **Fairy Trees:** In Ireland, it's not uncommon to see lone trees standing in the middle of fields, often adorned with ribbons or other decorations. These are known as "fairy trees" and are believed to be sacred spots where fairies reside. Farmers will often avoid cutting down or disturbing these trees for fear of bad luck.
- **Blarney Stone:** The Blarney Stone, located at Blarney Castle in County Cork, is said to give anyone who kisses it the gift of eloquence, or the "gift of gab." However, to reach the stone, one must lean backwards over the edge of the castle battlements – a daring feat that has been performed by visitors for centuries.
- **Puck Fair:** Held annually in the town of Killorglin, County Kerry, Puck Fair is one of the oldest fairs in Ireland, dating back over 400 years. The highlight of the fair is the crowning of a wild mountain goat as the "King of the Puck," who reigns over the festivities for three days.
- **The Burren:** This unique landscape in County Clare is often described as lunar-like due to its vast expanses of exposed limestone pavement. Despite its barren appearance, the Burren is home to a surprisingly diverse array of flora, including many rare and endangered plant species.
- **Giant's Causeway:** While most famous for its location in Northern Ireland, the Giant's Causeway actually extends into County Antrim in the Republic of Ireland. This UNESCO World Heritage Site is composed of around 40,000 interlocking basalt columns, the result of an ancient volcanic eruption.
- **Skellig Michael:** Located off the coast of County Kerry, Skellig Michael is an ancient monastic site perched atop a steep, rocky island. Dating back to the 6th century, the site is renowned for its well-preserved beehive huts and dramatic scenery. It gained widespread recognition after featuring in the "Star Wars" film series.
- **Connemara Marble:** Found exclusively in the Connemara region of County Galway, Connemara marble is a rare and unique stone prized for its distinctive green coloration. It has been used for centuries in jewelry and decorative objects, and folklore attributes various mystical properties to the stone.
- **St. Patrick's Day Traditions:** While St. Patrick's Day is celebrated around the world, few may know that until the 1970s, it was actually a religious holiday in Ireland, with pubs and bars closed for the day. Today, it's a lively celebration of Irish culture, with parades, music, and plenty of green attire.

What you need to know before you visit

Before visiting Ireland, there are several important factors to consider to ensure a safe and enjoyable trip. Additionally, while Ireland is generally a safe destination for tourists, there are some health complaints that visitors may encounter. Here are some things you need to know:

- **Weather:** Ireland's weather can be unpredictable, with frequent rain and cool temperatures, even in the summer months. It's essential to pack appropriate clothing, including waterproof layers and sturdy shoes, to stay comfortable while exploring.
- **Currency:** Ireland uses the euro (€) as its currency. It's a good idea to have some cash on hand for smaller purchases, as not all establishments accept credit or debit cards, especially in rural areas.
- **Healthcare:** Ireland has a high standard of healthcare, with both public and private medical facilities available. EU citizens can access emergency healthcare services with a European Health Insurance Card (EHIC), while non-EU visitors should have travel insurance that covers medical expenses.
- **Travel Insurance:** It's highly recommended to purchase travel insurance before visiting Ireland to cover any unexpected medical expenses, trip cancellations, or lost/stolen belongings.
- **Vaccinations:** There are no specific vaccinations required for visiting Ireland. However, it's a good idea to ensure routine vaccinations are up to date before traveling.
- **Water:** Tap water in Ireland is safe to drink and of high quality. Bottled water is also widely available for purchase if preferred.
- **Food Safety:** Ireland has strict food safety standards, and foodborne illnesses are relatively rare. However, it's still essential to practice basic food hygiene and choose reputable dining establishments.
- **Common Health Complaints:** Some health complaints that tourists visiting Ireland may encounter include:
    - **Colds and Flu:** Due to the cool and damp climate, respiratory infections like colds and flu are common, especially during the winter months.
    - **Allergies:** Pollen allergies can be an issue for some travelers, particularly during the spring and summer when plants are in bloom.
    - **Motion Sickness:** If you're prone to motion sickness, be prepared for travel on winding roads, especially in rural areas or along coastal routes.
- **Sun Protection:** Despite Ireland's reputation for rain, the sun can still be strong, particularly in the summer months. It's important to protect your skin with sunscreen, sunglasses, and a hat, especially if spending time outdoors.
- **Emergency Numbers:** The emergency number in Ireland is 999 or 112 for police, fire, or medical emergencies. Save these numbers in your phone in case of an emergency.

Some of Ireland's Best Bargains

Irish Discount Passes

Membership cards such as the Heritage Card or National Parks and Wildlife Service Annual Pass offer significant savings for visitors exploring Ireland's national parks and heritage sites. These cards provide unlimited access to participating attractions, allowing travelers to save money on entrance fees and enjoy a wider range of experiences during their trip.

Pass Name	Description	Pros	Cons	Starting Price
Heritage Card	Provides unlimited access to OPW-managed heritage sites and national parks in Ireland for a year.	- Unlimited access to over 80 heritage sites and national parks. - Cost-effective for frequent visitors.	- Valid for one year only. - Does not include all attractions in Ireland.	€25 (adult)
Dublin Pass	Grants access to over 30 attractions and tours in Dublin, including museums, historic sites, and sightseeing tours.	- Offers skip-the-line entry to popular attractions. - Includes hop-on-hop-off bus tours.	- Limited to attractions in Dublin only. - May not be cost-effective for those visiting other parts of Ireland.	€79 (1-day adult)
OPW Heritage Card	Provides unlimited access to OPW-managed heritage sites, including castles, gardens, and historic houses, for a year.	- Offers access to over 80 heritage sites. - Cost-effective for those interested in Ireland's historical sites.	- Valid for one year only. - Does not include all attractions in Ireland.	€40 (adult)
Dublin City Card	Offers discounts on attractions, tours, and dining in Dublin, as well as free public transportation within the city.	- Provides discounts on a variety of activities and services in Dublin. - Includes free public transportation within the city center.	- Limited to discounts within Dublin. - May not be suitable for those not planning to spend much time in the city.	€35 (adult, 1-day pass)
Ireland Heritage Pass	Allows access to a selection of heritage sites and attractions across Ireland, including castles, gardens, and historic houses.	- Provides access to a range of heritage sites across Ireland. - Flexibility to choose which attractions to visit.	- Limited selection of attractions compared to other passes. - Not as widely accepted as other passes.	€49 (adult)

| Wild Atlantic Way Pass | Grants access to attractions and experiences along the Wild Atlantic Way, including scenic drives, outdoor activities, and cultural sites. | - Offers discounts on a variety of attractions and activities along the Wild Atlantic Way. - Provides access to unique experiences. | - Limited to attractions along the Wild Atlantic Way. - May not be suitable for those not traveling the entire route. | €30 (adult) |

Island Stays

There are over 80 islands off the coast of Ireland and staying on several of them is super cheap! Embarking on an island stay in Ireland offers a unique opportunity to immerse yourself in the rich culture, stunning landscapes, and tranquil surroundings that these remote locations have to offer. From the rugged coastlines of County Mayo to the picturesque charm of County Cork and the breathtaking vistas of the Aran Islands, each island has its own distinct character and attractions waiting to be explored.

Each island in Ireland offers its own unique appeal, whether it's the rugged beauty of Inishturk Island, the peaceful seclusion of Bere Island, or the rich cultural heritage of Inis Mór in the Aran Islands. Island stays provide an opportunity to disconnect from the hustle and bustle of everyday life and immerse yourself in the natural beauty and tranquility of island living. Whether you're seeking outdoor adventures like hiking, kayaking, and birdwatching, or simply looking to relax and unwind surrounded by stunning scenery, an island stay in Ireland offers something for everyone.

Island	Location	Accommodation Type	Starting Price (per night)
Inishturk Island	County Mayo	Homestay	€30 - €50
Bere Island	County Cork	B&Bs or Self-catering cottages	€40 - €80
Inis Mór, Aran Islands	County Galway	Hostels or Guesthouses	€20 - €50

How to Get There

Getting to Ireland's islands typically involves taking a ferry or boat from the mainland. Ferry services operate from various ports depending on the island you wish to visit. For example, Inishturk Island in County Mayo is accessible via ferry from Roonagh Pier near Louisburgh. Bere Island in County Cork can be reached by ferry from the village of Castletownbere. The Aran Islands, including Inis Mór, are accessible by ferry from Rossaveal in County Galway or Doolin in County Clare. It's essential to check ferry schedules and book tickets in advance, especially during peak tourist seasons when services may be limited.

Heritage Walks

Many towns and villages in Ireland offer free guided heritage walks, allowing you to explore local history and culture with knowledgeable volunteer guides. Here's a list of some of the best free heritage walks in Ireland:

- Dublin Literary Pub Crawl (Dublin City)
    - Explore the literary history of Dublin with knowledgeable guides, visiting famous literary pubs and landmarks such as Trinity College Dublin and Dublin Castle.
    - No fee for the walk, but participants may need to purchase drinks or food at the pubs visited.
- Galway Historic Walking Tour (Galway City)
    - Discover the rich history of Galway City, including its medieval streets and iconic landmarks like the Spanish Arch and Galway City Museum.
    - Free to join the walking tour, though donations may be appreciated.
- Cork City Heritage Walking Tour (Cork City)
    - Explore the historic streets of Cork City, learning about its fascinating heritage and architecture, including landmarks like St. Fin Barre's Cathedral and the English Market.
    - Free to join the walking tour, with no required fee.
- Kilkenny Medieval Mile Walking Tour (Kilkenny City)
    - Take a journey through time along Kilkenny's Medieval Mile, discovering the city's medieval past and iconic sites such as Kilkenny Castle and St. Canice's Cathedral.
    - Free guided tours are available, though donations are welcome to support the preservation of heritage sites.
- Derry Walls Heritage Trail (Derry/Londonderry)
    - Walk along the historic walls of Derry/Londonderry, one of the best-preserved walled cities in Europe, while learning about its turbulent history and cultural significance.

Boat Cruises

The waters surrounding Ireland are rich in marine biodiversity, making them a popular habitat for various species of cetaceans, including dolphins and whales. Some of the most commonly spotted species include bottlenose dolphins, common dolphins, harbor porpoises, minke whales, and occasionally even larger species like humpback whales and fin whales. When it comes to affordable dolphin or whale watching experiences in Ireland, there are several options available that offer great value for money. Here are some of the best:

- **Mulranny Sea Tours - County Mayo:**
    - Price: €20-€25 per person (prices may vary depending on the tour)
    - Specifics: Mulranny Sea Tours offer budget-friendly boat trips along the stunning coastline of Clew Bay, where you can spot dolphins, seals, and a variety of seabirds. The tours typically last around 2 hours and provide an intimate and eco-friendly way to observe marine wildlife.
- **Dingle Dolphin Tours - County Kerry:**
    - Price: €20-€25 per person (prices may vary depending on the tour operator)

- Specifics: Dingle Dolphin Tours offer affordable boat trips to see Fungie, the famous resident bottlenose dolphin of Dingle Bay. The tours usually last around 1-1.5 hours and provide excellent opportunities to spot Fungie playing in the bay's waters.
- **Galway Bay Boat Tours - County Galway:**
  - Price: €25-€30 per person (prices may vary depending on the tour)
  - Specifics: Galway Bay Boat Tours offer reasonably priced cruises along the stunning Galway Bay, where you can encounter a variety of marine life, including dolphins, seals, and seabirds. The tours typically last around 1.5-2 hours and provide informative commentary from experienced guides.
- **Shore-based Whale Watching - Various Locations:**
  - Price: Free or minimal cost
  - Specifics: While boat tours can be a fantastic way to see dolphins and whales up close, shore-based whale watching can also be a rewarding and budget-friendly alternative. Head to coastal spots with elevated viewpoints, such as cliffs or headlands, and bring a pair of binoculars for the best chance of spotting marine mammals. Locations like Loop Head in County Clare or the Cliffs of Moher in County Clare offer excellent vantage points for shore-based whale watching.
- **Wildlife Watching from Ferry Crossings:**
  - Price: Varies depending on the ferry route
  - Specifics: If you're traveling between coastal destinations by ferry, keep an eye out for dolphins and whales during the journey. Ferry crossings between locations like Rathlin Island and Ballycastle in Northern Ireland or between the Aran Islands and the mainland in County Galway can offer unexpected wildlife sightings as you traverse the open sea.

Churches

Ireland is home to many stunning churches with rich histories and architectural beauty. You can bypass their entrance fees by attending any religious services Here are some of the best churches in Ireland, along with a glimpse into their histories and notable features:

- **St. Patrick's Cathedral, Dublin**: Built in honor of Ireland's patron saint, St. Patrick's Cathedral is one of Dublin's most iconic landmarks. Founded in 1191, it stands on the site where St. Patrick is believed to have baptized converts to Christianity. Inside, visitors can marvel at the intricate stained glass windows, elaborate Gothic architecture, and the tomb of Jonathan Swift, the author of "Gulliver's Travels," who served as the Dean of the cathedral. Entrance fee for adults is €8, with discounts for seniors and students. However, attending a service or Mass is free, allowing visitors to experience the cathedral's beauty and atmosphere without charge.
- **Christ Church Cathedral, Dublin**: Another architectural gem in Dublin, Christ Church Cathedral dates back to the 11th century and is one of the city's oldest buildings. Highlights include the medieval crypt, the largest in Ireland, which houses historical artifacts and the mummified remains of a cat and a rat found in the organ pipes. The cathedral's soaring nave and stunning stained glass windows are also worth admiring. Admission for adults is €7, with discounts available for seniors, students, and families. Attending a choral evensong service is a free way to experience the cathedral's stunning acoustics and architecture.
- **St. Canice's Cathedral, Kilkenny**: Located in the heart of Kilkenny, St. Canice's Cathedral is a magnificent example of medieval architecture. Built in the 13th century, it boasts a striking tower that offers panoramic views of the city and surrounding countryside. Inside, visitors can explore the beautifully preserved interior, including the intricately carved choir stalls and the ornate High Altar.
- **St. Mary's Cathedral, Limerick**: Known for its imposing Gothic facade and soaring spire, St. Mary's Cathedral is one of the oldest buildings in Limerick. Founded in 1168, it is the oldest building in continuous use in the city. Inside, visitors can admire the impressive stained glass windows, medieval tombs, and the ornate stone carvings that adorn the interior.
- **Kylemore Abbey Chapel, County Galway**: Nestled in the scenic Connemara region, Kylemore Abbey is a stunning neo-Gothic mansion set against the backdrop of the Twelve Bens mountain range. The abbey's charming chapel, with its intricate woodwork and colorful stained glass windows, is a serene oasis of tranquility. Visitors can attend daily Mass or simply soak in the peaceful atmosphere of this historic place of worship.
- **St. Nicholas' Collegiate Church, Galway**: Founded in 1320, St. Nicholas' Collegiate Church is the largest medieval parish church still in use in Ireland. Its impressive interior features a beautiful oak roof, medieval wall paintings, and a magnificent 17th-century organ. The church is also known for its connection to the famous Christmas carol, "The Wexford Carol," which is said to have been first performed here.

- **Rock of Cashel, County Tipperary:** While not a traditional church, the Rock of Cashel is a historic site that includes a collection of medieval buildings, including a cathedral, chapel, and round tower. Perched atop a limestone outcrop, it offers breathtaking views of the surrounding countryside. Visitors can explore the ruins and learn about the site's rich history through guided tours and interactive exhibits. Admission to the Rock of Cashel site, which includes access to the cathedral and other ruins, is €8 for adults. However, the site can be viewed from the exterior free of charge, allowing visitors to appreciate its impressive architecture and panoramic views without paying an entrance fee.

Performing Arts

The Arts Council of Ireland provides funding to numerous opera companies, theaters, and performing arts organizations across the country. As a result, you can often find affordable tickets to opera productions, theater performances, dance shows, and musical concerts, particularly for students, seniors, and members of the arts community. with starting prices for tickets. Here are some specific examples with starting prices for tickets:

- **Irish National Opera (INO):**
    - Description: Irish National Opera is the national opera company of Ireland, producing a diverse repertoire of operatic works ranging from classic to contemporary.
    - Starting Price: Tickets for INO productions typically start at around €20-€30 for standard seats, with discounted rates available for students, seniors, and members of the arts community.
- **Abbey Theatre:**
    - Description: The Abbey Theatre, located in Dublin, is Ireland's national theater and one of the country's premier cultural institutions. It showcases a mix of classic and contemporary plays, as well as new works by Irish playwrights.
    - Starting Price: Tickets for Abbey Theatre productions start at approximately €15-€25 for standard seats, with special offers and discounts for students and seniors.
- **Dublin Dance Festival:**
    - Description: Dublin Dance Festival is an annual event that celebrates contemporary dance and choreography, featuring performances by leading Irish and international dance artists.
    - Starting Price: Tickets for Dublin Dance Festival performances vary depending on the venue and production, but they often start at around €15-€20 for standard admission, with concessions available for students and seniors.
- **National Concert Hall (NCH):**
    - Description: National Concert Hall in Dublin is Ireland's premier venue for classical music, hosting a wide range of concerts, recitals, and performances by acclaimed orchestras, ensembles, and soloists.
    - Starting Price: Tickets for NCH concerts and recitals start at approximately €15-€20 for standard seating, with discounted rates offered to students and seniors.
- **Galway International Arts Festival (GIAF):**
    - Description: Galway International Arts Festival is one of Ireland's leading cultural events, featuring a diverse program of theater, music, visual arts, and street performances.
    - Starting Price: Tickets for GIAF events and performances vary depending on the program and venue, but they often start at around €15-€25 for standard admission, with concessions available for students and seniors.

- **Cork Opera House:**
  - Description: Cork Opera House is a historic theater in Cork City, hosting a wide range of productions including opera, musicals, concerts, and comedy shows.
  - Starting Price: Tickets for Cork Opera House performances start at approximately €20-€30 for standard seats, with discounts offered to students, seniors, and members of the arts community.

Seaweed Baths

Historically, seaweed baths were a common practice among coastal communities in Ireland, particularly in regions where seaweed was abundant along the shoreline. Seaweed was harvested from the sea and used for a variety of purposes, including as fertilizer for crops, food for livestock, and as a natural remedy for various ailments.

The therapeutic benefits of seaweed baths were well-known among the local population, who believed that soaking in seaweed-infused water could help alleviate aches and pains, soothe skin conditions, and promote overall health and well-being. Seaweed was prized for its high mineral content, including iodine, potassium, magnesium, and calcium, which were believed to have healing properties when absorbed through the skin.

Some coastal towns in Ireland offer public seaweed baths that are more affordable than private spa facilities. These baths often feature communal tubs filled with seaweed-infused water, allowing visitors to enjoy the experience at a lower cost. One example is the Kilcullen Seaweed Baths in County Sligo, where visitors can soak in communal seaweed baths overlooking the Atlantic Ocean. The cost of a public seaweed bath typically ranges from €15 to €25 per person for a single session, making it a budget-friendly option.

Free Tours

Ireland is home to a host of completely free entry tours. Here are my favourites:

- **Dublin:**
  - **National Museum of Ireland:** Explore the National Museum of Ireland's three Dublin branches – Archaeology, Decorative Arts & History, and Natural History – which offer free admission to their permanent collections. Discover artifacts, artworks, and exhibits showcasing Ireland's rich cultural heritage and natural history.
  - **Chester Beatty Library:** Visit the Chester Beatty Library, located in Dublin Castle, which houses a renowned collection of manuscripts, rare books, and artworks from around the world. Admission to the library and its exhibitions is free of charge.
- **Galway:**
  - **Galway City Walking Tour:** Join a free guided walking tour of Galway city, led by local volunteers from the Galway Civic Trust. Explore the city's medieval streets, historic landmarks, and colorful shops, while learning about Galway's fascinating history and culture.
  - **Galway City Museum:** Visit the Galway City Museum, which offers free admission to its exhibitions showcasing the history and heritage of Galway city and county. Learn about Galway's maritime history, medieval past, and cultural traditions through artifacts, multimedia displays, and interactive exhibits.
- **Cork:**
  - **Crawford Art Gallery:** Discover the Crawford Art Gallery, located in the heart of Cork city, which offers free admission to its permanent collection of artworks, including paintings, sculptures, and decorative arts. Explore works by Irish and international artists spanning centuries of artistic expression.
- **Belfast:**
  - **Belfast City Hall:** Take a free guided tour of Belfast City Hall, a stunning architectural landmark in the heart of the city. Learn about Belfast's history, politics, and culture as you explore the grand halls, historic chambers, and ornate interiors of this iconic building.
  - **Ulster Museum:** Visit the Ulster Museum, Northern Ireland's largest museum, which offers free admission to its permanent galleries showcasing art, history, and natural science. Explore exhibits on Irish history, ancient artifacts, and local wildlife, including the famous Egyptian mummy, Takabuti.

Secret Beaches

Ireland is home to many hidden gems along its coastline, including secluded beaches and coves. Take the time to explore lesser-known beaches such as Silver Strand Beach in County Donegal or Coumeenoole Beach in County Kerry for a luxurious and tranquil experience.

- **Silver Strand Beach, County Mayo:**
    - Location: Near Louisburgh, County Mayo
    - Public Transport: Take Bus Éireann route 450 from Westport to Louisburgh. From there, it's about a 10-minute taxi ride to Silver Strand Beach.
    - Nearby Attractions: Visit Old Head Signal Tower for stunning views of Clew Bay and nearby islands. The town of Louisburgh offers charming cafes and pubs.
    - Cheap Eats: Try the local fish and chips from one of the seafood cafes in Louisburgh.
- **Coumeenoole Beach, County Kerry:**
    - Location: Near Slea Head Drive, Dingle Peninsula, County Kerry
    - Public Transport: Take Bus Éireann route 275 from Tralee to Dingle. From Dingle, you can hire a taxi or join a local tour to reach Coumeenoole Beach.
    - Nearby Attractions: Explore the rugged beauty of Slea Head Drive, visit Dunbeg Fort, and take a boat tour to see the Blasket Islands.

- Cheap Eats: Enjoy a hearty bowl of seafood chowder or a traditional Irish stew at one of the cozy pubs in Dingle.
- **Ballyquin Beach, County Waterford:**
  - Location: Near Ardmore, County Waterford
  - Public Transport: Take Bus Éireann route 40 from Waterford to Dungarvan. From Dungarvan, you can take a taxi to Ardmore, then walk to Ballyquin Beach.
  - Nearby Attractions: Explore the historic ruins of Ardmore Cathedral and Round Tower, visit the Ardmore Cliff Walk, and discover the art galleries and craft shops in Ardmore village.
  - Cheap Eats: Grab a sandwich or salad from a local deli in Dungarvan before heading to Ardmore.
- **Kilmurvey Beach, County Galway:**
  - Location: Inishmore, Aran Islands, County Galway
  - Public Transport: Take a ferry from Rossaveal (near Galway City) to Inishmore. Once on the island, rent a bike or take a minibus to Kilmurvey Beach.
  - Nearby Attractions: Visit the prehistoric stone fort of Dún Aonghasa, explore the Inishmore Heritage Museum, and admire the scenic views from the Worm Hole.
  - Cheap Eats: Pick up some freshly baked pastries or sandwiches from a local bakery in Kilronan village before heading to Kilmurvey Beach.
- **Keem Bay, County Mayo:**
  - Location: Achill Island, County Mayo
  - Public Transport: Take Bus Éireann route 440 from Westport to Achill Sound. From there, you can hire a taxi or join a local tour to Keem Bay.
  - Nearby Attractions: Explore the stunning cliffs of Achill Island along the Atlantic Drive, visit Keel Beach for surfing or windsurfing, and hike up Croaghaun Mountain for panoramic views.
  - Cheap Eats: Grab a hearty seafood pie or a bowl of chowder from a local cafe in Keel village before heading to Keem Bay.

You can also rent ocean view apartments in Ireland cheaply. Here are a list of towns with Airbnbs year-round with great ocean views and low prices.

Location	Price (per night)	Sea View
Clifden, County Galway	€50	Yes
Ballycotton, County Cork	€60	Yes
Dingle, County Kerry	€55	Yes
Bundoran, County Donegal	€40	Yes
Lahinch, County Clare	€50	Yes

Oyster Happy Hours

Oysters hold a significant place in Irish culinary history, with evidence of their consumption dating back thousands of years. They still love them and you can enjoy them cheaply too:

- **The Oyster Tavern - Cork City:**
  - Description: Located in the heart of Cork City, The Oyster Tavern is renowned for its fresh seafood and vibrant atmosphere. During happy hour, patrons can enjoy discounted oysters served with classic accompaniments like lemon wedges and shallot vinegar.
  - Happy Hour: Typically held on weekday evenings from 5 PM to 7 PM.
  - Price: Oyster prices may vary, but happy hour discounts often make them more affordable, with prices ranging from €1-€2 per oyster.
- **The Cliff Townhouse - Dublin:**
  - Description: Situated in a historic Georgian building overlooking St. Stephen's Green, The Cliff Townhouse is a stylish seafood restaurant and oyster bar. Their happy hour specials feature freshly shucked oysters served with mignonette sauce and Tabasco.
  - Happy Hour: Usually available during weekday evenings from 5 PM to 7 PM.
  - Price: Oyster prices are discounted during happy hour, typically ranging from €2-€3 per oyster.
- **The Exchequer Wine Bar - Dublin:**
  - Description: The Exchequer Wine Bar is a cozy and chic spot in Dublin's city center, offering an extensive selection of wines and small plates. Their happy hour deals often include discounted oysters sourced from local oyster farms along Ireland's coastline.
  - Happy Hour: Happy hour times may vary, so it's advisable to check with the venue for specific details.
  - Price: Oyster prices during happy hour can be quite reasonable, with specials often priced at €1-€2 per oyster.
- **Kelly's Oysters - Galway:**
  - Description: Nestled in the heart of Galway's bustling Latin Quarter, Kelly's Oysters is a popular seafood bar known for its fresh oysters and friendly atmosphere. During happy hour, visitors can enjoy special discounts on a selection of oysters from nearby Galway Bay.
  - Happy Hour: Typically held in the late afternoon or early evening, but times may vary.
  - Price: Oyster prices are often discounted during happy hour, with specials ranging from €1.50-€2.50 per oyster.
- **O'Connors Seafood Restaurant - Bantry, County Cork:**
  - Description: Located on the picturesque Bantry Bay in County Cork, O'Connors Seafood Restaurant is celebrated for its superb seafood offerings, including locally sourced oysters. Their happy hour specials provide an excellent opportunity to sample fresh oysters at discounted prices.
  - Happy Hour: Specific happy hour times may vary, so it's recommended to inquire with the restaurant directly.
  - Price: Oyster prices during happy hour are typically discounted, with specials priced around €1.50-€2.50 per oyster.

Hidden Waterfalls

Ireland boasts numerous waterfalls tucked away in its lush countryside. Seek out lesser-known waterfalls for a peaceful and enchanting escape. Here's a chart highlighting some of the hidden waterfalls in Ireland, along with details on their locations, accessibility via public transport, and nearby attractions and options for affordable dining:

Waterfall Name	Location	Public Transport	Nearby Attractions	Cheap Eats Nearby
Torc Waterfall	County Kerry	Bus from Killarney Town	Killarney National Park	Paddywagon Irish Pub
			Muckross House	(Killarney Town)
Glenoe Waterfall	County Antrim	Train from Belfast to	Glenoe Village	The Ballygally Castle Hotel
		Larne, then bus/taxi	The Gobbins Coastal Path	(Ballygally)

Private Gardens

Some of Ireland's most beautiful gardens are privately owned and offer free or low-cost entry to the public. Visit hidden gems like Lismore Castle Gardens in County Waterford or Belleek Castle Gardens in County Mayo for a luxurious stroll amidst stunning landscapes. Here's a chart featuring some of the most enchanting private gardens in Ireland, along with information on their locations, accessibility via public transport, and nearby attractions and affordable dining options:

Garden Name	Location	Public Transport	Nearby Attractions	Cheap Eats Nearby
Powerscourt Gardens	County Wicklow	Bus from Dublin City Center	Powerscourt House	Avoca Powerscourt Café
			Enniskerry Village	(Enniskerry)
Mount Congreve Gardens	County Waterford	Train from Waterford to	Waterford Greenway	The Reg Waterford
		Waterford, then bus/taxi	Mount Congreve Arboretum	(Waterford)

Free Workshops

In Ireland, there are various free workshops available across different cities and towns, covering a wide range of interests and topics. Here are some examples along with any associated costs:

- **Creative Writing Workshops**: Many libraries and community centers offer free creative writing workshops facilitated by experienced writers or authors. These workshops provide aspiring writers with valuable insights, feedback, and techniques to improve their writing skills. Costs: Usually free, but some may require pre-registration.
- **Art and Craft Workshops**: Local art galleries, museums, and cultural centers often host free art and craft workshops for people of all ages. These workshops cover various art mediums such as painting, drawing, pottery, and sculpture, allowing participants to explore their creativity in a supportive environment. Costs: Generally free, but some may charge a nominal fee for materials.
- **Language Learning Workshops**: Language schools and cultural organizations sometimes offer free language learning workshops to introduce beginners to a new language or help learners practice their language skills. These workshops typically include vocabulary building exercises, pronunciation practice, and basic conversation sessions. Costs: Free, but advanced workshops or courses may require a fee.
- **Cooking and Culinary Workshops**: Food festivals, farmers' markets, and community kitchens often host free cooking and culinary workshops led by local chefs or food enthusiasts. These workshops cover a range of topics such as seasonal cooking, international cuisines, and healthy eating, allowing participants to learn new recipes and cooking techniques. Costs: Generally free, but some may charge for ingredients or equipment rental.
- **Yoga and Wellness Workshops**: Yoga studios, wellness centers, and community centers frequently offer free yoga and wellness workshops focused on relaxation, mindfulness, and stress management. These workshops may include guided yoga sessions, meditation practices, and wellness talks led by certified instructors or health professionals. Costs: Typically free, but donations may be appreciated.

Hiking

Ireland offers some breathtaking hiking opportunities, showcasing its stunning landscapes and diverse terrain. Here are some of the best hikes, along with their difficulty levels and rewarding sights:

- **Cliffs of Moher Coastal Walk (County Clare)**:
- Difficulty: Easy to Moderate
- The Cliffs of Moher Coastal Walk offers awe-inspiring views of Ireland's rugged west coast. The trail stretches for about 18 kilometers from Doolin to Hags Head, passing by the iconic Cliffs of Moher along the way. Hikers can enjoy panoramic vistas of the Atlantic Ocean, sea cliffs towering over 200 meters high, and seabird colonies. Nearby, visitors can explore the visitor center at the Cliffs of Moher, as well as the charming village of Doolin known for its traditional music scene.
- **Croagh Patrick (County Mayo)**:
- Difficulty: Moderate to Strenuous
- Croagh Patrick is one of Ireland's most famous pilgrimage sites, known for its association with Saint Patrick, Ireland's patron saint. The hike to the summit is challenging, with steep ascents and rocky terrain, but the effort is rewarded with stunning views of Clew Bay and the surrounding countryside. At the top, hikers can visit the small chapel and enjoy a sense of accomplishment. Nearby, the town of Westport offers amenities for hikers, including accommodations and restaurants.
- **The Wicklow Way (County Wicklow)**:

- Difficulty: Moderate to Strenuous
- The Wicklow Way is Ireland's oldest waymarked long-distance trail, stretching for 132 kilometers through the Wicklow Mountains. Hikers can choose to tackle the entire route or opt for shorter sections. Highlights along the way include lush forests, picturesque valleys, and serene lakes. The trail passes by historical sites such as Glendalough, a medieval monastic settlement with scenic hiking trails and ancient ruins. Nearby, the charming villages of Laragh and Roundwood offer accommodation and dining options.
- **Slieve League Cliffs (County Donegal)**:
- Difficulty: Moderate
- Slieve League Cliffs are among the highest sea cliffs in Europe, offering breathtaking views of the Atlantic Ocean and the rugged Donegal coastline. The hike to the summit is moderately challenging, with well-defined trails and some steep sections. At the top, hikers can marvel at the sheer cliffs plunging into the sea and explore the remains of an ancient hill fort. Nearby, visitors can explore the Slieve League Cultural Centre and the charming village of Carrick.

Surfing or Kayaking

Ireland offers some fantastic locations for surfing and kayaking, with breathtaking coastlines and scenic rivers.

Surfing:

County Clare:
- **Lahinch**: A popular surfing destination with consistent waves suitable for all levels.
- Surfboard Hire: Approximately €15-20 per day.
- Wetsuit Hire: Approximately €10-15 per day.

County Sligo:
- **Strandhill**: Known for its consistent surf breaks and stunning scenery.
- Surfboard Hire: Approximately €15-25 per day.
- Wetsuit Hire: Approximately €10-20 per day.

County Donegal:
- **Bundoran**: A mecca for surfers, offering a variety of breaks for all skill levels.
- Surfboard Hire: Approximately €15-25 per day.
- Wetsuit Hire: Approximately €10-20 per day.

Kayaking:

County Kerry:
- **Dingle Peninsula**: Explore sea caves, cliffs, and secluded beaches along the rugged coastline.
- Kayak Hire: Approximately €30-40 for a half-day guided tour.

County Galway:
- **Connemara**: Paddle through scenic lakes, rivers, and coastal areas in this stunning wilderness region.
- Kayak Hire: Approximately €25-35 for a half-day rental.

County Cork:
- **West Cork**: Discover hidden coves, sea stacks, and marine wildlife along the stunning coastline.
- Kayak Hire: Approximately €30-40 for a half-day guided tour.

Additional Tips:
- It's advisable to book in advance, especially during peak season, to ensure availability.
- Don't forget to inquire about safety equipment such as life jackets and helmets, which are often included in the hire price.

Irish Sports

Irish sports have a rich history and cultural significance, with Gaelic games, rugby, and soccer holding a special place in the hearts of the Irish people. Whether you're watching a local Gaelic football match or cheering on the national rugby team, experiencing Irish sports is a memorable and exciting part of Irish culture. To see Irish sports games on the cheap, there are several strategies you can consider:

- **Local Club Matches**: Attend local club matches for sports like Gaelic football, hurling, and rugby. These matches often have lower entry fees compared to professional or national games and many times are free.
- **Early Bird Tickets**: Look out for early bird ticket offers for larger events. Booking tickets well in advance can sometimes result in discounted prices.

Gaelic Games:

- **Gaelic Football**: One of Ireland's native sports, Gaelic football is played by teams of 15 players kicking or punching a round ball into the opponent's goal.
- **Hurling**: Often described as the fastest field sport in the world, hurling is played with a small ball (sliotar) and a stick (hurley), and players score points by hitting the ball between the opponent's goalposts.
- **Camogie**: The female equivalent of hurling, camogie is played by women and follows similar rules to hurling, though with some differences in equipment and gameplay.

Rugby:

- **Rugby Union**: Rugby has a long history in Ireland, with the Irish Rugby Football Union (IRFU) founded in 1874. The Irish national rugby team competes in international tournaments like the Six Nations Championship and the Rugby World Cup.

Soccer (Football):

- **Association Football (Soccer)**: Soccer is hugely popular in Ireland, with the Football Association of Ireland (FAI) overseeing the sport. The Irish national soccer team competes in international competitions such as the UEFA European Championship and the FIFA World Cup.

Interesting Facts:

- **Croke Park**: The largest stadium in Ireland, Croke Park in Dublin, is the headquarters of the Gaelic Athletic Association (GAA) and hosts major Gaelic games events, as well as concerts and other cultural events.
- **The GAA**: The Gaelic Athletic Association (GAA) was founded in 1884 to promote Irish sports and culture. It remains one of the largest amateur sporting organizations in the world.
- **Lansdowne Road**: The Aviva Stadium in Dublin, formerly known as Lansdowne Road Stadium, is the home of Irish rugby and soccer, hosting international matches for both sports.

- **Triple Crown**: In rugby, winning the Triple Crown involves defeating the other three "Home Nations" (England, Scotland, and Wales) in the Six Nations Championship. Ireland has won the Triple Crown numerous times throughout its rugby history.

Irish Literature

The oldest surviving manuscript in Ireland is the "Book of the Dun Cow" (Leabhar na hUidhre), which dates back to the 11th century. This manuscript contains a collection of early Irish sagas and legends, making it a valuable resource for scholars of medieval Irish literature. With the arrival of Christianity in Ireland, monastic scribes began to record and preserve Irish literature in written form. Monasteries such as Clonmacnoise and Glendalough became centers of learning and scholarship, producing illuminated manuscripts like the "Book of Kells" and the "Book of the Dun Cow," which contained early Irish sagas, religious texts, and historical chronicles. You can explore Irish literature on a budget easily:

Visit Literary Landmarks: Explore the places associated with famous Irish writers, such as James Joyce, W.B. Yeats, and Oscar Wilde. Many of these landmarks, including writers' homes, museums, and literary pubs, offer free or low-cost admission. For example, you can visit the Dublin Writers Museum to learn about Ireland's literary giants or take a self-guided walking tour of literary Dublin, tracing the footsteps of Joyce's characters in "Ulysses."

Attend Literary Events and Festivals: Keep an eye out for literary events and festivals happening throughout Ireland. Many of these events feature readings, book launches, panel discussions, and workshops, often with free or affordable admission. Examples include the Dublin International Literary Festival, Cork International Short Story Festival, and Belfast Book Festival. These events provide opportunities to engage with contemporary Irish writers and discover new voices in Irish literature.

Visit Libraries and Bookshops: Explore Ireland's public libraries and independent bookshops, where you can immerse yourself in Irish literature without spending a dime. Libraries often host literary events, book clubs, and author talks, while bookshops offer a treasure trove of Irish literary works, both classic and contemporary. Take your time browsing the shelves and discovering new authors and titles.

Join Literary Walking Tours: Many cities and towns in Ireland offer literary walking tours led by knowledgeable guides who share insights into local literary history and landmarks. While some guided tours may have a fee, you can often find free self-guided walking tours online or through tourist information centers. These tours allow you to explore literary sites at your own pace and on a budget.

Utilize Public Resources: Many libraries offer free access to e-books, audiobooks, and digital databases of Irish literature and literary journals. Additionally, websites like Project Gutenberg and Open Library provide free access to classic Irish texts that are in the public domain.

Attend Literary Readings and Open Mic Nights: Keep an eye out for literary readings and open mic nights happening at cafes, bookshops, and cultural centers. These events often showcase emerging writers and provide opportunities for aspiring writers to share their work in a supportive environment. Admission is typically free or may involve a nominal cover charge, making it an affordable way to experience Irish literature firsthand.

Stargazing

Ireland's dark skies offer excellent opportunities for stargazing, especially in remote rural areas. Pack a blanket, find a secluded spot away from city lights, and marvel at the beauty of the night sky for a truly luxurious experience under the stars. Best Places to Go:

- **Kerry International Dark Sky Reserve:** Located in County Kerry, this reserve is one of the best places in Ireland for stargazing due to its low light pollution levels. The reserve offers designated stargazing spots and guided tours for visitors.
- **Mayo Dark Sky Park:** Situated in County Mayo, this park is Ireland's first International Dark Sky Park. It provides excellent opportunities for stargazing with its dark skies and clear visibility.
- **Connemara National Park:** Located in County Galway, Connemara National Park offers stunning landscapes and relatively low light pollution, making it a great spot for stargazing. The park occasionally hosts stargazing events and guided walks.
- **Burren National Park:** Found in County Clare, Burren National Park is renowned for its unique limestone landscapes. Visitors can enjoy stargazing opportunities amidst this rugged terrain with relatively low light pollution.
- **Wicklow Mountains National Park:** Situated in County Wicklow, this national park offers breathtaking scenery and relatively dark skies, especially away from urban areas. It's a great spot for both beginners and experienced stargazers.

Film

In Ireland, film screenings, festivals, and cultural events celebrating Irish cinema are abundant, offering opportunities to immerse yourself in the rich tapestry of Irish filmmaking. Thanks to the support provided by government bodies such as the Irish Film Board and Culture Ireland, many of these events are accessible to audiences at affordable prices or even free of charge. Here are some specific examples:

- **Galway Film Fleadh:**
  - Description: The Galway Film Fleadh is one of Ireland's most prestigious film festivals, showcasing the best in Irish and international cinema. The festival features a diverse program of feature films, documentaries, shorts, and animations, with screenings held in venues across Galway City.
  - Starting Price: Ticket prices for screenings at the Galway Film Fleadh vary depending on the film and venue, but they often start at around €10-€12 for standard admission, with discounts available for students and seniors.
- **Dublin International Film Festival (DIFF):**
  - Description: The Dublin International Film Festival is an annual event that celebrates the art of filmmaking from around the world. The festival presents a curated selection of acclaimed films, premieres, and special events, attracting filmmakers, industry professionals, and cinephiles from near and far.
  - Starting Price: Ticket prices for DIFF screenings range from €10-€15 for standard admission, with discounted rates offered for students, seniors, and festival passes available for multiple screenings.
- **Irish Film Institute (IFI):**
  - Description: The Irish Film Institute is a cultural institution dedicated to promoting and preserving Irish and international film heritage. The IFI screens a wide range of films throughout the year, including classic cinema, contemporary releases, and special retrospectives.
  - Starting Price: Ticket prices for screenings at the IFI start at approximately €9-€11 for standard admission, with discounts available for IFI members, students, and seniors.
- **Cinema on the Square (Merrion Square, Dublin):**
  - Description: During the summer months, Dublin's Merrion Square transforms into an outdoor cinema venue, hosting free screenings of classic films, family favorites, and cult classics. Cinema on the Square offers a unique and relaxed atmosphere, with audiences picnicking on the grass while enjoying cinematic delights under the stars.
  - Starting Price: Free entry; bring your own picnic or purchase snacks from on-site vendors.
- **Culture Night:**
  - Description: Culture Night is an annual nationwide celebration of arts and culture, with thousands of free events and activities taking place across Ireland. As part of Culture Night, many venues, including theaters, cinemas,

and cultural centers, host free film screenings, discussions, and exhibitions, allowing audiences to experience the best of Irish culture.
- Starting Price: Free entry to participating events; check the Culture Night website for program details and schedules.

Ireland Today

Population:
- Ireland's population is estimated to be around 4.9 million people.
- The population of Ireland has been steadily increasing in recent years, driven by factors such as natural population growth and immigration.

Politics:
- Ireland is a parliamentary democracy with a system of government based on the Westminster model.
- Ireland has a bicameral parliament known as the Oireachtas, consisting of the Dáil Éireann (House of Representatives) and the Seanad Éireann (Senate).

Economy:
- Ireland has a diverse and open economy, with key sectors including technology, pharmaceuticals, finance, agriculture, and tourism.
- Dublin, the capital city, is a major financial hub and home to many multinational corporations' European headquarters.
- Ireland has a relatively low corporate tax rate, which has attracted significant foreign investment and contributed to economic growth.
- The cost of living in Ireland, particularly in urban areas like Dublin, can be relatively high compared to other European countries, with housing costs being a significant factor.

Culture and Society:
- Ireland has a rich cultural heritage, with traditions in music, literature, dance, and folklore deeply ingrained in society.
- The Irish language (Gaeilge) is recognized as the first official language of Ireland, alongside English, and efforts are ongoing to promote its use and preservation.
- Traditional Irish music sessions can be found in pubs and cultural venues across the country, showcasing the country's musical heritage.
- Ireland has made significant progress in recent years in social issues such as LGBTQ+ rights, gender equality, and immigration policy.
-

How to Enjoy ALLOCATING Money in Ireland

'Money's greatest intrinsic value—and this can't be overstated—is its ability to give you control over your time.' - Morgan Housel

Notice I have titled the chapter how to enjoy allocating money in Ireland. I'll use saving and allocating interchangeably in the book, but since most people associate saving to feel like a turtleneck, that's too tight, I've chosen to use wealth language. Rich people don't save. They allocate. What's the difference? Saving can feel like something you don't want or wish to do and allocating has your personal will attached to it.

And on that note, it would be helpful if you considered removing the following words and phrase from your vocabulary for planning and enjoying your Ireland trip:

- Wish
- Want
- Maybe someday

These words are part of poverty language. Language is a dominant source of creation. Use it to your advantage. You don't have to wish, want or say maybe someday to Ireland. You can enjoy the same things millionaires enjoy in Ireland without the huge spend.

'People don't like to be sold-but they love to buy.' - Jeffrey Gitomer.

Every good salesperson who understands the quote above places obstacles in the way of their clients' buying. Companies create waiting lists, restaurants pay people to queue outside in order to create demand. People reason if something is so in demand, it must be worth having but that's often just marketing. Take this sales maxim 'People don't like to be sold-but they love to buy and flip it on its head to allocate your money in Ireland on things YOU desire. You love to spend and hate to be sold. That means when something comes your way, it's not 'I can't afford it,' it's 'I don't want it' or maybe 'I don't want it right now'.

Saving money doesn't mean never buying a latte, never taking a taxi, never taking vacations (of course, you bought this book). Only you get to decide on how you spend and on what. Not an advice columnist who thinks you can buy a house if you never eat avocado toast again.

I love what Kate Northrup says about affording something: "If you really wanted it you would figure out a way to get it. If it were that VALUABLE to you, you would make it happen."

I believe if you master the art of allocating money to bargains, it can feel even better than spending it! Bold claim, I know. But here's the truth: Money gives you freedom and options. The more you keep in your account and or invested the more freedom and options you'll have. The principal reason you should save and allocate money is TO BE FREE! Remember, a trip's main purpose is relaxation, rest and enjoyment, aka to feel free.

When you talk to most people about saving money on vacation. They grimace. How awful they proclaim not to go wild on your vacation. If you can't get into a ton of debt enjoying your once-in-a-lifetime vacation, when can you?

When you spend money 'theres's a sudden rush of dopamine which vanishes once the transaction is complete. What happens in the brain when you save money? It increases feelings of security and peace. You don't need to stress life's uncertainties. And having a greater sense of peace can actually help you save more money.' Stressed out people make impulsive financial choices, calm people don't.'

The secret to enjoying saving money on vacation is very simple: never save money from a position of lack. Don't think 'I wish I could afford that'. Choose not to be marketed to. Choose not to consume at a price others set. Don't save money from the flawed premise you don't have enough. Don't waste your time living in the box that society has created, which says saving money on vacation means sacrifice. It doesn't.

Traveling to Ireland can be an expensive endeavor if you don't approach it with a plan, but you have this book which is packed with tips. The biggest other asset is your perspective.

Winning the Vacation Game

The inspiration for these books struck me during a Vipassana meditation retreat. As I contemplated the excitement that precedes a vacation, I couldn't help but wish that we could all carry that same sense of anticipation in our daily lives. It was from this introspection that the concept of indulging in luxurious trips on a budget was born. The driving force behind this idea has always been the prevalence of disregarded inequalities.

A report from the Pew Charitable Trusts unveiled a stark reality: only about 4% of individuals born into the lowest income quintile, the bottom 20%, in the United States manage to ascend to the top income quintile during their lifetime. This trend is mirrored in many parts of Europe, underscoring the immense hurdles faced by those from disadvantaged backgrounds, including myself, in their pursuit of financial security.

To compound this, a comprehensive study conducted by researchers at Stanford University and published in the Journal of Personality and Social Psychology illuminated a compelling connection between career choices, personal fulfillment, and income. It revealed that individuals who prioritize intrinsic factors like passion often find themselves with lower average incomes, highlighting the intricate dynamics at play in the pursuit of one's dreams. Either you're in a low-income career, believing you can't afford to travel, or you're earning well but desperately need a vacation due to your work being mediocre at best. Personally, I believe it's better to do what you love and take time to plan a luxury trip on a budget. Of course, that, in itself, is a luxurious choice not all of us have. I haven't even mentioned Income, education, and systemic inequalities that can lock restrict travel opportunities for many.

Despite these challenging realities, I firmly believe that every individual can have their dream getaway. I am committed to providing practical insights and strategies that empower individuals to turn their dream vacations into a tangible reality without breaking the bank.

The key to acquiring anything is belief. But how do you believe in something you don't currently believe in? I've addressed this in detail in the bonus tips section entitled How to Believe Something You Don't Believe.

How to feel RICH in Ireland

You don't need millions in your bank to **feel rich**. Feeling rich feels different to every person."Researchers have pooled data on the relationship between money and emotions from more than 1.6 million people across 162 countries and found that **wealthier people feel more positive "self-regard emotions" such as confidence, pride and determination."**

Here are things to see, do and taste in Ireland, that will have you overflowing with gratitude for your luxury trip to Ireland.

- Achieving a Michelin Star rating is the most coveted accolade for restaurants but those that obtain a Michelin Star are synonymous with high cost, but in Ireland there are restaurants with Michelin-stars offering lunch menus for 15 euros or less! If you want to taste the finest seasonal local dishes while dining in pure luxury, have Lunch at Chapter One in Dublin. It offers a two-course lunch menu that is an unforgettable treat. If fine dining isn't your thing, don't worry further on in the guide you will find a range of delicious cheap eats in Ireland that deserve a Michelin-Star.
- While money can't buy happiness, it can buy cake and isn't that sort of the same thing? Jokes aside, Bretzel Bakery in Dublin has turned cakes and pastries into edible art. Visit to taste the most delicious Bretzel in Ireland.
- While you might not be staying in a penthouse, you can still enjoy the same views. Visit rooftop bars in Ireland, like The Dáil Bar in Galway to enjoy incredible sunset views for the price of just one drink. And if you want to continue enjoying libations, head over to The Front Door Pub for a dirt-cheap happy hour, lots of reasonably priced (and delicious) cocktails and cheap delicious snacks.
- Join a TV audience. Shows that have offered audience tickets in the past include "The Late Late Show," "The Tommy Tiernan Show," "The Ray D'Arcy Show," and "The Graham Norton Show." Visit the official websites of TV networks for the shows you're interested in attending. Fill in a form and then go be part of the action.

Those are just some ideas for you to know that visiting Ireland on a budget doesn't have to feel like sacrifice or constriction. Now let's get into the nuts and bolts of Ireland on the super cheap.

How to use this book

Google and TripAdvisor are your on-the-go guides while traveling, a travel guide adds the most value during the planning phase, and if you're without Wi-Fi. Always download the google map for your destination - having an offline map will make using this guide much more comfortable. For ease of use, we've set the book out the way you travel, booking your flights, arriving, how to get around, then on to the money-saving tips. The tips we ordered according to when you need to know the tip to save money, so free tours and combination tickets feature first. We prioritized the rest of the tips by how much money you can save and then by how likely it was that you could find the tip with a google search. Meaning those we think you could find alone are nearer the bottom. I hope you find this layout useful. If you have any ideas about making Super Cheap Insider Guides easier to use, please email me philgattang@gmail.com

A quick note on How We Source Super Cheap Tips
We focus entirely on finding the best bargains. We give each of our collaborators $2,000 to hunt down never-before-seen deals. The type you either only know if you're local or by on the ground research. We spend zero on marketing and a little on designing an excellent cover. We do this yearly, which means we just keep finding more amazing ways for you to have the same experience for less.

Now let's get started with juicing the most pleasure from your trip to Ireland with the least possible money!

Planning your trip

When to visit

The first step in saving money on your Ireland trip is timing. If you are not tied to school holidays, the **best time to visit is during the shoulder-season months of March, April and October and November.**

Traveling in the off-season offers a host of benefits. You will have less of a chance to be jostled by large crowds and your hotel bookings will be much cheaper and you won't need to buy skip the line tickets. Plus, during these shoulder months, there is a chance of seeing tulips in bloom. In addition, you will find some of the Netherlands' most scenic beaches and small towns.

The High season starts in April and goes until September and prices DOUBLE so if you're planning to come then book accommodation ahead of time to save money on price hikes.

If you are visiting during the peak season, you should expect to pay higher rates for hotels and airfare. You will also have to cope with long lines at some of the city's most popular attractions but don't despair there are innumerable hacks to save on accommodation in Ireland which we will go into detail on. Plus if you visit in summer, Ireland is awash with free festivals. From the Robeco Zomerconcerten series to the Vondelpark Open Air Theater, there's something for everyone.

Whats on?

Free Festivals in Ireland

Festival Name	Date	Location
St. Patrick's Festival	March 17	Dublin
Galway International Arts Festival	July 11 - 24	Galway
Spraoi International Street Arts Festival	August 5 - 7	Waterford
Culture Night	September 16	Nationwide

What's On Month by Month in Ireland

Here's a month-by-month guide to some of the vibrant and diverse events and festivals that take place throughout the year in Ireland:

January:

- **Temple Bar TradFest in Dublin:** Kick off the new year with a celebration of traditional Irish music and culture in Dublin's historic Temple Bar district. The festival features live performances, sessions, workshops, and more.

- **First Fortnight Mental Health Arts Festival:** Raise awareness about mental health issues through artistic expression at this unique festival, which showcases a variety of events including music, theatre, film, and visual arts.

February:

- **Jameson Dublin International Film Festival:** Film enthusiasts gather in Dublin for this prestigious event, which features screenings of Irish and international films, Q&A sessions with filmmakers, and special events.
- **Smithwick's Kilkenny Roots Festival:** Enjoy a weekend of live music in the picturesque city of Kilkenny, with performances from top folk, blues, and Americana artists in various venues across the city.

March:

- **St. Patrick's Festival in Dublin:** Experience the world-famous St. Patrick's Day celebrations in Dublin, featuring parades, concerts, street performances, and cultural events showcasing Irish heritage and creativity.
- **Cork International Choral Festival:** Immerse yourself in the harmonious sounds of choirs from around the world at this renowned choral festival in Cork, with competitions, workshops, and concerts.

April:

- **West Waterford Festival of Food:** Foodies flock to Dungarvan for this gastronomic extravaganza, which celebrates the best of local produce with tastings, cookery demonstrations, markets, and culinary events.
- **Clifden Traditional Music Festival:** Join musicians and music lovers in the scenic town of Clifden for a weekend of traditional Irish music sessions, concerts, workshops, and dancing.

May:

- **Féile na Bealtaine in Dingle:** Experience the creative spirit of Dingle at this multidisciplinary arts festival, featuring music, literature, theatre, visual arts, and more, set against the stunning backdrop of the Dingle Peninsula.
- **Galway Early Music Festival:** Journey back in time with a celebration of medieval, renaissance, and baroque music in Galway, with concerts, workshops, and talks showcasing historical musical styles and instruments.

June:

- **Bloomsday Festival in Dublin:** Celebrate James Joyce's iconic novel "Ulysses" with a series of literary events, walking tours, readings, performances, and themed activities inspired by the book and its characters.
- **Sea Sessions Surf Music Festival in Donegal:** Combine your love of music and surfing at this unique festival on the shores of Bundoran, featuring live music, surfing competitions, beach sports, and seaside entertainment.

July:

- **Galway International Arts Festival:** Experience the vibrant cultural scene of Galway with a diverse program of theatre, dance, music, visual arts, street performances, and special events, attracting artists and audiences from around the world.

- **Willie Clancy Summer School in Clare:** Immerse yourself in the rich tradition of Irish music at this renowned summer school in Miltown Malbay, featuring workshops, masterclasses, sessions, and concerts celebrating the legacy of uilleann piper Willie Clancy.

August:

- **Spraoi International Street Arts Festival in Waterford:** Be amazed by spectacular street performances, circus acts, music, and visual arts at Ireland's largest street arts festival in the historic city of Waterford, attracting performers and audiences of all ages.
- **Puck Fair in Kerry:** Join the lively festivities in Killorglin for one of Ireland's oldest fairs, where a wild mountain goat is crowned king for three days of music, parades, entertainment, and family fun.

September:

- **Dublin Fringe Festival:** Experience the cutting edge of Irish and international theatre, dance, comedy, music, and visual arts at this dynamic festival, which showcases emerging artists and innovative performances in venues across Dublin.
- **Lisdoonvarna Matchmaking Festival:** Discover the art of matchmaking in the charming town of Lisdoonvarna, with music, dancing, and social events bringing singles together in search of love and romance.

October:

- **Cork Jazz Festival:** Get into the groove at Ireland's largest jazz festival, with an eclectic lineup of performances by local and international artists in venues throughout Cork City, along with workshops, masterclasses, and jam sessions.
- **Bram Stoker Festival in Dublin:** Embrace the Halloween spirit with a celebration of the life and works of Bram Stoker, author of "Dracula," featuring gothic-themed events, performances, tours, and immersive experiences in Dublin.

November:

- **Cork Film Festival:** Discover the best of Irish and international cinema at one of Ireland's oldest film festivals, with screenings, premieres, discussions, and events showcasing a diverse range of cinematic styles and genres.
- **Dublin Book Festival:** Celebrate literature and storytelling at this annual festival, which features book launches, author readings, panel discussions, workshops, and literary events for readers of all ages and interests.

December:

- **Winter Solstice at Newgrange:** Witness the ancient tradition of the winter solstice alignment at the Neolithic passage tomb of Newgrange in County Meath, where sunlight illuminates the chamber on the shortest day of the year.
- **Galway Christmas Market:** Experience the festive atmosphere of Galway's Christmas market, with stalls selling artisan crafts, seasonal treats, and gifts, along with entertainment, carol singing, and family activities in the heart of the city.

Festival Name	Location	Highlights	Dates	Cost to Attend	Best Affordable Luxury Accommodation	Starting Price
St. Patrick's Festival	Dublin	Parades, concerts, fireworks, cultural events	March 17th	Free	The Morrison Hotel	€120 per night
Galway Oyster Festival	Galway	Oyster tastings, live music, seafood delights	Late September	Varies	The Connacht Hotel	€80 per night
Dublin Fringe Festival	Dublin	Theatre, dance, music, comedy, and visual arts	September	Varies	The Croke Park Hotel	€100 per night
Galway International Arts Festival	Galway	Theatre, dance, music, visual arts, street performances	July-August	Varies	Jurys Inn Galway	€90 per night
Bloomsday Festival	Dublin	Celebrates James Joyce's Ulysses with readings, tours	June 16th	Free	The Gresham Hotel	€150 per night
Electric Picnic	County Laois	Music, arts, food, and holistic experiences	September	Varies	The Midlands Park Hotel	€100 per night
Cork Jazz Festival	Cork	Jazz performances, street parties, and workshops	October	Varies	The River Lee Hotel	€120 per night
Kilkenny Arts Festival	Kilkenny	Theatre, music, dance, visual arts, and literary events	August-September	Varies	Pembroke Hotel	€110 per night
Lisdoonvarna Matchmaking Festival	County Clare	Traditional matchmaking, music, dancing, and events	August-September	Varies	The Hydro Hotel	€90 per night

The seasons in Ireland and what to pack for each

Ireland experiences a temperate maritime climate, characterized by mild winters and cool summers. The weather can be changeable and unpredictable, with frequent rainfall throughout the year. Here's a breakdown of the seasons in Ireland and what to pack for each:

- **Spring (March to May):**
    - Weather: Spring in Ireland is generally mild, with temperatures ranging from 6°C to 13°C (43°F to 55°F). There can be a mix of sunny days and occasional rain showers.
        - What to Pack:
        - Lightweight, breathable layers: Long-sleeved shirts, sweaters, and jackets.
        - Waterproof jacket or coat.
        - Comfortable walking shoes or boots for exploring.
        - Scarf and gloves for cooler days.
        - Umbrella or raincoat for unexpected showers.
        - Hat and sunglasses for sunny days.
        - Casual attire for sightseeing and outdoor activities.
- **Summer (June to August):**
    - Weather: Summer is the warmest and driest season in Ireland, with temperatures averaging between 10°C to 20°C (50°F to 68°F). Days are long, with up to 18 hours of daylight in June.
        - What to Pack:
        - Light, breathable clothing: T-shirts, shorts, skirts, and dresses.
        - Layers for cooler evenings: Sweaters or light jackets.
        - Waterproof jacket or poncho for occasional rain showers.
        - Comfortable walking shoes or sandals.
        - Sunscreen with a high SPF and sun hat.
        - Sunglasses to protect your eyes from the sun.
        - Swimwear if you plan to visit beaches or go swimming.
        - Insect repellent for outdoor activities.
- **Autumn (September to November):**
    - Weather: Autumn in Ireland brings cooler temperatures and more frequent rainfall. Average temperatures range from 8°C to 14°C (46°F to 57°F).
        - What to Pack:
        - Layers for variable weather: Sweaters, long-sleeved shirts, and light jackets.
        - Waterproof and windproof outerwear.
        - Closed-toe shoes or boots for walking in damp conditions.
        - Scarf, gloves, and hat for cooler days.
        - Umbrella or raincoat for rainy days.
        - Casual attire suitable for sightseeing and outdoor activities.
        - Daypack or backpack for carrying essentials during day trips.
- **Winter (December to February):**

- Weather: Winter in Ireland is mild but damp, with temperatures averaging between 4°C to 9°C (39°F to 48°F). Rainfall is common, and occasional frost or snow may occur, particularly in higher elevations.
    - What to Pack:
    - Warm layers: Sweaters, thermal underwear, and heavy coats.
    - Waterproof and windproof outerwear.
    - Insulated, waterproof boots with good traction.
    - Hat, scarf, and gloves for cold weather.
    - Umbrella or waterproof hat for rainy days.
    - Warm socks and thermal clothing for outdoor activities.
    - Indoor attire for cozy evenings, such as lounge pants and slippers.
    - Travel adapter for charging electronic devices.

Regardless of the season, it's always a good idea to pack versatile clothing that can be layered to accommodate changing weather conditions. Don't forget to check the weather forecast before your trip and adjust your packing list accordingly.

Not surprisingly, the Irish language has several words to describe different types of rain, the varying intensity and characteristics of rain but also reflect the nuanced relationship that the Irish people have with the weather

- **Báisteach:** This is the most common word for "rain" in Irish.
- **Fuar báisteach:** This translates to "cold rain," reflecting the chilly nature of the precipitation.
- **Téad báistí:** This phrase is used to describe a "downpour" or heavy rain.
- **Ceobhrán:** This word refers to a "fine mist" or light drizzle.
- **Cíochán:** This term is used for "showers" or intermittent rain.
- **Tuirseach:** This word means "tiring rain," indicating a prolonged or exhausting period of wet weather.

Booking Flights

How to Find Heavily Discounted Private Jet Flights to or from Ireland

If you're dreaming of travelling to Ireland on a private jet you can accomplish your dream for a 10th of the cost.

Empty leg flights, also known as empty leg charters or deadhead flights, are flights operated by private jet companies that do not have any passengers on board. These flights occur when a private jet is chartered for a one-way trip, but the jet needs to return to its base or another location without passengers.

Rather than flying empty, private jet companies may offer these empty leg flights for a reduced price to travelers who are flexible and able to fly on short notice. Because the flight is already scheduled and paid for by the original charter, private jet companies are willing to offer these flights at a discounted rate in order to recoup some of the cost.

Empty leg flights can be a cost-effective way to experience the luxury and convenience of private jet travel.

Taking an empty leg private jet flight from America to Ireland

The New York City-Ireland route is one of the busiest private jet routes in the world, with many private jet operators offering regular flights between the two cities.

There are several websites that offer empty leg flights for booking. Here are a few:

JetSuiteX: This website offers discounted, last-minute flights on private jets, including empty leg flights.

PrivateFly: This website allows you to search for empty leg flights by location or date. You can also request a quote for a custom flight if you have specific needs.

Victor: This website offers a variety of private jet services, including empty leg flights.

Sky500: This website offers a variety of private jet services, including empty leg flights.

Air Charter Service: This website allows you to search for empty leg flights by location or date. You can also request a quote for a custom flight if you have specific needs.

Keep in mind that empty leg flights are often available at short notice, so it's a good idea to be flexible with your travel plans if you're looking for a deal. It's also important to do your research and read reviews before booking a flight with any company.

RECAP: To book an empty leg flight in Ireland, follow these steps:

1. Research and identify private jet companies and or brokers that offer empty leg flights departing from Ireland. You can use the websites mentioned earlier, such as JetSuiteX, PrivateFly, Victor, Sky500, or Air Charter Service, to search for available flights.

2. Check the availability and pricing of empty leg flights that match your travel dates and destination. Empty leg flights are often available at short notice.

3. Contact the private jet company or broker to inquire about booking the empty leg flight. Be sure to provide your travel details, including your preferred departure and arrival times, number of passengers, and any special requests.

4. Confirm your booking and make payment. Private jet companies and brokers typically require full payment upfront, so be prepared to pay for the flight in advance.

5. Arrive at the airport at least 30 minutes before the scheduled departure time.

6. Check in at the private jet terminal and go through any necessary security checks. Unlike commercial airlines, there is typically no long queue or security checks for private jet flights.

7. Board the private jet and settle into your seat. You will have plenty of space to stretch out and relax, as well as access to amenities such as Wi-Fi, entertainment systems, and refreshments.

How to Find CHEAP FIRST-CLASS Flights to Ireland

Upgrade at the airport

Airlines are extremely reluctant to advertise price drops in first or business class tickets so the best way to secure them is actually at the airport when airlines have no choice but to decrease prices dramatically because otherwise they lose money. Ask about upgrading to business or first-class when you check-in. If you check-in online look around the airport for your airlines branded bidding system.

Use Air-miles

When it comes to accruing air-miles for American citizens **Chase Sapphire Reserve card** ranks top. If you put everything on there and pay it off immediately you will end up getting free flights all the time, aside from taxes.

Get 2-3 chase cards with sign up bonuses, you'll have 200k points in no time and can book with points on multiple airlines when transferring your points to them.

Please note, this is only applicable to those living in the USA. In the Bonus Section we have detailed the best air-mile credit cards for those living in other countries.

How many miles does it take to fly first class?
New York City to Dublin could require anywhere from 70,000 to 120,000 frequent flyer miles, depending on the airline and the time of year you plan to travel.

Every Friday I send out an email featuring business and first class flights under $500. If you'd like to sign-up, you can do so here - form.jotform.com/philgtang/fly Enter your name and your closest airport.

How to Fly Business Class to Ireland cheaply

Aer Lingus is a popular airline that operates flights from New York City to Ireland with the cheapest business class options. In low season this route typically started at around $1,000-$1,500 per person for a round-trip ticket.

The average cost for a round-trip flight from New York City to Ireland typically ranged from around $400 to $1200 for an economy seat, so if travelling business class is important to you, Aer LingusI is likely to be the best bang for your buck.

To find the best deals on business class flights to Ireland, follow these steps:

1. Use travel search engines: Start by searching for flights on popular travel search engines like Google Flights, Kayak, or Skyscanner. These sites allow you to compare prices from different airlines and book the cheapest available business option.
2. Sign up for airline newsletters: Airlines often send out exclusive deals and promotions to their email subscribers. Sign up for TAP Air Portugal's newsletter to receive notifications about special offers and discounts on business class flights.
3. Book in advance: Booking your flight well in advance can help you secure a better deal on business class tickets. Aim to book your flight at least two to three months before your travel date.

How to ALWAYS Find Super Cheap Flights to Ireland

If you're just interested in finding the cheapest flight to Ireland here is here to do it!

Luck is just an illusion.

Anyone can find incredible flight deals. If you can be flexible you can save huge amounts of money. In fact, the biggest tip I can give you for finding incredible flight deals is simple: find a flexible job. Don't despair if you can't do that theres still a lot you can do.

Book your flight to Ireland on a Tuesday or Wednesday

Tuesdays and Wednesdays are the cheapest days of the week to fly. You can take a flight to Ireland on a Tuesday or Wednesday for less than half the price you'd pay on a Thursday Friday, Saturday, Sunday or Monday.

Start with Google Flights (but NEVER book through them)

I conduct upwards of 50 flight searches a day for readers. I use google flights first when looking for flights. I put specific departure but broad destination (e.g Europe) and usually find amazing deals.

The great thing about Google Flights is you can search by class. You can pick a specific destination and it will tell you which time is cheapest in which class. Or you can put in dates and you can see which area is cheapest to travel to.

But be aware Google flights does not show the cheapest prices among the flight search engines but it does offer several advantages

1. You can see the cheapest dates for the next 8 weeks. Other search engines will blackout over 70% of the prices.
2. You can put in multiple airports to fly from. Just use a common to separate in the from input.
3. If you're flexible on where you're going Google flights can show you the cheapest destinations.
4. You can set-up price tracking, where Google will email you when prices rise or decline.

Once you have established the cheapest dates to fly go over to skyscanner.net and put those dates in. You will find sky scanner offers the cheapest flights.

Get Alerts when Prices to Ireland are Lowest

Google also has a nice feature which allows you to set up an alert to email you when prices to your destination are at their lowest. So if you don't have fixed dates this feature can save you a fortune.

Baggage add-ons

It may be cheaper and more convenient to send your luggage separately with a service like sendmybag.com Often the luggage sending fee is cheaper than what the airlines charge to check baggage. Visit Lugless.com or luggagefree.com in addition to sendmybag.com for a quotation.

Loading times

Anyone who has attempted to find a cheap flight will know the pain of excruciating long loading times. If you encounter this issue use google flights to find the cheapest dates and then go to skyscanner.net for the lowest price.

Always try to book direct with the airline

Once you have found the cheapest flight go direct to the airlines booking page. This is advantageous because if you need to change your flights or arrange a refund, its much easier to do so, than via a third party booking agent.

That said, sometimes the third party bookers offer cheaper deals than the airline, so you need to make the decision based on how likely you think it is that disruption will impede you making those flights.

More Fight Tricks and Tips

www.secretflying.com/usa-deals offers a range of deals from the USA and other countries. For example you can pick-up a round trip flight non-stop from from the east coast to johannesburg for $350 return on this site

Scott's cheap flights, you can select your home airport and get emails on deals but you pay for an annual subscription. A free workaround is to download Hopper and set search alerts for trips/price drops.

Premium service of Scott's cheap flights.
They sometime have discounted business and first class but in my experience they are few and far between.

JGOOT.com has 5 times as many choices as Scott's cheap flights.

kiwi.com allows you to be able to do radius searches so you can find cheaper flights to general areas.

Finding Error Fares

Travel Pirates (www.travelpirates.com) is a gold-mine for finding error deals. Subscribe to their newsletter. I recently found a reader an airfare from Montreal-Brazil for a $200 round trip (mistake fare!). Of course these error fares are always certain dates, but if you can be flexible you can save a lot of money.

Things you can do that might reduce the fare to Ireland:

- Use a VPN (if the booker knows you booked one-way, the return fare will go up)
- Buy your ticket in a different currency

If all else fails...

If you can't find a cheap flight for your dates I can find one for you. I do not charge for this nor do I send affiliate links. I'll send you a screenshot of the best options I find as airlines attach cookies to flight links. To use this free service please review this guide and send me a screenshot of your review - with your flight hacking request. I aim to reply to you within 12 hours. If it's an urgent request mark the email URGENT in the subject line and I will endeavour to reply ASAP.

A tip for coping with Jet-lag

Jetlag is primarily caused by disruptions to the body's circadian rhythm, which is the internal "biological clock" that regulates many of the body's processes, including sleep-wake cycles. When you travel across multiple time zones, your body's clock is disrupted, leading to symptoms like fatigue, insomnia, and stomach problems.

Eating on your travel destination's time before you travel can help to adjust your body's clock before you arrive, which can help to mitigate the effects of jetlag. This means that if you're traveling to a destination that is several hours ahead of your current time zone, you should try to eat meals at the appropriate times for your destination a few days before you leave. For example, if you're traveling from New York to Ireland, which is seven hours ahead, you could start eating dinner at 9pm EST (which is 3am Ireland time) a few days before your trip.

By adjusting your eating schedule before you travel, you can help to shift your body's clock closer to the destination's time zone, which can make it easier to adjust to the new schedule once you arrive.

Accommodation

Your two biggest expenses when travelling to Ireland are accommodation and food. This section is intended to help you cut these costs dramatically without compromising on those luxury feels:

How to Book a Five-star Hotel consistently on the Cheap in Ireland

The cheapest four and five-star hotel deals are available when you 'blind book'. Blind booking is a type of discounted hotel booking where the guest doesn't know the name of the hotel until after they've booked and paid for the reservation. This allows hotels to offer lower prices without damaging their brand image or cannibalizing their full-price bookings.

Here are some of the best platforms for blind booking a hotel in Ireland:

1. Hotwire - This website offers discounted hotel rates for blind booking. You can choose the star rating, neighborhood, and amenities you want, but the actual hotel name will not be revealed until after you've booked.
2. Priceline - Once you've made the reservation, the hotel name and location will be revealed.
3. Secret Escapes - This website offers luxury hotel deals at discounted rates. You can choose the type of hotel you want and the general location, but the hotel name and exact location will be revealed after you book.
4. Lastminute.com - You can select the star rating and general location, but the hotel name and exact location will be revealed after booking. Using the Top Secret hotels you can find a four star hotel from $60 a night in Ireland - consistently! Most of the hotels featured are in the Grange Group. If in doubt, simply copy and paste the description into Google to find the name before booking.

Where to stay?

Where to Stay for Different Groups:

- **Solo Travelers**:
    - Hostels: Ideal for meeting other travelers and budget-friendly stays.
    - Boutique hotels or guesthouses: Offers a more personalized experience and a chance to connect with locals.
- **Couples**:
    - Romantic B&Bs: Provides a cozy and intimate atmosphere.
    - Boutique hotels: Offers luxury and privacy for a romantic getaway.
- **Families**:
    - Serviced apartments: Provides more space and flexibility for families.
    - Hotels with family-friendly amenities such as playgrounds or swimming pools.
- **Groups of Friends**:
    - Vacation rentals: Offers shared spaces and cost savings for larger groups.
    - Hostels with private rooms: Allows for group bookings while still having the option for privacy.
- **Business Travelers**:
    - Business hotels: Provides amenities like conference rooms, Wi-Fi, and proximity to business districts.
    - Serviced apartments: Offers more space and a home-like environment for longer stays.

Irish Bed and Breakfasts are often cheaper when booked direct or on these two websites:

IrishTourism.com: This website specifically focuses on travel to Ireland and includes a section dedicated to bed and breakfast accommodations. You can browse listings by region, view photos, and find contact information to make reservations.

GoIreland.com: GoIreland.com offers a selection of bed and breakfast accommodations across Ireland, with options to search by location, price range, and amenities. They also provide travel guides and tips for exploring the country.

Ireland is divided into 32 counties. Here's a brief overview of what each offers any potential drawbacks, and the average starting price of hotels:

County	What Each Offers Travelers	Cons	Average Starting Price of Hotels
Carlow	Scenic countryside, ancient ruins, outdoor activities	Limited public transportation options	€70-100
Cavan	Lakes, forests, outdoor recreation	Limited nightlife and dining options	€60-90
Clare	Cliffs of Moher, Burren National Park, traditional music	Crowded tourist attractions during peak season	€80-120
Cork	Scenic coastline, historic cities, culinary delights	Traffic congestion in urban areas	€80-150
Donegal	Wild Atlantic Way, Slieve League Cliffs, rugged landscapes	Remote locations may require longer travel times	€70-120
Dublin	Historic sites, vibrant nightlife, cultural attractions	High cost of accommodation and dining	€100-200
Galway	Connemara National Park, Aran Islands, Galway City	Crowded streets and traffic congestion in Galway City	€80-150
Kerry	Ring of Kerry, Killarney National Park, Dingle Peninsula	Crowded tourist attractions during peak season	€90-150
Kildare	Historic castles, equestrian activities, shopping	Limited public transportation options	€80-120
Kilkenny	Medieval architecture, Kilkenny Castle, cultural festivals	Crowded tourist attractions during peak season	€90-130
Laois	Historic sites, outdoor activities, scenic drives	Limited nightlife and dining options	€70-100
Leitrim	Glencar Waterfall, Shannon-Erne Waterway, scenic landscapes	Limited public transportation options	€60-90
Limerick	King John's Castle, River Shannon, cultural events	Some areas may have higher crime rates	€80-120
Longford	Corlea Trackway Visitor Center, outdoor activities	Limited tourist attractions and amenities	€60-80
Louth	Historic sites, scenic coastlines, medieval town of Drogheda	Limited public transportation options	€80-120
Mayo	Croagh Patrick, Achill Island, Westport House	Remote locations may require longer travel times	€70-120
Meath	Bru na Boinne, Trim Castle, scenic countryside	Limited public transportation options	€80-120

Monaghan	Castle Leslie Estate, Patrick Kavanagh Centre, outdoor activities	Limited nightlife and dining options	€60-90
Offaly	Birr Castle, Slieve Bloom Mountains, outdoor recreation	Limited public transportation options	€70-100
Roscommon	Lough Key Forest Park, Strokestown Park, outdoor activities	Limited tourist attractions and amenities	€60-90
Sligo	Benbulbin, Yeats Country, Strandhill Beach	Limited public transportation options	€70-120
Tipperary	Rock of Cashel, Glen of Aherlow, scenic landscapes	Limited public transportation options	€80-120
Waterford	Waterford Greenway, Copper Coast Geopark, historic sites	Limited nightlife and dining options	€80-120
Westmeath	Belvedere House, Athlone Castle, outdoor activities	Limited public transportation options	€70-100
Wexford	Hook Lighthouse, Irish National Heritage Park, sandy beaches	Crowded tourist attractions during peak season	€80-120
Wicklow	Wicklow Mountains, Glendalough, Powerscourt Estate	Crowded tourist attractions during peak season	€80-130
Northern Ireland	Giant's Causeway, Carrick-a-Rede Rope Bridge, Belfast	Political tensions in some areas, potential for isolated incidents	£70-120

Enjoy the Finest Five-star Hotels for a 10th of the Cost

If you travel during the peak season or during a major event, you can still enjoy the finest hotels in Ireland for a 10th of the normal cost. With a day pass, you can enjoy all the amenities that the hotel has to offer, including the pool, spa, gym, and included lunches at fine restaurants. This can be a great way to relax and unwind for a day without having to spend money on an overnight stay.

Here are some of the best luxury day passes Ireland hotels:

The Marker Hotel - Dublin
Starting Price: From €50 per person
Amenities: Access to the rooftop terrace with stunning views of Dublin, outdoor infinity pool, sauna, and fitness center. The hotel also offers dining options and spa services.

The Shelbourne, Autograph Collection - Dublin
Starting Price: From €50 per person
Amenities: Access to the hotel's fitness center and swimming pool. Guests can also relax in the spa or enjoy dining options at the hotel's restaurants and bars.

Adare Manor - County Limerick
Starting Price: From €100 per person
Amenities: Access to the luxurious grounds of Adare Manor, including gardens, walking trails, and lakes. Guests can also enjoy dining options and recreational activities such as golf and falconry.

The Europe Hotel & Resort - County Kerry
Starting Price: From €75 per person
Amenities: Access to the hotel's leisure center with indoor pool, sauna, steam room, and fitness center. Guests can also explore the hotel's landscaped gardens and enjoy dining options overlooking Lake Lough Leane.

Ashford Castle - County Mayo
Starting Price: From €150 per person
Amenities: Access to the stunning grounds of Ashford Castle, including gardens, woodlands, and walking trails. Guests can also enjoy dining options and activities such as falconry and boat trips on Lough Corrib.

It's important to note that availability and pricing for day passes may vary depending on the hotel and time of year, so it's always a good idea to check directly with the hotel for the most up-to-date information and to pre-book before your trip to avoid disappointment.

TOP TIP: AVOID The weekend price hike

Hotel prices skyrocket during weekends in peak season (June, July, August and December). If you can, get out of Ireland for the weekend you'll save thousands on luxury hotels. For example a room at a popular five-star hotel costs $80 a night during the week when blind-booking. That price goes to $400 a night for Saturday's and Sundays. Amazing nearby weekend trips are featured further on and planning those on the weekends could easily save you a ton of money and make your trip more comfortable by avoiding crowds.

Cheapest Hotel Chains in Ireland:

- **Travelodge**: Known for budget-friendly accommodations with basic amenities, including locations in Dublin, Cork, Galway, and other cities across Ireland.
- **Premier Inn**: Offers affordable stays with comfortable rooms and convenient locations, including properties in Dublin and Belfast.
- **Ibis Budget**: Provides budget-friendly accommodations with modern facilities, including locations in Dublin, Cork, and other major cities.
- **Jurys Inn**: Offers mid-range accommodations at competitive prices with multiple properties in Dublin, Cork, Galway, and other cities.
- **Maldron Hotel**: Known for its affordable yet comfortable stays, with various locations across Ireland, including Dublin, Cork, and Galway.

Strategies to Book Five-Star Hotels for Two-Star Prices in Ireland

Use Time

There are two ways to use time. One is to book in advance. Three months will net you the best deal, especially if your visit coincides with an event. The other is to book on the day of your stay. This is a risky move, but if executed well, you can lay your head in a five-star hotel for a 2-star fee.

Before you travel to Ireland, check for big events using a simple google search 'What's on in Ireland', if you find no big events drawing travellers, risk showing up with no accommodation booked (If there are big events on demand exceeds supply and you should avoid using this strategy). If you don't want to risk showing up with no accommodation booked, book a cheap accommodation with free-cancellation.

Before I go into demand-based pricing, take a moment to think about your risk tolerance. By risk, I am not talking about personal safety. No amount of financial savings is worth risking that. What I am talking about is being inconvenienced. Do you deal well with last-minute changes? Can you roll with the punches or do you freak out if something changes? Everyone is different and knowing yourself is the best way to plan a great trip. If you are someone that likes to have everything pre-planned using demand-based pricing to get cheap accommodation will not work for you.

Demand-based pricing

Be they an Airbnb host or hotel manager; no one wants empty rooms. Most will do anything to make some revenue because they still have the same costs to cover whether the room is occupied or not. That's why you will find many hotels drastically slashing room rates for same-day bookings.

How to book five-star hotels for a two-star price

You will not be able to find these discounts when the demand exceeds the supply. So if you're visiting during the peak season, or during an event which has drawn many travellers again don't try this.

1. On the day of your stay, visit booking.com (which offers better discounts than Kayak and agoda.com). Hotel
Tonight individually checks for any last-minute bookings, but they take a big chunk of the action, so the better deals come from booking.com.
2. The best results come from booking between 2 pm and 4 pm when the risk of losing any revenue with no occupancy is most pronounced, so algorithms supporting hotels slash prices. This is when you can find rates that are not within the "lowest publicly visible" rate.

3. To avoid losing customers to other websites, or cheapening the image of their hotel most will only offer the super cheap rates during a two hour window from 2 pm to 4 pm. Two guests will pay 10x difference in price but it's absolutely vital to the hotel that neither knows it.

Takeaway: To get the lowest price book on the day of stay between 2 pm and 4 pm and extend your search radius to include further afield hotels with good transport connections.

There are several luxury hotels outside of Dublin's city center that offer good transport connections to the city, as well as easy access to other nearby attractions. Here are a few options to consider:

- **Castleknock Hotel**: Nestled in the leafy suburb of Castleknock, this modern hotel offers spacious rooms, a championship golf course, and a wellness center with a swimming pool and gym facilities. Starting prices: around €90 per night.
- **Talbot Hotel Stillorgan**: Located in the south Dublin suburb of Stillorgan, Talbot Hotel Stillorgan boasts stylish rooms, a leisure center, and easy access to nearby attractions such as Dundrum Town Centre and the Leopardstown Racecourse. Starting prices: around €80 per night.
- **Red Cow Moran Hotel**: Situated on the outskirts of Dublin, near the M50 motorway, Red Cow Moran Hotel offers contemporary accommodations with convenient access to Dublin city center and Dublin Airport. Starting prices: around €70 per night.

These are just a few examples of luxury hotels outside of Ireland's city center with good transport connections to the city and opportunities for last-minute discounts.

Priceline Hack to get a Luxury Hotel on the Cheap

Priceline.com has been around since 1997 and is an incredible site for sourcing luxury Hotels on the cheap in Ireland.

Priceline have a database of the lowest price a hotel will accept for a particular time and date. That amount changes depending on two factors:

1. Demand: More demand high prices.
2. Likelihood of lost revenue: if the room is still available at 3pm the same-day prices will plummet.

Obviously they don't want you to know the lowest price as they make more commission the higher the price you pay.

They offer two good deals to entice you to book with them in Ireland. And the good news is neither require last-minute booking (though the price will decrease the closer to the date you book).

'Firstly, 'price-breakers'. You blind book from a choice of three highly rated hotels which they name. Pricebreakers, travelers are shown three similar, highly-rated hotels, listed under a single low price.' After you book they reveal the name of the hotel.

Secondly, the 'express deals'. These are the last minute deals. You'll be able to see the name of the hotel before you book.

To find the right luxury hotel for you at a cheap price you should plug in the neighbourhoods you want to stay in, an acceptable rating (4 or 5 stars), and filter by the amenities you want.

You can also get an addition discount for your Ireland hotel by booking on their dedicated app.

How to trick travel Algorithms to get the lowest hotel price

Do not believe anyone who says changing your IP address to get cheaper hotels or flights does NOT work. If you don't believe us, download a Tor Network and search for flights and hotels to one destination using your current IP and then the tor network (a tor browser hides your IP address from algorithms. It is commonly used by hackers). You will receive different prices.

The price you see is a decision made by an algorithm that adjusts prices using data points such as past bookings, remaining capacity, average demand and the probability of selling the room or flight later at a higher price. If knows you've searched for the area before ip the prices high. To circumvent this, you can either use a different IP address from a cafe or airport or data from an international sim. I use a sim from Three, which provides free data in many countries around the world. When you search from a new IP address, most of the time, and particularly near booking you will get a lower price. Sometimes if your sim comes from a 'rich' country, say the UK or USA, you will see higher rates as the algorithm has learnt people from these countries pay more. The solution is to book from a local wifi connection - but a different one from the one you originally searched from.

Best Areas to Stay in an Airbnb in Ireland

While Airbnb's don't come with daily cleanings and room-service, they can be luxury. Ireland has a diverse range of neighborhoods, each with its own unique character and charm. Here are some areas that are great for cheap Airbnb stays:

Ireland's villages can offer travelers a charming and budget-friendly way to experience the country's rich culture and stunning landscapes. Among the cheapest villages in Ireland to rent an Airbnb, one may consider picturesque locations such as Sneem in County Kerry. Nestled along the Ring of Kerry, Sneem boasts breathtaking scenery of mountains and sea, along with colorful village streets lined with quaint shops and cozy pubs. Airbnb options here often include traditional Irish cottages or rooms in local homes, providing an authentic and affordable experience for travelers.

Similarly, in County Clare, the village of Doolin offers affordable Airbnb accommodations amidst the rugged beauty of the Wild Atlantic Way. Famous for its lively music scene and proximity to the Cliffs of Moher, Doolin provides an ideal base for exploring the stunning coastline and nearby attractions. Travelers can find budget-friendly options ranging from cozy cottages to guesthouses, all within walking distance of the village's pubs and restaurants.

Further north, the village of Clifden in Connemara, County Galway, offers affordable Airbnb rentals amidst the stunning landscapes of Ireland's west coast. Surrounded by rugged mountains and scenic coastal drives, Clifden provides an excellent starting point for exploring Connemara National Park and nearby beaches. Airbnb options here often include charming cottages or apartments with views of the surrounding countryside, providing a peaceful and budget-friendly retreat for travelers.

In County Donegal, the village of Ardara offers affordable Airbnb accommodations amidst the stunning landscapes of Ireland's northwest. Known for its traditional music and friendly locals, Ardara provides a warm welcome to travelers seeking an authentic Irish experience on a budget. Airbnb options here range from cozy cottages to guesthouses, all within easy reach of the village's pubs and shops.

Here are some more villages known for offering relatively affordable Airbnb options:

- **Clifden, County Galway**: Located in Connemara, Clifden offers stunning landscapes and is known for its reasonable Airbnb prices, particularly in the off-peak season.
- **Dingle, County Kerry**: Dingle is a picturesque village on the southwest coast of Ireland, famous for its traditional music, charming pubs, and scenic views. It often has affordable Airbnb options, especially outside of peak tourist times.
- **Westport, County Mayo**: Westport is a vibrant town with a range of shops, restaurants, and outdoor activities nearby, including the stunning Croagh Patrick mountain. It's known for having reasonably priced Airbnb accommodations.

- **Kenmare, County Kerry**: Nestled between the Ring of Kerry and the Ring of Beara, Kenmare is a quaint town with plenty of affordable Airbnb options, making it a great base for exploring the surrounding countryside.
- **Bantry, County Cork**: Bantry is a picturesque market town situated on the shores of Bantry Bay. It offers a range of affordable Airbnb accommodations and easy access to the nearby Sheep's Head Peninsula and Beara Peninsula.
- **Bundoran, County Donegal**: Known as a popular surfing destination, Bundoran offers a range of budget-friendly Airbnb options, particularly for travelers looking to enjoy outdoor activities along the Wild Atlantic Way.

Dangerous areas to approach with caution in Ireland

While Ireland is generally a safe and welcoming country for travelers, there are a few areas where visitors should exercise caution. In Dublin, the North Inner City, including areas around O'Connell Street and Parnell Street, have higher levels of street crime, including theft and opportunistic crime. Travelers should be vigilant and avoid walking alone late at night in these areas, particularly in poorly lit or deserted streets.

In Cork, around the McCurtain Street and Lower Glanmire Road areas, also have higher crime rates, particularly related to theft and anti-social behavior. While these areas are generally safe during the day, travelers should exercise caution, especially after dark, and avoid displaying valuables or walking alone in secluded areas.

In Limerick, the Moyross and Southill estates, have reputations for higher levels of crime and social deprivation. Travelers should exercise caution when visiting these areas and avoid walking alone, especially after dark. It's advisable to stay in well-populated areas and use reputable taxi services when traveling at night.

In Belfast, the Donegall Road and Shankill Road areas, have higher levels of sectarian tension and occasional incidents of violence, particularly around significant dates or events. Travelers should be aware of their surroundings and avoid getting involved in discussions or activities related to local politics or sectarian issues.

How to get last-minute discounts on owner rented properties

In addition to Airbnb, you can also find owner rented rooms and apartments on www.vrbo.com or HomeAway or a host of others.

Nearly all owners renting accommodation will happily give renters a "last-minute" discount to avoid the space sitting empty, not earning a dime.

Go to Airbnb or another platform and put in today's date. Once you've found something you like start the negotiating by asking for a 25% reduction. A sample message to an Airbnb host might read:

Dear HOST NAME,

I love your apartment. It looks perfect for me. Unfortunately, I'm on a very tight budget. I hope you won't be offended, but I wanted to ask if you would be amenable to offering me a 25% discount for tonight, tomorrow and the following day? I see that you aren't booked. I can assure you, I will leave your place exactly the way I found it. I will put bed linen in the washer and ensure everything is clean for the next guest. I would be delighted to bring you a bottle of wine to thank you for any discount that you could offer.

If this sounds okay, please send me a custom offer, and I will book straight away.

YOUR NAME.

In my experience, a polite, genuine message like this, that proposes reciprocity will be successful 80% of the time. Don't ask for more than 25% off, this person still has to pay the bills and will probably say no as your stay will cost them more in bills than they make. Plus starting higher, can offend the owner and do you want to stay somewhere, where you have offended the host?

In Practice

To use either of these methods, you must travel light. Less stuff means greater mobility, everything is faster and you don't have to check-in or store luggage. If you have a lot of luggage, you're going to have fewer of these opportunities to save on accommodation. Plus travelling light benefits the planet - you're buying, consuming, and transporting less stuff.

Blind-booking

If your risk tolerance does not allow for last-minute booking, you can use blind-booking. Many hotels not wanting to cheapen their brand with known low-prices, choose to operate a blind booking policy. This is where you book without knowing the name of the hotel you're going to stay in until you've made the payment. This is also sometimes used as a marketing strategy where the hotel is seeking to recover from past issues. I've stayed in plenty of blind book hotels. As long as you choose 4 or 5 star hotels, you will find them to be clean, comfortable and safe. priceline.com, Hot Rate® Hotels and Top Secret

Hotels (operated by lastminute.com) offer the best deals.

Hotels.com Loyalty Program

This is currently the best hotel loyalty program with hotels in Ireland. The basic premise is you collect 10 nights and get 1 free. hotels.com price match, so if booking.com has a cheaper price you can get hotel.com, to match. If you intend to travel more than ten nights in a year, its a great choice to get the 11th free.

Don't let time use you.

Rigidity will cost you money. You pay the price you're willing to pay, not the amount it requires a hotel to deliver. Therefore if you're in town for a big event, saving money on accommodation is nearly impossible so in such cases book three months ahead.

How to trick travel Algorithms to get the lowest hotel price

Do not believe anyone who says changing your IP address to get cheaper hotels or flights does NOT work. If you don't believe us, download a Tor Network and search for flights and hotels to one destination using your current IP and then the tor network (a tor browser hides your IP address from algorithms. It is commonly used by hackers). You will receive different prices.

The price you see is a decision made by an algorithm that adjusts prices using data points such as past bookings, remaining capacity, average demand and the probability of selling the room or flight later at a higher price. If knows you've searched for the area before ip the prices high. To circumvent this, you can either use a different IP address from a cafe or airport or data from an international sim. I use a sim from Three, which provides free data in many countries around the world. When you search from a new IP address, most of the time, and particularly near booking you will get a lower price. Sometimes if your sim comes from a 'rich' country, say the UK or USA, you will see higher rates as the algorithm has learnt people from these countries pay more. The solution is to book from a local wifi connection - but a different one from the one you originally searched from.

Unique Accommodation in Ireland

Camping Sites

- Wild Camping: Free (where permitted)
- Campsites: Starting from €10 - €20 per night for a pitch.
- Glamping Pods: Starting from €50 - €100 per night for a basic pod.

Wild camping, also known as free camping, is a popular and budget-friendly way to experience the stunning natural landscapes of Ireland. While wild camping is legal in many parts of Ireland, it's essential to follow certain guidelines and respect the environment to ensure a safe and enjoyable experience. One of the biggest advantages of wild camping is that it can save you a significant amount on accommodation, especially during the summer months when traditional campsites can be expensive and crowded.

While wild camping is generally permitted in remote and rural areas, it's essential to obtain landowner permission if camping on private land. Additionally, some areas may have restrictions or regulations in place to protect sensitive habitats or wildlife, so be sure to research and adhere to any guidelines provided by local authorities or land management agencies.

When packing for a wild camping trip in Ireland, it's essential to bring the necessary gear and supplies to ensure your comfort and safety. Some essential items to pack include a sturdy tent, sleeping bag, sleeping pad or mattress, cooking stove and utensils, food and water supplies, appropriate clothing and footwear for the weather conditions, a first aid kit, and a map and compass or GPS device for navigation. Additionally, it's crucial to practice Leave No Trace principles by minimizing your impact on the environment and packing out all trash and waste.

While wild camping is permitted in many areas of Ireland, there are also numerous campsites and designated camping areas available for those who prefer more amenities and facilities. These campsites often provide access to toilets, showers, and other amenities, making them suitable for travelers who prefer a more comfortable camping experience. Some popular campsites in Ireland include Glenmalure Hostel and Campsite in County Wicklow, Mannix Point Camping and Caravan Park in County Kerry, and Roundwood Caravan and Camping Park in County Wicklow.

When choosing a location for wild camping in Ireland, consider factors such as accessibility, terrain, and proximity to water sources. Some of the best places for wild camping in Ireland include remote mountainous areas, coastal cliffs and beaches, and scenic lakeside or riverside spots. Be sure to choose a flat and level campsite away from hazards such as steep slopes, unstable rocks, or areas prone to flooding. Additionally, it's essential to set up camp at least 200 meters away from roads, buildings, and water sources to minimize your impact on the environment and ensure your safety and privacy.

Farm Stays

- Farmhouses or B&Bs: Starting from €40 - €80 per night per person, including breakfast.
- Working Farm Stays: Starting from €50 - €100 per night, offering hands-on farm experiences.

Farm Stay	Location	Pros	Cons	Starting Price (per night)
Rock Farm	Slane, County Meath	- Eco-friendly accommodations in a scenic rural setting	- Limited availability may require booking well in advance	€80-100
Claddagh Farm	Dingle, County Kerry	- Stunning views of the Dingle Peninsula	- Basic amenities and rustic accommodations	€60-80
Kilmokea Country Manor	Campile, County Wexford	- Beautiful historic estate with gardens and orchards	- Remote location may require a car for transportation	€90-120
The Three Towers Eco House and Organic Kitchen	Loughrea, County Galway	- Sustainable living experience with organic meals	- Shared facilities and communal living may not suit all travelers	€70-90
Kilgraney House	Bagenalstown, County Carlow	- Gourmet dining featuring farm-to-table cuisine	- Higher-end pricing compared to other farm stays	€120-150
Kilgraney Organic Farm	Borris, County Carlow	- Authentic farm experience with opportunities to participate in farm activities	- Limited availability and booking restrictions may apply	€70-100
Green Farmhouse	Derry, County Londonderry	- Peaceful rural setting with access to scenic walks and bike trails	- Limited dining options and amenities nearby	£50-70
The Schoolhouse at Annaghmakerrig	Cootehill, County Cavan	- Historic setting with cultural and artistic activities	- Limited availability and may be booked for residencies or events	€80-100
Clonabreany House	Crossakiel, County Meath	- Elegant accommodations in a restored country estate	- Higher-end pricing compared to other farm stays	€120-150
Inish Beg Estate	Baltimore, County Cork	- Luxury estate with gardens, woodlands, and walking trails	- Higher-end pricing compared to other farm stays	€150-200

Castles

- Castle Hotels: Starting from €100 - €200 per night for a unique castle experience.
- Castle Stays: Some castles offer budget-friendly dormitory or hostel-style accommodations starting from €20 - €50 per night.

Castle	Location	Pros	Cons	Starting Price (per night)
Ashford Castle	Cong, County Mayo	- Luxurious accommodations in a historic castle setting	- Higher-end pricing compared to other accommodations	€300-500
Dromoland Castle	Newmarket-on-Fergus, County Clare	- Elegant rooms and suites with scenic views	- Higher-end pricing compared to other accommodations	€250-400
Lough Eske Castle	Donegal Town, County Donegal	- Beautiful castle hotel surrounded by picturesque landscapes	- Remote location may require a car for transportation	€200-350
Waterford Castle Hotel	Waterford City, County Waterford	- Island location with stunning views of the River Suir	- Limited dining and entertainment options on the island	€150-250

Ballynahinch Castle	Recess, County Galway	- Tranquil setting in Connemara National Park	- Remote location may require a car for transportation	€200-350
Kilkea Castle	Castledermot, County Kildare	- Historic castle with modern amenities and activities	- Limited dining and entertainment options nearby	€200-300
Castle Leslie Estate	Glaslough, County Monaghan	- Unique accommodations in a historic estate with extensive grounds	- Remote location may require a car for transportation	€200-350
Barberstown Castle	Straffan, County Kildare	- Charming castle hotel with period features and elegant dining options	- Limited availability for castle tours and events	€150-250
Ballyseede Castle	Tralee, County Kerry	- Authentic castle experience with cozy rooms and traditional Irish hospitality	- Limited dining options and amenities nearby	€150-250
Dungiven Castle	Dungiven, County Londonderry	- Historic castle with elegant accommodations and scenic views	- Limited dining and entertainment options nearby	£100-200

While many castles in Ireland primarily offer luxurious accommodations, there are a few that provide more budget-friendly options, including dormitory or hostel-style stays. Here are some places where you can find such accommodations:

- **Kinlay Hostel Galway** - While not a castle per se, Kinlay Hostel is located within a historic building in the heart of Galway City. The hostel provides dormitory-style accommodations with shared facilities and offers budget-friendly rates starting from around €20 - €50 per night.
- **Rowantree Hostel** - Located in the village of Ennis, County Clare, Rowantree Hostel is situated within a historic building and offers dormitory-style accommodations. Prices typically range from €20 - €50 per night, making it a budget-friendly option for travelers exploring the Wild Atlantic Way.
- **Ballyhoura Hostel** - Situated near the Ballyhoura Mountains in County Limerick, Ballyhoura Hostel offers dormitory-style accommodations in a picturesque rural setting. Prices start from around €20 - €50 per night, making it an affordable choice for those seeking budget-friendly accommodations.
- **Sleepzone Hostel Galway City** - Another hostel option in Galway City, Sleepzone Hostel offers dormitory-style accommodations within walking distance of Galway's attractions. Prices typically range from €20 - €50 per night, making it a convenient and affordable choice for travelers.
- **Dublin International Youth Hostel** - Located in a historic building near Dublin's city center, this hostel offers dormitory-style accommodations with budget-friendly rates starting from around €20 - €50 per night. It provides easy access to Dublin's attractions and is a popular choice for budget-conscious travelers.

Universities

During the summer months, several universities in Ireland offer dormitory accommodation for short-term stays, catering to tourists, conference attendees, and individuals visiting the country for various purposes. While availability and prices may vary depending on the university and specific dates, here are some examples of universities in Ireland that rent out dorm rooms in the summer, along with starting prices:

- **University College Dublin (UCD):**
    - Description: UCD offers modern and comfortable accommodation options on its campus, conveniently located just a short distance from Dublin city center. The university typically rents out student residences during the summer months.
    - Starting Price: Prices for dormitory rooms at UCD during the summer start at approximately €40-€50 per night for single rooms, with shared bathroom facilities. Prices may vary depending on the specific residence and room type.
- **University of Limerick (UL):**
    - Description: UL's campus is situated on the banks of the River Shannon, offering scenic surroundings and a range of amenities. The university provides accommodation options for short-term stays during the summer, including student residences and apartment-style accommodation.
    - Starting Price: Prices for dormitory rooms at UL during the summer typically start at around €30-€40 per night for single rooms, with shared facilities. Apartment-style accommodation may be available at higher rates.
- **Trinity College Dublin (TCD):**
    - Description: Trinity College Dublin, located in the heart of Dublin city center, offers accommodation in its historic campus during the summer months. The university provides a variety of room types, including single and twin rooms, with shared bathroom facilities.
    - Starting Price: Prices for dormitory rooms at TCD vary depending on the room type and facilities. Starting prices for single rooms typically range from €50-€70 per night, with discounts available for longer stays.
- **National University of Ireland, Galway (NUIG):**
    - Description: NUIG's campus is situated along the banks of the River Corrib, offering picturesque views and convenient access to Galway city center. The university offers accommodation options for short-term stays during the summer, including student residences and apartments.
    - Starting Price: Prices for dormitory rooms at NUIG during the summer start at approximately €30-€40 per night for single rooms, with shared facilities. Apartment-style accommodation may be available at higher rates.
- **University College Cork (UCC):**
    - Description: UCC's campus is located near Cork city center, offering easy access to local attractions and amenities. The university provides accommodation options for visitors during the summer months, including student residences and apartments.
    - Starting Price: Prices for dormitory rooms at UCC during the summer typically start at around €30-€40 per night for single rooms, with shared facilities. Apartment-style accommodation may be available at higher rates.

Saving money on Food in Ireland

If you walk-in to any Ireland restaurant without planning you can easily walk out with a bill for 50 euros plus per person, so it pays to know how to eat well cheaply.

Use 'Too Good To Go'

Ireland offers plenty of food bargains; if you know where to look. Thankfully the app 'Too Good to Go' is turning visitors into locals by showing them exactly where to find the tastiest deals. In Ireland you can pick up a $15 buy of baked goods for $2.99. You'll also find lots of fish and meat dishes on offer in Ireland from notable restaurants, which would normally be expensive.

How it works? You pay for a magic bag on the app and simply pick it up from the bakery or restaurant during the time they've selected. You can find extremely cheap breakfast, lunch, dinner and even groceries this way. Simply download the app and press 'my current location' to find the deals near you in Ireland. .What's not to love about driving down food waste?

Here are the best Too Good to Go Magic Bags in Ireland:

- **Cocu** - Cocu is a health-conscious café offering salads, sandwiches, and other freshly prepared meals. With Too Good To Go, you can expect to receive a selection of their delicious salads, wraps, or sandwiches at a discounted price.
- **Chopped** - Chopped is a chain of salad bars offering a variety of fresh salads, wraps, and smoothies. Through Too Good To Go, you may receive a selection of their signature salads, wraps, or healthy snacks.
- **Pita Pit** - Pita Pit offers a range of fresh and customizable pita sandwiches, salads, and smoothies. With Too Good To Go, you may receive a selection of their freshly made pitas or salads at a discounted price.
- **The Rolling Donut** - The Rolling Donut is a popular spot for freshly made donuts in a variety of flavors. Through Too Good To Go, you may receive a selection of their delicious donuts at a discounted price, allowing you to indulge in a sweet treat for less.
- **Insomnia Coffee Company** - Insomnia is a well-known chain of coffee shops offering a range of hot and cold beverages, as well as sandwiches and snacks. With Too Good To Go, you may receive a selection of their baked goods, sandwiches, or other snacks at a discounted price.
- **Sprout & Co** - Sprout & Co is a health-focused café offering a range of salads, wraps, juices, and smoothies made with fresh, organic ingredients. Through Too Good To Go, you may receive a selection of their nutritious and delicious offerings at a discounted price.
- **Itsa Bagel** - Itsa Bagel is a café specializing in freshly baked bagels with a variety of toppings and fillings. With Too Good To Go, you may receive a selection of their freshly baked bagels, sandwiches, or salads at a discounted price.

An oft-quoted parable is 'There is no such thing as cheap food. Either you pay at the cash registry or the doctor's office'. This dismisses the fact that good nutrition is a choice; we all make every-time we eat. Cheap eats are not confined to hotdogs and kebabs. The great thing about using Too Good To Go is you can eat nutritious food cheaply: fruits, vegetables, fish and nut dishes are a fraction of their supermarket cost.

Japan has the longest life expectancy in the world. A national study by the Japanese Ministry of Internal Affairs and Communications revealed that between January and May 2019, a household of two spent on average ¥65,994 a month, that's $10 per person per day on food. You truly don't need to spend a lot to eat nutritious food. That's a marketing gimmick hawkers of overpriced muesli bars want you to believe.

Opt for early bird dinner menus

You'll see them all over the Ireland. Three courses for under €10.

Use delivery services on the cheap.

Take advantage of local offers on food delivery services. Most platforms including Uber Eats and Just Eat offer $10 off the first order in Ireland.

Cheapest supermarkets in Ireland

In Ireland, several supermarket chains offer competitive prices and are known for being budget-friendly. Here are some of the cheapest supermarkets in Ireland:

- **Aldi**: Aldi is known for its low prices and focus on discount groceries. They offer a range of own-brand products at competitive prices, including fresh produce, meat, and household essentials.
- **Lidl**: Similar to Aldi, Lidl is a discount supermarket chain offering affordable groceries and household items. They often have weekly specials on various products, including fresh produce, bakery items, and pantry staples.
- **Tesco**: While not exclusively a discount supermarket, Tesco is one of the largest grocery retailers in Ireland and offers a range of budget-friendly options. They have regular promotions and discounts on own-brand products, as well as a value range for budget-conscious shoppers.
- **SuperValu**: SuperValu is a popular supermarket chain in Ireland that focuses on offering competitive prices on a wide range of products. They often have special offers and discounts, particularly on fresh produce and Irish-made products.
- **Londis**: Londis is a convenience store chain that offers a selection of affordable groceries, including own-brand products and household essentials. While prices may vary depending on the location, Londis stores generally offer competitive prices for everyday items.
- **Centra**: Centra is another convenience store chain that provides a range of affordable groceries and household items. They often have promotions and special offers on selected products, making them a budget-friendly option for shoppers.

You can also find these supermarkets on Too Good To Go so instead of spending $50 on groceries, you can spend $5.

Cheapest Take Away Coffee Ireland

A great way to start your morning in Ireland is to grab a fresh cup of coffee at one of the many great take away coffee shops in town but it doesn't have to set you back €6 like Starbucks will.

Insomnia coffee offer coffees from €2. This chain of restaurants has several locations around cities and they have decent loyalty discounts.

IKEA
Ikea offers free coffee (with a FAMILY CARD). To access the restaurant, you must first go to the IKEA store at Hullenbergweg 2 in south-east Ireland. From there, take the metro 50 or 54 to station Bullewijk. Its menu includes a 1 euro breakfast, which includes a boiled egg, croissant, jam, and filter coffee.

20 cheap eats in Ireland and where to eat them

Here are 20 cheap eats in Ireland along with tips on where to eat them:

- **Fish and Chips**:
  - Tip: Look for local fish and chip shops near coastal towns or fishing villages for fresh and affordable options.
- **Irish Breakfast (Full Irish)**:
  - Tip: Visit local cafes or B&Bs for budget-friendly versions of this hearty meal, often available all day.
- **Irish Stew**:
  - Tip: Seek out traditional pubs or local eateries in rural areas for authentic and affordable Irish stew.
- **Boxty**:
  - Tip: Visit local cafes or farmers' markets for budget-friendly boxty, often served with various fillings like bacon or cheese.
- **Colcannon**:
  - Tip: Look for traditional Irish restaurants or pubs for affordable colcannon, especially during festive occasions like Halloween.
- **Seafood Chowder**:
  - Tip: Coastal towns and fishing villages often offer affordable seafood chowder in pubs or seafood shacks.
- **Bacon and Cabbage**:
  - Tip: Seek out traditional Irish restaurants or local pubs for budget-friendly versions of this classic dish.
- **Potato Bread (Farl)**:
  - Tip: Look for bakeries or cafes specializing in Irish cuisine for affordable potato bread served with butter or jam.
- **Soda Bread**:
  - Tip: Visit local bakeries or farmers' markets for freshly baked soda bread at affordable prices.
- **Barmbrack**:
  - Tip: Visit local bakeries or supermarkets for budget-friendly barmbrack, a traditional Irish fruitcake.
- **Irish Sausage Roll**:
  - Tip: Look for bakeries or delis offering freshly baked Irish sausage rolls at affordable prices.
- **Coddle**:
  - Tip: Seek out traditional pubs or local eateries in Dublin for budget-friendly coddle, a hearty stew-like dish.
- **Boxty Pancakes**:
  - Tip: Visit local cafes or breakfast spots for budget-friendly boxty pancakes served with sweet or savory toppings.
- **Cheese and Onion Sandwich**:
  - Tip: Look for cafes or delis offering affordable cheese and onion sandwiches, a simple yet satisfying option.

- **Apple Tart**:
    - Tip: Visit local bakeries or farmers' markets for budget-friendly apple tarts made with fresh, seasonal apples.
- **Guinness Beef Pie**:
    - Tip: Seek out traditional Irish pubs or restaurants for affordable Guinness beef pies, often served with mashed potatoes.
- **Irish Lamb Curry**:
    - Tip: Look for Indian restaurants or curry houses offering budget-friendly Irish lamb curry with a local twist.
- **Irish Apple Crumble**:
    - Tip: Visit local cafes or bakeries for budget-friendly Irish apple crumble served with custard or ice cream.
- **Black Pudding**:
    - Tip: Seek out local butcher shops or food markets for affordable black pudding, often served as part of a full Irish breakfast.
- **Irish Coffee**:
    - Tip: Visit traditional Irish pubs or cafes for budget-friendly Irish coffee, a warming blend of coffee, whiskey, sugar, and cream.

Traditional Irish Cuisine:
- **Irish Stew**: A hearty dish made with lamb or beef, potatoes, carrots, onions, and herbs.
- **Boxty**: A type of potato pancake, often served with various toppings or fillings.
- **Colcannon**: Mashed potatoes mixed with cabbage or kale, butter, and sometimes scallions.
- **Soda Bread**: A quick bread made with flour, baking soda, salt, and buttermilk.
- **Seafood**: Ireland's coastal location means fresh seafood is abundant, with favorites like smoked salmon, Dublin Bay prawns, and oysters.
- **Irish Breakfast**: A traditional Irish breakfast typically includes bacon, sausages, eggs, black and white pudding, tomatoes, mushrooms, and toast.
- **Guinness**: While not a food, Guinness is an integral part of Irish culture and is often enjoyed alongside a meal or as an ingredient in cooking.

Modern Irish Cuisine:
- **Farm-to-Table Restaurants**: Many Irish restaurants emphasize locally-sourced ingredients, showcasing the country's diverse agricultural produce.
- **Creative Fusion**: Chefs are blending traditional Irish ingredients with international flavors, resulting in innovative dishes that reflect Ireland's multicultural influences.
- **Craft Beer and Distilleries**: Ireland has a booming craft beer and whiskey scene, with many restaurants offering locally-produced brews and spirits.

Types of Restaurants:

Pub/Bar:
- Pubs in Ireland often serve food alongside drinks, ranging from traditional pub grub to gourmet cuisine.
- Casual atmosphere, ideal for socializing and enjoying live music.

Fine Dining Restaurants:

- Upscale establishments offering refined cuisine, often with a focus on seasonal and locally-sourced ingredients.
- Elegant ambiance, attentive service, and extensive wine lists.

Casual Dining/Cafés:
- Relaxed settings offering a diverse range of dishes, from sandwiches and salads to soups and hearty meals.
- Perfect for a leisurely meal or a quick bite on the go.

Dining Etiquette:
- **Tipping**: While not obligatory, tipping around 10-15% is appreciated for good service.
- **Reservations**: Recommended for fine dining restaurants, especially during peak hours.
- **Table Manners**: It's customary to wait until everyone at the table has been served before beginning to eat. Bread and butter are usually served as a starter.
- **Politeness**: Saying "please" and "thank you" to servers is considered polite and appreciated.

Popular Irish Seafood:

1. **Salmon**: Ireland is known for its high-quality salmon, which is often smoked or served fresh. Look for Irish smoked salmon on menus or in local markets for a delicious and iconic Irish seafood experience.

2. **Oysters**: Ireland's pristine coastal waters are home to some of the finest oysters in the world. Enjoy them freshly shucked with a squeeze of lemon or a dash of Tabasco sauce for a briny and indulgent treat.

3. **Mussels**: Irish mussels are plump, flavorful, and abundant along the coast. They're often steamed with white wine, garlic, and herbs or served in a rich tomato broth for a comforting and satisfying meal.

4. **Brown Crab**: Brown crab, also known as Dublin Bay crab, is a prized delicacy in Ireland. Enjoy it in dishes like crab claws with garlic butter or in a creamy seafood chowder for a taste of coastal luxury.

5. **Haddock and Cod**: Ireland's fishing industry also produces excellent white fish like haddock and cod. Look for fish and chips shops or seafood restaurants offering these fresh catches for a classic Irish seafood meal.

How to Eat Irish Seafood Cheaply:

1. **Visit Local Fish Markets**: Skip the fancy restaurants and head to local fish markets or seafood stalls where you can purchase fresh seafood at more affordable prices. You can often find deals on less popular or lesser-known varieties of fish and shellfish.

3. **Lunch Specials and Early Bird Menus**: Many seafood restaurants offer lunch specials or early bird menus with discounted prices compared to dinner service. Take advantage of these deals to enjoy a seafood meal at a more affordable rate.

4. **Explore Coastal Towns**: Visit coastal towns and villages where seafood is abundant and often more reasonably priced than in urban areas. Look for family-owned seafood restaurants or fishmongers catering to locals and visitors alike.

5. **Seasonal Specials**: Keep an eye out for seasonal seafood specials, as prices may fluctuate depending on the availability of certain species. Visit during peak seasons for seafood like crab or mussels to enjoy them at their freshest and most affordable.

6. **BYOB Restaurants**: Look for restaurants that allow you to bring your own alcohol (BYOB), as this can help reduce the overall cost of dining out. Pair your favorite seafood dishes with a bottle of wine or beer from a local shop for a budget-friendly meal.

Irish Beer Culture

Beer has a long and storied history in Ireland, dating back thousands of years to ancient Celtic times. Early Irish beer, known as ale, was brewed using traditional methods and ingredients such as barley, water, and wild herbs. With the arrival of Christianity in Ireland, monasteries played a significant role in the brewing industry, refining brewing techniques and producing high-quality beers for religious ceremonies and everyday consumption.

In the Middle Ages, brewing became more widespread across Ireland, with towns and cities developing their own breweries and brewing traditions. Irish beer styles such as stout, porter, and red ale emerged during this period, catering to the tastes of local communities. By the 18th century, Dublin had become a major brewing center, with iconic breweries like Guinness, founded in 1759, shaping the city's brewing legacy and exporting Irish stout around the world.

Today, Ireland boasts a thriving craft beer scene alongside its renowned breweries, with microbreweries and brewpubs producing a diverse range of innovative and flavorful beers. From traditional Irish stouts to experimental IPAs and sour ales, Irish beer continues to evolve while honoring its rich brewing heritage.

Traditional Irish Beer Styles:

- **Stout**: Ireland is renowned for its stouts, with Guinness being the most famous example. Stouts are characterized by their dark color, creamy texture, and roasted malt flavors.
- **Red Ale**: Irish red ales are known for their reddish-brown hue, malty sweetness, and subtle hop bitterness.
- **Irish Pale Ale**: Ales brewed with Irish malt and hops, featuring a balanced flavor profile with notes of caramel, citrus, and floral hops.
- **Irish Craft Beer**: In recent years, Ireland has seen a surge in craft breweries producing a wide variety of beer styles, from IPAs and porters to sour ales and barrel-aged beers.

Beer Drinking Etiquette:

- **Cheers:** When clinking glasses for a toast, it's customary to make eye contact and say "Sláinte" (pronounced slawn-cha), which means "health" or "cheers" in Irish.
- **Buying Rounds:** In Ireland, it's common for friends to take turns buying rounds of drinks for each other, known as "shouting a round."

Interesting Facts:

- **Arthur Guinness**: Arthur Guinness signed a 9,000-year lease for the St. James's Gate brewery in Dublin in 1759, laying the foundation for the iconic Guinness brand.
- **Black and Tan**: A popular beer cocktail made by layering stout and pale ale, named after the paramilitary force that operated during the Irish War of Independence.
- **Irish Beer Day**: The first Thursday in September is celebrated as "National Beer Day" in Ireland, honoring the country's rich brewing heritage.

Ireland's cheapest beer tours:

- **Franciscan Well Brewery (Cork):**
  - Starting Price: €15.00
  - Description: Take a guided tour of the Franciscan Well Brewery in Cork, where you'll learn about the brewing process and the history of the brewery. The tour includes tastings of Franciscan Well beers.
- **Smithwick's Experience (Kilkenny):**
  - Starting Price: €15.00
  - Description: Explore the history of Smithwick's, one of Ireland's oldest beer brands, on a guided tour of the Smithwick's Experience in Kilkenny. Learn about the brewing process, enjoy interactive exhibits, and sample Smithwick's beers.
- **Hooker Brewery (Galway):**
  - Starting Price: €10.00
  - Description: Visit the Hooker Brewery in Galway for a behind-the-scenes tour of the brewing facilities. Learn about the brewing process, ingredients, and the history of Hooker beers. The tour includes tastings of Hooker beers.

Irish Whiskey Culture

The Irish word for whiskey, "uisce beatha," translates to "water of life," reflecting the reverence and importance placed on this beloved spirit. Monks in Irish monasteries are credited with the early distillation of whiskey, using barley-based mash and copper pot stills to produce a potent and flavorful spirit.

By the late Middle Ages, whiskey production had become more widespread across Ireland, with distilleries emerging in towns and regions throughout the country. Irish whiskey gained popularity both domestically and internationally, becoming known for its smoothness, complexity, and distinctive flavor profile.

In the 19th century, Irish whiskey experienced a golden age, with Dublin emerging as a global hub for whiskey production and innovation. The city was home to numerous distilleries, including iconic names such as Jameson, Powers, and Bushmills, which exported Irish whiskey to markets around the world.

However, the Irish whiskey industry faced significant challenges in the 20th century, including Prohibition in the United States, economic downturns, and the decline of traditional distilleries. Despite these setbacks, Irish whiskey has experienced a remarkable resurgence in recent years, with new distilleries opening and old ones being revived. Today, Irish whiskey is celebrated for its craftsmanship, heritage, and unique flavor profile, attracting whiskey enthusiasts from around the globe to savor the spirit of Ireland.

Traditional Irish Whiskey Styles:

- **Single Malt**: Made from 100% malted barley and distilled in pot stills, resulting in a smooth and complex flavor profile.
- **Single Pot Still**: A uniquely Irish style made from a mix of malted and unmalted barley, offering spicy, fruity, and creamy notes.
- **Blended Whiskey**: Blends of malt and grain whiskeys, offering a balanced and approachable flavor profile.
- **Cask Finish**: Some Irish whiskeys are finished in various casks, such as sherry, port, or wine casks, adding layers of complexity to the final product.

Whiskey Tasting Etiquette:

- **Glassware**: Use a tulip-shaped glass or a Glencairn whiskey glass to concentrate aromas and enhance the tasting experience.
- **Nosing**: Take time to smell the whiskey before tasting, noting the aromas of fruits, spices, oak, and caramel.
- **Sipping**: Take small sips, allowing the whiskey to coat your palate and fully appreciate its flavors.
- **Adding Water**: Some whiskey enthusiasts add a few drops of water to their whiskey to open up the flavors and release more aromas.

Types of Distilleries:

Large Distilleries:

- Established distilleries like Jameson, Bushmills, and Midleton produce iconic Irish whiskey brands known around the world.
- Many large distilleries offer guided tours where visitors can learn about the whiskey-making process, from mashing and fermentation to distillation and maturation.

Craft Distilleries:
- Ireland has seen a resurgence in craft distilleries in recent years, producing small-batch and artisanal whiskeys.
- Craft distilleries often offer personalized tours and tastings, allowing visitors to interact with the distillers and learn about their unique production methods

Interesting Facts:

- **Oldest Licensed Distillery**: Bushmills Distillery in County Antrim is the oldest licensed distillery in Ireland, dating back to 1608.
- **Triple Distillation**: Many Irish whiskeys undergo triple distillation, resulting in a smoother and lighter spirit compared to Scotch whisky, which is typically distilled twice.
- **Powerscourt Distillery**: Located in County Wicklow, Powerscourt Distillery offers a luxury whiskey experience, including guided tours, tastings, and access to the historic Powerscourt Estate.

Ireland's cheapest whiskey tours

- **Tullamore DEW Visitor Centre (Tullamore):**
    - Starting Price: €14.00
    - Description: Explore the history and heritage of Tullamore DEW Irish whiskey at the Tullamore DEW Visitor Centre. The tour includes a guided visit to the distillery, interactive exhibits, and a whiskey tasting.
- **Bushmills Distillery (County Antrim):**
    - Starting Price: £10.00
    - Description: Visit the Bushmills Distillery in County Antrim for a guided tour of one of Ireland's oldest distilleries. Learn about the whiskey-making process, explore the distillery's historic buildings, and enjoy a tasting of Bushmills whiskey.
- **Old Bushmills Distillery (County Antrim):**
    - Starting Price: £10.00
    - Description: Discover the secrets of Bushmills Irish whiskey on a guided tour of the Old Bushmills Distillery. Learn about the craftsmanship and tradition behind Bushmills whiskey, and enjoy a tasting of their award-winning spirits.
- **Midleton Distillery (County Cork):**
    - Starting Price: €20.00
    - Description: Take a guided tour of the Midleton Distillery, home to some of Ireland's most renowned whiskey brands, including Jameson. Learn about the whiskey-making process, explore the distillery's warehouses, and enjoy a tasting of premium Irish whiskeys.

First-day Itinerary

Morning:

- **Arrival at Dublin Airport:** Arrive at Dublin Airport and make your way to your accommodation in the city center. Consider staying in the Temple Bar area for a lively atmosphere and convenient access to many attractions.
- **Breakfast in a Café:** Start your day with a hearty Irish breakfast at a local café or restaurant. Enjoy traditional dishes like Irish bacon, sausage, black pudding, eggs, and grilled tomatoes, accompanied by a cup of freshly brewed tea or coffee.
- **Visit Trinity College:** After breakfast, head to Trinity College, Ireland's oldest university. Take a guided tour of the campus and visit the iconic Long Room in the Old Library, home to the famous Book of Kells, an illuminated manuscript dating back to the 9th century.

Midday:

- **Explore Dublin Castle:** Walk to Dublin Castle, a historic fortress located in the heart of the city. Join a guided tour to learn about its fascinating history and explore the State Apartments, Chapel Royal, and Gothic Revival-style gardens.
- **Lunch in Temple Bar:** Head to the lively Temple Bar district for lunch. Explore the cobblestone streets lined with colorful pubs, restaurants, and shops. Enjoy a traditional Irish meal like fish and chips or a hearty stew, accompanied by a pint of Guinness or a glass of Irish whiskey.

Afternoon:

- **Stroll along the River Liffey:** Take a leisurely stroll along the banks of the River Liffey, Dublin's main waterway. Admire the historic bridges, bustling quaysides, and iconic landmarks like the Ha'penny Bridge and the Custom House.
- **Visit St. Stephen's Green:** Spend some time relaxing in St. Stephen's Green, a beautiful Victorian park located in the city center. Explore its manicured lawns, colorful flowerbeds, tranquil ponds, and charming pathways.

Evening:

- **Dinner and Traditional Music:** In the evening, enjoy dinner at a local restaurant or pub. Choose from a wide range of dining options, from modern Irish cuisine to international fare. After dinner, experience the vibrant Irish music scene with a traditional music session at a nearby pub, where you can listen to live performances of traditional tunes played on fiddles, tin whistles, and bodhráns.
- **Return to Accommodation:** After a full day of exploring Dublin's sights and sounds, return to your accommodation for a well-deserved rest and relaxation, ready to embark on more adventures in Ireland the next day.

The Best of Ireland in One week

Day 1: Arrival in Dublin

- Arrive in Dublin and check into a budget-friendly yet centrally located accommodation, such as a hostel or budget hotel. Starting price: €50 per night.
- Spend the day exploring Dublin's highlights on foot or using public transportation, including Trinity College, Temple Bar, Dublin Castle, and St. Stephen's Green.
- Enjoy a pint of Guinness at a traditional pub in Temple Bar, soaking in the lively atmosphere without overspending. Price: €5-7.

Day 2: Dublin to Galway

- Take a bus or train from Dublin to Galway, enjoying scenic views of the Irish countryside along the way. Starting price: €15-20.
- Check into a budget-friendly guesthouse or Airbnb in Galway city center. Starting price: €60 per night.
- Explore Galway's charming streets, colorful shops, and lively pubs. Visit Eyre Square, Spanish Arch, and Galway Cathedral.
- Treat yourself to a seafood dinner at one of Galway's affordable yet delicious restaurants. Price: €15-20.

Day 3: Day Trip to Connemara

- Take a bus tour or rent a bike to explore the stunning Connemara region, known for its rugged landscapes, pristine beaches, and picturesque villages.
- Visit Kylemore Abbey and Gardens, a beautiful estate set against the backdrop of the Twelve Bens mountain range. Admission price: €13.
- Explore Connemara National Park, where you can hike scenic trails and enjoy panoramic views of the Connemara wilderness. Free admission.

Day 4: Galway to Killarney

- Travel from Galway to Killarney by bus or train, admiring the scenery along the way. Starting price: €20-25.
- Check into a budget-friendly accommodation in Killarney town center, such as a guesthouse or budget hotel. Starting price: €50 per night.
- Explore Killarney National Park, home to stunning lakes, forests, and mountains. Visit Muckross House and Gardens, admission price: €9.
- Enjoy a traditional Irish music session at a local pub in Killarney. Price: Free (with purchase of a drink).

Day 5: Ring of Kerry Tour

- Take a bus tour or rent a car to explore the scenic Ring of Kerry, one of Ireland's most iconic driving routes. Enjoy breathtaking views of mountains, coastline, and ancient ruins.
- Stop at picturesque villages along the way, such as Sneem, Waterville, and Cahersiveen. Explore local shops and cafes.

- Visit the Skellig Experience Visitor Center to learn about the history and wildlife of the Skellig Islands. Admission price: €5.

Day 6: Killarney to Cork

- Travel from Killarney to Cork by bus or train, enjoying the convenience of public transportation. Starting price: €15-20.
- Check into a budget-friendly accommodation in Cork city center, such as a hostel or budget hotel. Starting price: €50 per night.
- Explore Cork's vibrant English Market, where you can sample local delicacies and browse artisanal products. Free admission.
- Visit Cork City Gaol, a historic former prison turned museum. Admission price: €10.

Day 7: Cork to Dublin

- Travel back to Dublin from Cork by bus or train, reflecting on the memorable experiences of your week in Ireland. Starting price: €15-20.
- Spend your final day in Dublin exploring any remaining sights or indulging in last-minute shopping.
- Enjoy a farewell dinner at a cozy restaurant in Dublin, savoring the flavors of Irish cuisine one last time. Price: €20-25.

The Best of Ireland in Two weeks

Day 1-3: Dublin

- Arrive in Dublin and spend three days exploring the capital city.
- Visit Trinity College and see the Book of Kells.
- Explore Dublin Castle and its gardens.
- Wander through the vibrant streets of Temple Bar.
- Learn about Ireland's history at Kilmainham Gaol.
- Enjoy a pint of Guinness at the Guinness Storehouse.
- Take a day trip to Howth or Malahide for coastal views and fresh seafood.

Day 4-5: Galway

- Travel to Galway, known for its lively atmosphere and traditional music.
- Explore the colorful streets of Galway's Latin Quarter.
- Visit Eyre Square and the Spanish Arch.
- Take a day trip to the Aran Islands or the Cliffs of Moher.
- Sample fresh seafood at one of Galway's many restaurants.

Day 6-7: Connemara

- Discover the rugged beauty of Connemara National Park.
- Visit Kylemore Abbey and its stunning gardens.
- Explore the quaint villages of Clifden and Roundstone.
- Go hiking, fishing, or horseback riding in the Connemara countryside.

Day 8-9: County Kerry

- Drive or take a bus to County Kerry, stopping in charming villages along the way.
- Explore Killarney National Park and its famous lakes.
- Drive the scenic Ring of Kerry, stopping at viewpoints and historical sites.
- Visit the Skellig Islands, weather permitting, to see ancient monastic ruins and seabird colonies.

Day 10-11: County Cork

- Travel to Cork, Ireland's second-largest city.
- Explore the English Market and sample local delicacies.
- Visit the historic port town of Cobh, known for its maritime history.
- Take a day trip to the picturesque town of Kinsale for its colorful streets and gourmet food scene.
- Visit the Rock of Cashel and Cahir Castle on the way to Cork.

Day 12-13: County Clare

- Drive or take a bus to County Clare.
- Explore the Burren region, known for its unique karst landscape and ancient monuments.
- Visit the Cliffs of Moher, one of Ireland's most iconic natural attractions.
- Explore the charming villages of Doolin and Lahinch.

- Take a boat trip to the Aran Islands and experience traditional Irish culture.

Day 14: Return to Dublin

- Travel back to Dublin for your departure.
- Spend your last day shopping for souvenirs or visiting any attractions you missed.
- Enjoy a farewell dinner in Dublin, reminiscing about your two weeks of adventure in Ireland.

Snapshot: How to have a $10,000 trip to Ireland for $1,000

Cost saving	Information	Money-Saving Tips
Transportation	Public transportation (buses and trains) available, rental cars an option.	- Use public transportation where possible to save on rental and fuel costs. - Look for discounted transportation passes or fares for additional savings.
Accommodations	Hostels, guesthouses, budget hotels available.	- Consider staying in hostels or guesthouses for affordable accommodations. - Look for deals and discounts on booking platforms, especially for off-peak seasons.
Dining	Wide range of dining options, from pubs to restaurants.	- Opt for budget-friendly dining options such as local pubs or cafes. - Take advantage of lunch specials and early bird menus for discounted meals.
Attractions and Tours	Numerous attractions and tours available, some offering discounts for advance booking or group rates.	- Plan your itinerary in advance to take advantage of discounts for attractions and tours. - Look for combo tickets or passes for multiple attractions to save money.
Entertainment	Music sessions, festivals, cultural events, and outdoor activities abundant.	- Seek out free or low-cost entertainment options such as outdoor concerts or local festivals. - Check for discounted tickets or special offers for cultural events and performances.
Shopping	Variety of shopping experiences, from markets to boutiques.	- Shop at local markets or outlets for unique souvenirs at lower prices. - Look for sales, discounts, and tax-free shopping opportunities, especially in tourist areas.
Travel Insurance	Highly recommended for medical coverage, trip cancellations, and lost belongings.	- Compare prices and coverage options from different insurance providers to find the best value for your needs. - Consider purchasing an annual policy if you plan to travel frequently for potential long-term savings.
Off-peak Travel	Consider traveling during off-peak seasons for lower prices and fewer crowds.	- Research the best times to visit Ireland for lower prices on accommodations and attractions. - Be flexible with travel dates to take advantage of off-peak deals and discounts.
Local Deals and Discounts	Keep an eye out for special offers, promotions, and local discounts.	- Check tourism websites, visitor centers, and local publications for deals and discounts on attractions, dining, and activities. - Ask locals for recommendations on hidden gems and budget-friendly options in the area.

OUR SUPER CHEAP TIPS…

Here are our specific super cheap tips for enjoying a $10,000 trip to Ireland for just $1,000.

Cheapest route to Ireland from America

At the time of writing Aer Lingus and or Norse Atlantics Airways are flying to Ireland with a stop in Dublin for around $200 return.

How to Find Super Cheap Flights to Ireland

Luck is just an illusion. Anyone can find incredible flight deals. If you can be flexible you can save huge amounts of money. In fact, the biggest tip I can give you for finding incredible flight deals is simple: find a flexible job. Don't despair if you can't do that theres still a lot you can do.

Book your flight to Ireland on a Tuesday or Wednesday

Tuesdays and Wednesdays are the cheapest days of the week to fly. You can take a flight to Ireland on a Tuesday or Wednesday for less than half the price you'd pay on a Thursday Friday, Saturday, Sunday or Monday.

Start with Google Flights (but NEVER book through them)

I conduct upwards of 50 flight searches a day for readers. I use google flights first when looking for flights. I put specific departure but broad destination (e.g Europe) and usually find amazing deals.

The great thing about Google Flights is you can search by class. You can pick a specific destination and it will tell you which time is cheapest in which class. Or you can put in dates and you can see which area is cheapest to travel to.

But be aware Google flights does not show the cheapest prices among the flight search engines but it does offer several advantages

1. You can see the cheapest dates for the next 8 weeks. Other search engines will blackout over 70% of the prices.
2. You can put in multiple airports to fly from. Just use a common to separate in the from input.
3. If you're flexible on where you're going Google flights can show you the cheapest destinations.
4. You can set-up price tracking, where Google will email you when prices rise or decline.

Once you have established the cheapest dates to fly go over to skyscanner.net and put those dates in. You will find sky scanner offers the cheapest flights.

Get Alerts when Prices to Ireland are Lowest

Google also has a nice feature which allows you to set up an alert to email you when prices to your destination are at their lowest. So if you don't have fixed dates this feature can save you a fortune.

Baggage add-ons

It may be cheaper and more convenient to send your luggage separately with a service like sendmybag.com Often the luggage sending fee is cheaper than what the airlines charge to check baggage. Visit Lugless.com or luggagefree.com in addition to sendmybag.com for a quotation.

Loading times

Anyone who has attempted to find a cheap flight will know the pain of excruciating long loading times. If you encounter this issue use google flights to find the cheapest dates and then go to skyscanner.net for the lowest price.

Always try to book direct with the airline

Once you have found the cheapest flight go direct to the airlines booking page. This is advantageous in the current covid cancellation climate, because if you need to change your flights or arrange a refund, its much easier to do so, than via a third party booking agent.

That said, sometimes the third party bookers offer cheaper deals than the airline, so you need to make the decision based on how likely you think it is that disruption will impede you making those flights.

More flight tricks and tips

www.secretflying.com/usa-deals offers a range of deals from the USA and other countries. For example you can pick-up a round trip flight non-stop from from the east coast to johannesburg for $350 return on this site

Scott's cheap flights, you can select your home airport and get emails on deals but you pay for an annual subscription. A free workaround is to download Hopper and set search alerts for trips/price drops.

Premium service of Scott's cheap flights.
They sometime have discounted business and first class but in my experience they are few and far between.

JGOOT.com has 5 times as many choices as Scott's cheap flights.

kiwi.com allows you to be able to do radius searches so you can find cheaper flights to general areas.

Finding Error Fares

Travel Pirates (www.travelpirates.com) is a gold-mine for finding error deals. Subscribe to their newsletter. I recently found a reader an airfare from Montreal-Brazil for a $200 round trip (mistake fare!). Of course these error fares are always certain dates, but if you can be flexible you can save a lot of money.

Things you can do that might reduce the fare to Ireland:--
• Use a VPN (if the booker knows you booked one-way, the return fare will go up)
• Buy your ticket in a different currency

If all else fails…

If you can't find a cheap flight for your dates I can find one for you. I do not charge for this nor do I send affiliate links. I'll send you a screenshot of the best options I find as airlines attach cookies to flight links. To use this free service please review this guide and send me a screenshot of your review - with your flight hacking request. I aim to reply to you within 12 hours. If it's an urgent request mark the email URGENT in the subject line and I will endeavour to reply ASAP.

How to Find CHEAP FIRST-CLASS Flights to Ireland

Upgrade at the airport
Airlines are extremely reluctant to advertise price drops in first or business class tickets so the best way to secure them is actually at the airport when airlines have no choice but to decrease prices dramatically because otherwise they lose money. Ask about upgrading to business or first-class when you check-in. If you check-in online look around the airport for your airlines branded bidding system. KLM have terminals where you can bid on upgrades.

Use Air-miles

When it comes to accruing air-miles for American citizens **Chase Sapphire Reserve card** ranks top. If you put everything on there and pay it off immediately you will end up getting free flights all the time, aside from taxes.

Get 2-3 chase cards with sign up bonuses, you'll have 200k points in no time and can book with points on multiple airlines when transferring your points to them.

Please note, this is only applicable to those living in the USA. In the Bonus Section we have detailed the best air-mile credit cards for those living in the UK, Canada, Germany, Austria, Ireland and Australia.

Arriving

In Ireland, there are several airports serving different regions, with transportation options available to get from them to the city centers at varying prices. Here are the main airports in Ireland and some affordable transportation options to reach the city centers:

- **Dublin Airport (DUB)**:
    - Airlink Express Bus: Operated by Dublin Bus, the Airlink Express (routes 747 and 757) offers direct service from Dublin Airport to the city center, including stops at major hotels. Tickets start from around €6 one way.
    - Dublin Bus: Several regular bus routes connect Dublin Airport to the city center and surrounding areas. Single tickets start from around €3.
    - Taxis and Ride-Sharing: Taxis and ride-sharing services like Uber are available at Dublin Airport. Prices vary depending on the destination and time of day but typically start from €25 to €35 to the city center.
- **Cork Airport (ORK)**:
    - Aircoach: Aircoach operates a service from Cork Airport to Cork city center, with tickets starting from around €10 one way.
    - Bus Éireann: Bus Éireann operates several routes connecting Cork Airport to the city center and surrounding areas. Single tickets start from around €3.
    - Taxis and Ride-Sharing: Taxis and ride-sharing services are available at Cork Airport, with prices starting from around €15 to €25 to the city center.
- **Shannon Airport (SNN)**:
    - Bus Éireann: Bus Éireann operates a service from Shannon Airport to Limerick city center, with tickets starting from around €8 one way.
    - Taxis: Taxis are available at Shannon Airport, with prices starting from around €30 to €40 to Limerick city center.
- **Knock Airport (NOC)**:
    - Bus Éireann: Bus Éireann operates a service from Knock Airport to various destinations, including Galway and Sligo, with tickets starting from around €10 one way.
    - Taxis: Taxis are available at Knock Airport, with prices varying depending on the destination.
- **Belfast International Airport (BFS)**:
    - Airport Express 300: Airport Express 300 offers direct service from Belfast International Airport to Belfast city center, with tickets starting from around £8 one way.
    - Taxis and Ride-Sharing: Taxis and ride-sharing services are available at Belfast International Airport, with prices starting from around £30 to £40 to Belfast city center.

Getting Around

One of the first challenges you'll encounter is the sheer diversity of options available. From trains to buses to ferries, there's no shortage of ways to get around. But with so many choices, figuring out the most efficient route can feel like solving a complex puzzle. Should you hop on a train to Cork or catch a bus to Galway? And what about those scenic coastal routes that seem to beckon from every corner?

Then there's the issue of timing. Public transport schedules in Ireland can sometimes be a bit...fluid, let's say. Buses may run on "Irish time," which is to say they might arrive a few minutes early or fashionably late. And don't even get me started on trying to catch the last ferry to the Aran Islands - it's like a race against the setting sun, with no guarantees of making it onboard in time. Tthe challenges of traveling around Ireland with public transport are all part of the adventure. Yes, you may encounter the occasional hiccup or delay, but isn't that what makes the journey memorable? So pack your sense of humor, embrace the unpredictability of Irish Transportation Options:

- **Bus Services**:
    - **Bus Éireann**: National bus service connecting major cities and towns across Ireland.
    - **CityLink**: Offers intercity bus services between major cities and towns.
    - **Local Bus Services**: Operated by various companies in cities and towns, providing affordable transportation within urban areas.

- **Train Services**:
    - **Irish Rail (Iarnród Éireann)**: National train service connecting major cities and towns.
    - **DART (Dublin Area Rapid Transit)**: Commuter rail service serving Dublin and surrounding areas.
    - **LUAS**: Light rail system serving Dublin city and suburbs.

- **Ferries**:
    - **Irish Ferries** and **Stena Line**: Operate ferry services between Ireland and the UK, with frequent sailings and competitive prices.
    - **Interislander Ferries**: Connects Ireland to nearby islands such as the Aran Islands and Inishmore.

- **Bike Rentals**:
    - **Dublin Bike**: Public bike-sharing scheme available in Dublin city, with affordable rental rates for short trips. You can use the leap card to access them.

Travel Passes and Discounts:

- **Leap Card**:
    - Prepaid smart card offering discounted fares on buses, trains, and trams in Dublin and surrounding areas.
    - Available for purchase at various locations, including train stations, convenience stores, and online.

- **Rambler Tickets**:
    - Offered by Bus Éireann and Irish Rail, providing unlimited travel within specified zones for a set duration.
    - Available for 1-day, 3-day, and 7-day periods, offering flexibility for travelers.
- **Explorer Passes**:
    - Offered by Irish Rail and providing unlimited travel on certain routes for a set duration.
    - Available for different regions, such as the Dublin Area, Cork and Kerry, and the West of Ireland.
- **Student and Senior Discounts**:
    - Students and seniors are eligible for discounted fares on most public transportation services in Ireland.
    - Valid ID required to avail of these discounts.

Pass/Ticket	Starting Price	Benefits
Leap Visitor Card	€10	Unlimited travel on Dublin Bus, Luas (tram), and DART/Commuter Rail in Dublin for 1, 3, or 7 consecutive days
Explorer Ticket	€30	Unlimited travel on Irish Rail services for 1, 3, or 7 consecutive days
Dublin Bus Rambler	€7	Unlimited travel on Dublin Bus services for 1 day
Luas Day Saver	€7	Unlimited travel on Luas (tram) services for 1 day
Irish Rail Flexi-Pass	€100	10 single tickets valid for travel between any two destinations on Irish Rail services
Bus Éireann City Direct	€2.20 - €3.30 (varies)	Discounted fares for single journeys on Bus Éireann services within major cities
Student Leap Card	€10	Discounted fares for students on Dublin Bus, Luas, DART, and Commuter Rail services

Comparison of Transportation Costs:

Mode of Transportation	Cost (€)	Notes
Dublin Bus (Single Fare)	2.50	Valid for 90 minutes of travel
Leap Card (Daily Cap)	7.00	Maximum daily fare on Dublin Bus and LUAS
Irish Rail (Dublin-Cork)	19.99	Off-peak fare for one-way ticket
Intercity Bus (Galway-Dublin)	13.00	Standard single fare
Dublin Bike (Day Pass)	5.00	Unlimited 30-minute rides within 24 hours
Car Rental (Per Day)	30.00	Economy car rental, excluding fuel and insurance

Tips for Cheap Travel:

- **Book in Advance**: Many transportation services offer discounted fares for bookings made in advance.
- **Off-Peak Travel**: Traveling during off-peak hours can result in lower fares and less crowded services.

- **Use Travel Apps**: Apps like Moovit, Rome2rio, and National Journey Planner provide real-time information on routes, schedules, and fares.
- **Explore Multi-Day Passes**: Consider purchasing multi-day passes or tickets for unlimited travel within a specified period.
- **Consider Alternative Modes**: Walking, cycling, and ridesharing can be cost-effective alternatives for short trips within cities and towns.

Irish Rail:

- **Book in Advance:** Irish Rail often offers discounted fares for tickets booked in advance, especially for off-peak travel times. Look out for online promotions and early bird discounts.
- **Check Timetables:** Be sure to check the timetable for your desired route in advance, as train frequencies can vary depending on the time of day and day of the week. Plan your journey accordingly to avoid long wait times.
- **Seat Reservations:** While seat reservations are not mandatory on Irish Rail, they can be a good idea, especially during peak travel times or on longer journeys. Consider reserving a seat for added comfort and peace of mind.
- **Pack Snacks:** While Irish Rail does have onboard catering services on some routes, it's a good idea to pack some snacks and drinks for your journey, especially if you have dietary restrictions or preferences.
- **Stay Informed:** Keep an eye on Irish Rail's official website and social media channels for service updates, disruptions, and special offers. Follow them on Twitter for real-time updates on delays and cancellations.

Bus Éireann:

- **Use Leap Card:** If you're traveling within Dublin or other major cities served by Bus Éireann, consider using a Leap Card for discounted fares. Leap Cards can also be used on other modes of public transportation, including Dublin Bus and Luas.
- **Arrive Early:** Bus stops can sometimes be crowded, especially during peak travel times. Arrive at your bus stop early to ensure you have enough time to board the bus and find a seat.
- **Check Routes:** Bus Éireann operates a comprehensive network of routes covering both urban and rural areas. Be sure to check the route map and timetable for your desired destination to ensure you catch the right bus.
- **Be Prepared for Delays:** While Bus Éireann strives to maintain punctuality, delays can sometimes occur due to traffic, roadworks, or other unforeseen circumstances. Allow extra time for your journey, especially if you have connecting travel arrangements.
- **Ask the Driver:** If you're unsure about which bus to take or where to get off, don't hesitate to ask the bus driver for assistance. They are usually happy to help and can provide information about routes, stops, and landmarks.

Carpooling

In Ireland, several carpooling services offer convenient and cost-effective transportation options for travelers. Here are some of the best carpooling services available:

- **GoCarShare:** GoCarShare connects drivers with spare seats to passengers heading in the same direction. Users can search for rides or offer seats for their journeys. The platform also emphasizes sustainability and reducing carbon emissions.
- **Liftshare:** Liftshare is a popular carpooling platform that matches drivers with passengers traveling on similar routes. Users can search for rides or offer seats in their vehicles, making it a flexible and eco-friendly transportation option.
- **BlaBlaCar:** BlaBlaCar is a leading long-distance carpooling service that connects drivers with empty seats to passengers traveling between cities or regions. The platform offers a range of rideshare options and allows users to read reviews and ratings before booking.
- **Carma Carpooling:** Carma Carpooling facilitates ridesharing for commuters and travelers, helping to reduce traffic congestion and carbon emissions. Users can find and share rides for regular commutes or one-time trips.
- **Gocarshare.ie:** Gocarshare.ie is another platform that matches drivers with passengers traveling to the same destination. Users can search for rides or offer seats in their vehicles, making it easy to find cost-effective transportation options.

Driving

- **Stay Left:** In Ireland, vehicles drive on the left side of the road. If you're accustomed to driving on the right, take extra caution when navigating roundabouts and turning at intersections.
- **Road Conditions:** While major highways are generally well-maintained, rural roads may be narrow and winding. Be prepared for single-lane roads, especially in remote areas, and watch out for potholes, particularly after heavy rainfall.
- **Speed Limits:** Speed limits in Ireland are measured in kilometers per hour (km/h). The standard speed limits are 50 km/h in urban areas, 80 km/h on rural roads, and 120 km/h on motorways. Pay attention to posted signs indicating speed limits, especially in built-up areas and near schools.
- **Traffic Signs:** Familiarize yourself with Irish road signs, which may differ from those in your home country. Pay close attention to warning signs, such as sharp bends, narrow roads, and pedestrian crossings.
- **Roundabouts:** Ireland has numerous roundabouts, especially in urban areas. Remember to give way to traffic approaching from your right and use your turn signals to indicate your intended exit.
- **Parking:** When parking in towns and cities, look for designated parking areas or pay-and-display parking meters. Avoid parking in restricted zones or blocking driveways to prevent fines or towing.
- **Toll Roads:** Some major highways in Ireland are tolled, including sections of the M1, M4, M6, M7, and M50 motorways. Be prepared to pay tolls at toll booths or via electronic tolling systems such as EazyPass or VideoPay.
- **Drink Driving Laws:** Ireland has strict laws regarding driving under the influence of alcohol. The legal blood alcohol limit is lower than in many other countries, so it's safest to avoid alcohol entirely if you plan to drive.
- **Weather Conditions:** Irish weather can be unpredictable, with rain and fog common throughout the year. Exercise caution when driving in adverse weather conditions, and reduce your speed to maintain control of your vehicle.
- **Local Etiquette:** Be courteous to other road users, including cyclists, pedestrians, and horse-drawn vehicles, which are more common in rural areas. Use your horn sparingly and always yield to emergency vehicles.
- **Car Rentals**:
    - **Budget Car Rental, Avis, Europcar, Hertz**, etc.: Major car rental companies operate in Ireland, offering competitive rates for short-term and long-term rentals.
    - **Comparison Websites**: Use websites like Rentalcars.com or Kayak to compare prices across multiple rental companies and find the best deals.

Top 20 attractions in Ireland with money saving tips

Attractions	Money-Saving Tips	Starting Prices
1. Guinness Storehouse	- Book tickets online in advance for discounts	Starting at €20
2. Cliffs of Moher	- Visit during off-peak hours to avoid crowds	Starting at €8
3. Dublin Castle	- Attend free events or festivals for free entry	Starting at €8
4. Trinity College	- Book combined tickets for discounts	Starting at €14
5. Temple Bar District	- Enjoy lunch specials or happy hour deals	Free (prices vary)
6. National Museum of Ireland		Free (donations appreciated)
7. Dublin Zoo	- Book tickets online for discounted rates	Starting at €17.50
8. St. Patrick's Cathedral	- Attend a service or concert for free entry	Starting at €8
9. Ring of Kerry	- Explore by public transport or join group tours	Free (prices vary)
10. Blarney Castle	- Book tickets online in advance for discounts	Starting at €18
11. Killarney National Park	- Take advantage of free admission	Free (donations appreciated)
12. Giant's Causeway	- Purchase visitor passes or combination tickets	Starting at £12.50
13. Glenveagh National Park	- Entry is free, bring a picnic for affordable dining	Free
14. Titanic Belfast	- Look for discounted tickets or combination packages	Starting at £19
15. Carrick-a-Rede Rope Bridge	- Visit during off-peak hours to avoid crowds	Starting at £9.90
16. Dark Hedges	- Explore independently on self-guided tours	Free
17. Derry/Londonderry	- Take advantage of free walking tours or explore independently	Free
18. Glendalough	- Entry to the visitor center is free, guided tours may have fees	Free
19. Powerscourt Estate	- Book online for discounts, enjoy free gardens entry	Starting at €12.50
20. Bunratty Castle	- Look for combined tickets or family discounts	Starting at €18

The Major Attractions Minus the crowds

To enjoy Ireland minus the crowds, consider visiting top attractions during less busy times such as early mornings, weekdays, or during the off-peak season. Here are some recommendations for visiting popular attractions with fewer crowds:

Cliffs of Moher:

- Beat the crowds by arriving early in the morning or visiting in the late afternoon when tour buses are less likely to be present. For an even quieter experience, plan your visit during the shoulder seasons of spring or autumn when tourist numbers are lower. Insider tip: Consider exploring the lesser-known Cliffs of Moher Coastal Walk for stunning views without the crowds.

Giant's Causeway:

- Escape the midday rush by visiting early in the morning or late in the afternoon. Another option is to plan your visit during the winter months when tourist numbers decrease significantly. Insider tip: Take advantage of the visitor center's audio guides or downloadable app to learn more about the geological marvels of the Giant's Causeway at your own pace.

Blarney Castle:

- Avoid the crowds by arriving early in the morning or later in the afternoon, especially on weekdays when tour groups are less common. Weekdays tend to be quieter than weekends, so plan your visit accordingly. Insider tip: To skip the line, purchase your tickets online in advance and consider exploring the picturesque Blarney Castle Gardens for a tranquil experience away from the crowds.

Trinity College and the Book of Kells:

- Start your day early and visit Trinity College in the morning on weekdays when there are fewer tourists, particularly during the academic year. Avoid weekends and peak tourist seasons to experience the Book of Kells and the Long Room Library with fewer crowds. Insider tip: Purchase tickets online in advance to bypass ticket queues and maximize your time exploring the historic campus.

Ring of Kerry:

- Beat the crowds by driving the Ring of Kerry in the early morning or late afternoon when tour buses are less prevalent. For a quieter experience, consider visiting during the shoulder seasons when roads and accommodations are less crowded. Insider tip: Take your time to explore hidden gems along the route, such as the Skellig Ring and the Kerry Cliffs, to escape the main tourist trail.

Dublin Castle:

- Plan your visit for weekday mornings when there are fewer tour groups and visitors. Avoid weekends and peak tourist seasons to experience Dublin Castle's history and architecture without the crowds. Insider tip: Consider joining a guided tour to learn more about the castle's fascinating past and hidden treasures, including the State Apartments and the Chapel Royal.

Kylemore Abbey:

- Enjoy a peaceful visit by arriving early in the day or later in the afternoon to avoid crowds. Midweek visits are typically quieter than weekends, offering a more serene experience. Insider tip: Explore the extensive Victorian Walled Garden and tranquil woodland trails surrounding Kylemore Abbey for a tranquil escape from the hustle and bustle.

Killarney National Park:

- Explore the park's natural beauty in the early morning or later in the evening to avoid peak visitor times. For a quieter experience, consider visiting during the off-peak season when crowds are sparse. Insider tip: Rent a bike or hike to lesser-known areas of the park, such as Torc Waterfall or the Gap of Dunloe, for a peaceful nature experience away from the main tourist attractions.

National Parks

Entry to Ireland's National Parks is mainly free! And there are often free guided tours. Check the individual parks websites for availability.

- **Killarney National Park**
    - **Pros:** Stunning scenery with lakes, mountains, and woodlands. Rich biodiversity, including rare and protected species. Abundance of hiking trails and outdoor activities.
    - **Cons:** Can get crowded during peak tourist seasons. Limited parking at popular trailheads.
    - **How to Get There:** Located near Killarney town in County Kerry. Accessible by car, bus, or train from major cities like Dublin and Cork.
    - **Starting Price:** Entry to the park is free, but there may be fees for parking and certain attractions within the park, such as Muckross House and Gardens (€9).
- **Connemara National Park**
    - **Pros:** Unspoiled landscapes with mountains, bogs, and coastal habitats. Scenic hiking trails with panoramic views. Rich cultural heritage and archaeological sites.
    - **Cons:** Limited facilities within the park. Weather can be unpredictable, with frequent rain and wind.
    - **How to Get There:** Located near Letterfrack in County Galway. Accessible by car, bus, or bike from Galway city.
    - **Starting Price:** Entry to the park is free. Guided tours and special events may have additional fees.
- **The Burren National Park**
    - **Pros:** Unique karst limestone landscape with rare flora and fauna. Fascinating geological formations and archaeological sites. Great opportunities for hiking, birdwatching, and photography.
    - **Cons:** Limited visitor facilities and amenities. Terrain can be rugged and challenging for some visitors.
    - **How to Get There:** Located in County Clare, near the villages of Ballyvaughan and Corofin. Accessible by car or bus from Galway or Limerick.
    - **Starting Price:** Entry to the park is free. Guided tours and educational programs may have additional fees.
- **Wicklow Mountains National Park**
    - **Pros:** Picturesque landscapes with mountains, lakes, and forests. Extensive network of hiking trails, including the Wicklow Way. Rich cultural heritage and historic sites.
    - **Cons:** Can be crowded on weekends and during peak hiking season. Weather can change rapidly, so come prepared.
    - **How to Get There:** Located in County Wicklow, south of Dublin. Accessible by car or bus from Dublin city.
    - **Starting Price:** Entry to the park is free. Some visitor centers and guided tours may have fees.

- **Glenveagh National Park**
    - **Pros:** Spectacular scenery with mountains, lakes, and gardens. Home to Glenveagh Castle and its beautiful gardens. Abundance of wildlife, including golden eagles and red deer.
    - **Cons:** Remote location may require a longer journey. Limited public transportation options.
    - **How to Get There:** Located in County Donegal, near the town of Letterkenny. Accessible by car, bus, or bike from Letterkenny.
    - **Starting Price:** Entry to the park is free. Guided tours of Glenveagh Castle and gardens have a fee (€6).

Ireland's fauna and flora, offer a rich tapestry of biodiversity, shaped by the island's diverse landscapes and temperate climate. Here's a guide to some of the remarkable wildlife found in Ireland:

Fauna:

The largest land mammal in Ireland, the red deer can be found in woodlands and upland areas across the country. A native species of hare found throughout Ireland, often spotted in open countryside and grasslands. Found in rivers, lakes, and coastal areas, the otter is a semi-aquatic mammal known for its playful behavior and sleek, waterproof fur. A beloved seabird with its distinctive colorful beak, the Atlantic puffin breeds in colonies along the coastal cliffs of western and northern Ireland. Frequently seen off the coast of Ireland, especially in the warmer summer months, common dolphins are known for their acrobatic displays and playful nature. An iconic breed of dog with a long history in Ireland, the Irish wolfhound is known for its size, strength, and gentle temperament. Native to Ireland, the red squirrel is a charming woodland dweller known for its russet-red fur and bushy tail. Commonly found along Ireland's coastlines, harbor seals can often be seen basking on rocks or swimming in the sea.

Flora:

A dominant species in Ireland's native woodlands, the Irish oak is a symbol of strength and endurance, with its distinctive acorns providing food for wildlife. Blanketing Ireland's uplands and heathlands with vibrant purple hues, common heather is a hardy plant that thrives in acidic soils. A delicate white flower that carpets Ireland's peatlands and boggy landscapes, bog cotton adds a touch of ethereal beauty to the countryside. With its bright yellow flowers and coconut-scented blooms, gorse is a common sight in Ireland's hedgerows, coastal cliffs, and heathlands. Growing in coastal areas and rocky shores, sea thrift produces clusters of pink or white flowers, adding splashes of color to Ireland's coastal landscapes. A native evergreen tree with dark green foliage and red berries, the Irish yew is often found in churchyards and ancient woodland sites. The Burren in County Clare is renowned for its unique limestone pavement landscape and diverse flora, including rare alpine and Mediterranean plants that thrive in its rocky terrain.

Castles

Carlow

Ireland's abundance of castles is rooted in its turbulent history, characterized by invasions, power struggles, and territorial disputes. Throughout the medieval period, Gaelic clans erected fortified strongholds to defend against rival factions and foreign invaders amidst political instability. The Anglo-Norman invasion in the 12th century further fueled castle construction, as Norman lords sought to consolidate control over Irish territories and suppress indigenous resistance.

Ireland is renowned for its storied castles, each with its own rich history and architectural beauty. Here are some of Ireland's most famous castles along with their entry fees:

- **Blarney Castle** (County Cork): Home to the famous Blarney Stone, visitors can explore the medieval fortress, lush gardens, and enjoy panoramic views from the top of the castle's tower. Entry Fee: €18 for adults, €8 for children.
- **Dublin Castle** (Dublin): This historic castle dates back to the 13th century and served as the seat of British rule in Ireland for centuries. Visitors can take guided

tours to learn about its fascinating history and explore the State Apartments, Chapel Royal, and gardens. Entry Fee: €8 for adults, €6 for seniors and students, €4 for children.
- **Kylemore Abbey** (County Galway): Set amidst the stunning Connemara landscape, Kylemore Abbey is a beautiful Victorian mansion with a captivating history. Visitors can tour the abbey, explore the Gothic church, and wander through the walled gardens. Entry Fee: €16 for adults, €13 for seniors and students, €10 for children.
- **Bunratty Castle and Folk Park** (County Clare): Experience medieval life at Bunratty Castle, where costumed guides lead tours through the atmospheric interiors. The adjacent Folk Park offers a glimpse into traditional Irish village life with reconstructed buildings and craft demonstrations. Entry Fee: €15 for adults, €9 for children.
- **Rock of Cashel** (County Tipperary): Perched atop a limestone hill, the Rock of Cashel is a striking archaeological site with a complex of medieval buildings including a round tower, cathedral, and high crosses. Visitors can explore the ruins and enjoy panoramic views of the surrounding countryside. Entry Fee: €8 for adults, €4 for seniors and students, €2 for children.
- **Cahir Castle** (County Tipperary): One of Ireland's largest and best-preserved castles, Cahir Castle boasts impressive defensive features and well-preserved interiors. Visitors can take self-guided tours to explore the castle's towers, halls, and courtyards. Entry Fee: €6 for adults, €4 for seniors and students, €2 for children.

Regions of Ireland

Ireland's Regions by most visited

County	Pros	Cons	Highlights
Dublin	Vibrant city life, rich history and culture, diverse attractions	Crowded tourist areas, high cost of living	Dublin City, Trinity College, Guinness Storehouse, Temple Bar, Phoenix Park
Galway	Stunning scenery, vibrant arts scene, traditional music	Can be busy during peak tourist season, weather can be unpredictable	Galway City, Connemara National Park, Cliffs of Moher, Kylemore Abbey, Galway Bay
Kerry	Breathtaking landscapes, charming towns and villages, outdoor activities	Crowded during summer months, narrow roads can be challenging for drivers	Killarney National Park, Ring of Kerry, Dingle Peninsula, Skellig Michael, Gap of Dunloe
Cork	Rich history and culture, beautiful coastline, gourmet food scene	Traffic congestion in Cork City, weather can be wet	Blarney Castle, Cork City, Kinsale, Cobh, Ring of Beara, Fota Wildlife Park
Clare	Stunning natural attractions, rich heritage and history, friendly locals	Crowded at popular attractions, weather can be unpredictable	Cliffs of Moher, The Burren, Bunratty Castle, Loop Head Peninsula, Doolin, Spanish Point
Donegal	Untouched landscapes, outdoor adventures, traditional music and culture	Remote locations may require longer travel times, weather can be unpredictable	Glenveagh National Park, Slieve League Cliffs, Donegal Town, Fanad Head Lighthouse, Donegal Bay

County	Pros	Cons	Highlights
Wicklow	Scenic beauty, outdoor activities, historic sites	Can be crowded on weekends, weather can be wet	Glendalough, Wicklow Mountains, Powerscourt Estate, Brittas Bay, Avoca
Mayo	Diverse landscapes, rich heritage, friendly locals	Limited public transportation options, remote areas may require longer travel times	Croagh Patrick, Westport, Achill Island, Cong, Ceide Fields, Wild Atlantic Way
Waterford	Rich history and culture, stunning coastline, outdoor activities	Crowded during peak tourist season, weather can be unpredictable	Waterford City, Copper Coast, Waterford Greenway, Dunmore East, Comeragh Mountains, Lismore Castle
Limerick	Historic sites, cultural attractions, picturesque countryside	Traffic congestion in Limerick City, limited public transportation options	King John's Castle, Lough Gur, Adare Village, Thomond Park, Foynes Flying Boat Museum, Shannon Estuary
Kilkenny	Medieval architecture, cultural heritage, lively arts scene	Can be crowded during peak tourist season, limited parking options	Kilkenny Castle, Rock of Cashel, Jerpoint Abbey, Dunmore Cave, Butler Gallery
Tipperary	Historic sites, scenic landscapes, outdoor activities	Limited public transportation options, weather can be unpredictable	Rock of Cashel, Cahir Castle, Mitchelstown Cave, Holycross Abbey, Glen of Aherlow
Wexford	Beautiful beaches, historic sites, family-friendly attractions	Crowded during summer months, weather can be unpredictable	Hook Lighthouse, Irish National Heritage Park, Johnstown Castle, Dunbrody Abbey, Kilmore Quay

County	Pros	Cons	Highlights
Sligo	Stunning scenery, cultural attractions, outdoor adventures	Limited public transportation options, weather can be wet	Benbulben, Strandhill, Carrowmore Megalithic Cemetery, Yeats Country, Lough Gill
Cavan	Peaceful countryside, outdoor activities, historical sites	Limited nightlife options, remote locations may require longer travel times	Marble Arch Caves, Cavan Burren Park, Belturbet, Crom Estate, Cuilcagh Boardwalk
Meath	Ancient history, historic sites, family-friendly attractions	Crowded during peak tourist season, limited public transportation options	Newgrange, Trim Castle, Hill of Tara, Bru na Boinne, Kells, Slane Castle
Kildare	Equestrian heritage, historic sites, shopping	Traffic congestion in some areas, limited nightlife options	Irish National Stud, Kildare Village Outlet Shopping, Curragh Racecourse, Castletown House, Donadea Forest Park,
Donegal	Untouched landscapes, outdoor adventures, traditional music and culture	Remote locations may require longer travel times, weather can be unpredictable	Glenveagh National Park, Slieve League Cliffs, Donegal Town, Fanad Head Lighthouse, Donegal Bay
Louth	Historic sites, scenic countryside, charming villages	Traffic congestion in Dundalk, limited public transportation options	Carlingford, Cooley Peninsula, Drogheda, Monasterboice, Mellifont Abbey
Laois	Rural landscapes, outdoor activities, heritage sites	Limited public transportation options, fewer tourist attractions compared to other counties	Portlaoise, Emo Court, Rock of Dunamase, Slieve Bloom Mountains, Heywood Gardens, Stradbally

County	Pros	Cons	Highlights
Carlow	Historic sites, outdoor activities, scenic beauty	Limited public transportation options, fewer tourist attractions compared to other counties	Altamont Gardens, Brownshill Dolmen, Carlow County Museum, Duckett's Grove, Borris House
Longford	Tranquil countryside, outdoor activities, heritage sites	Limited nightlife options, fewer tourist attractions compared to other counties	Corlea Trackway Visitor Centre, Strokestown Park House, Lough Ree, Ardagh Heritage Village, Royal Canal Greenway
Westmeath	Lakes and waterways, historic sites, outdoor activities	Limited public transportation options, fewer tourist attractions compared to other counties	Athlone, Lough Ree, Belvedere House and Gardens, Mullingar, Fore Abbey, Tullynally Castle
Offaly	Historic sites, outdoor activities, rural landscapes	Limited public transportation options, fewer tourist attractions compared to other counties	Birr Castle, Clonmacnoise, Tullamore, Slieve Bloom Mountains, Lough Boora Parklands, Charleville Castle
Roscommon	Lakes and rivers, outdoor activities, heritage sites	Limited public transportation options, fewer tourist attractions compared to other counties	Lough Key Forest Park, Strokestown Park House, Roscommon Town, Athlone Castle, Boyle Abbey, Arigna Mining Experience
Monaghan	Rural landscapes, historic sites, outdoor activities	Limited public transportation options, fewer tourist attractions compared to other counties	Castle Leslie Estate, Rossmore Forest Park, Clones, Patrick Kavanagh Centre, Lough Muckno

County	Pros	Cons	Highlights
Leitrim	Peaceful countryside, outdoor activities, scenic beauty	Limited public transportation options, fewer tourist attractions compared to other counties	Carrick-on-Shannon, Glencar Waterfall, Lough Allen, Drumshanbo, Leitrim Village, Sliabh an Iarainn
Kilkenny	Medieval architecture, cultural heritage, lively arts scene	Can be crowded during peak tourist season, limited parking options	Kilkenny Castle, Rock of Cashel, Jerpoint Abbey, Dunmore Cave, Butler Gallery
Tipperary	Historic sites, scenic landscapes, outdoor activities	Limited public transportation options, weather can be unpredictable	Rock of Cashel, Cahir Castle, Mitchelstown Cave, Holycross Abbey, Glen of Aherlow
Wexford	Beautiful beaches, historic sites, family-friendly attractions	Crowded during summer months, weather can be unpredictable	Hook Lighthouse, Irish National Heritage Park, Johnstown Castle, Dunbrody Abbey, Kilmore Quay
Fermanagh	Peaceful lakes, outdoor activities, historic sites	Limited public transportation options, fewer tourist attractions compared to other counties	Enniskillen, Marble Arch Caves, Crom Estate, Devenish Island, Belleek Pottery, Lough Erne
Antrim	Stunning coastline, historic sites, vibrant cities	Crowded during peak tourist season, traffic congestion in Belfast	Giant's Causeway, Belfast City, Carrick-a-Rede Rope Bridge, Titanic Belfast, Bushmills Distillery, Dunluce Castle

We will cover how to experience a luxury trip in each Irish city by those most visited.

Irish Slang

It will come in very useful to familiarise yourself with Irish slang words. Irish slang is a fascinating effusion of both English and Gaelic, reflecting the complex linguistic heritage and cultural dynamics of Ireland. Many Irish slang terms have direct Gaelic origins, either borrowed directly from the Irish language or Anglicized versions of Gaelic words. For example:

- **Craic**: From the Gaelic word "craic" meaning fun or entertainment.
- **Banshee**: From the Gaelic "bean sí" meaning woman of the fairy mound.
- **Sláinte**: A toast meaning health, often used when raising a glass.

- **Anglicized Gaelic Phrases**: Some Irish slang incorporates Gaelic phrases that have been adapted or Anglicized over time, blending seamlessly with English. For instance:
  - **Árd rí**: Pronounced "ard ree," meaning a big boss or important person.
  - **Bád**: Pronounced "bawd," meaning boat or ship.
  - **Craic agus ceol**: Pronounced "crack ah-gus kay-ol," meaning fun and music.

- **English Words with Irish Twist**: Many English words used in Irish slang are pronounced or spelled in a distinctively Irish manner, adding a Gaelic flair to the vocabulary. Examples include:
  - **Quare**: Meaning very or extremely, derived from the Irish word "quare" meaning strange or peculiar.
  - **Yoke**: Referring to a thing or object, with roots in both English and Irish usage.
  - **Bog**: Meaning marsh or wetland, derived from the Irish word "bog."

- **Phonetic Adaptations**: Some Gaelic-influenced slang terms are phonetic adaptations of English words, reflecting the Irish accent and pronunciation. For example:
  - **Sound**: Meaning good or reliable, pronounced with an Irish lilt.
  - **Cute hoor**: Referring to someone sly or cunning, with "hoor" being an adaptation of "whore" but used in a different context in Irish slang.

Greetings and Expressions:

- **How's the craic?** - A common way to ask how someone is doing or what's happening.
- **Grand** - Meaning good, okay, or fine.
- **Sound** - Used to describe someone who is reliable, trustworthy, or friendly.
- **Deadly** - Great, fantastic, amazing.

Everyday Phrases:

- **Feck** - A milder version of the word "fuck," often used for emphasis or frustration.
- **Craic** - Fun or enjoyment, as in "What's the craic?"
- **Gobshite** - A foolish or annoying person.
- **Eejit** - A fool or idiot.

- **Gas** - Funny or amusing.
- **Yoke** - A thing or object, often used when the name of the object is unknown or forgotten.
- **Cute hoor** - Someone who is sly or cunning, often used in a humorous or affectionate way.

Food and Drink:

- **Pint of the black stuff** - A pint of Guinness.
- **Tay** - Tea.
- **Biscuit** - Cookie.
- **Crisps** - Potato chips.
- **Munch** - Food, particularly snacks or a meal.

People and Relationships:

- **Your wan/your man** - Referring to someone whose name you don't know or can't remember.
- **Shift** - To kiss or make out with someone.
- **Ride** - A sexual encounter or an attractive person.
- **Banjaxed** - Broken or ruined.
- **Gobdaw** - A foolish or stupid person.

Weather and Nature:

- **Baltic** - Extremely cold.
- **Lashing** - Raining heavily.
- **Soft day** - Light rain or drizzle.
- **Gaff** - House or home.
- **Bog** - Marsh or wetland.

Good to know:

- **Craic house** - A place known for its lively atmosphere and entertainment. NOT a place to buy or use drugs.
- **Sesh** - A drinking session or party.
- **Mortified** - Extremely embarrassed or ashamed.
- **Scarlet** - Embarrassed or mortified.
- **Savage** - Excellent or impressive.

Now you know some of the lingo, we are ready to delve in to the cities, towns and regions and their bargains!

Dublin

Dublin, the capital city of Ireland, is a vibrant metropolis teeming with history, culture, and charm. Nestled on the east coast of Ireland, Dublin boasts a rich tapestry of architectural wonders, picturesque landscapes, and a lively atmosphere that captivates visitors from around the globe.

Steeped in history dating back over a millennium, Dublin has evolved from a Viking settlement to a medieval stronghold and eventually into the bustling cosmopolitan hub it is today. Its historic streets are lined with Georgian townhouses, medieval castles, and grand cathedrals, each telling stories of the city's past.

One of the city's most iconic landmarks is Dublin Castle, a symbol of Ireland's medieval heritage and former seat of British rule. Visitors can explore its opulent State Apartments, stroll through the scenic Dubh Linn Gardens, and delve into centuries of history within its walls.

Trinity College Dublin stands as a testament to Ireland's intellectual legacy, housing the famous Book of Kells and the stunning Long Room Library, a bibliophile's paradise adorned with countless rare manuscripts and literary treasures.

Dublin's vibrant cultural scene is exemplified by its lively pubs, where traditional Irish music fills the air and friendly locals gather for a pint of Guinness or a dram of whiskey. From the historic Temple Bar district to the trendy streets of St. Stephen's Green, Dublin offers a plethora of dining, shopping, and entertainment options to suit every taste and budget.

Insider Tips:

- **Public Transport**: Use the Leap Card for discounted fares on buses, trams, and the DART train system.
- **Free Attractions**: Take advantage of free attractions like parks, museums with free admission days, and walking tours.
- **Dining**: Look for early bird menus and lunch specials at restaurants to enjoy fine dining at lower prices.
- **Accommodation**: Book accommodations in advance and consider staying in budget-friendly hostels, guesthouses, or Airbnb properties.
- **City Passes**: Consider purchasing a Dublin Pass or Heritage Card for discounted entry to multiple attractions. examples of heritage sites in Dublin that typically accept the Heritage Card for entry:
- **Kilmainham Gaol**: This historic former prison, located west of Dublin city center, offers guided tours that provide insight into Ireland's political and social history, including its role in the struggle for independence.
- **Dublin Castle**: Situated in the heart of Dublin, Dublin Castle is a symbol of the city's history and heritage. Visitors can explore the castle grounds, State Apartments, and exhibitions showcasing Ireland's past and present.
- **Collins Barracks - National Museum of Ireland**: Collins Barracks is home to the National Museum of Ireland's Decorative Arts and History collection. Visitors can discover exhibitions on Irish design, decorative arts, and military history.
- **St. Audoen's Church**: This medieval church, located in Dublin's historic city center, is one of the oldest churches in the city. It features architectural highlights such as its Norman tower and medieval tombs.
- **Rathfarnham Castle**: This 16th-century castle, located south of Dublin city center, offers visitors the chance to explore its elegant interiors, landscaped gardens, and historical exhibitions.
- **Dublinia**: Located near Christ Church Cathedral, Dublinia is an interactive museum that explores Dublin's Viking and medieval past through immersive exhibits and experiences.
- **The Casino at Marino**: This 18th-century neoclassical villa, located north of Dublin city center, is renowned for its architectural beauty and intricate design. Visitors can explore the interior rooms and landscaped gardens.

Luxury but Affordable Accommodation in Dublin

Accommodation	Pros	Cons	Starting Price
The Morrison Hotel	Central location, modern amenities	Can be noisy due to city center	€100 per night
The Dean Hotel	Stylish design, rooftop bar	Limited dining options on-site	€120 per night
The Harding Hotel	Historic charm, friendly staff	Some rooms may be small	€80 per night

DIY TOUR

You don't need to do the hop on and hop off bus. You can see all the sights on the 123 route. A single journey on the Dublin Bus Route 123 typically costs around €3.30 for an adult ticket, with options for cheaper fares if you have a Leap Card or purchase a return ticket.

Now, let's embark on a virtual journey aboard the Dublin Bus Route 123. First up, we cruise through the vibrant streets of O'Connell Street, Dublin's bustling main thoroughfare. Look out for the towering Spire of Dublin, a modern architectural marvel soaring 120 meters into the sky. Its sleek design and striking presence make it a must-see landmark.

Next, we pass by the historic General Post Office (GPO), a symbol of Irish independence and resilience. During the Easter Rising of 1916, the GPO served as the headquarters of the rebels, who bravely proclaimed Ireland's independence from British rule. The bullet holes on its façade are a reminder of the courage and sacrifice of those who fought for freedom.

As we continue our journey, we arrive at Trinity College, Ireland's oldest and most prestigious university. Founded in 1592, Trinity College boasts a rich academic tradition and a stunning campus filled with architectural treasures. Be sure to catch a glimpse of the iconic Campanile, a landmark tower that has stood tall for centuries.

Now, we venture into the lively neighborhood of Temple Bar, known for its vibrant atmosphere and eclectic charm. Cobblestone streets lined with colorful pubs, quirky shops, and lively street performers create an unforgettable vibe that's quintessentially Dublin.

As we make our way through the city, we catch sight of Dublin Castle, a historic fortress dating back to the 13th century. Over the centuries, the castle has served as a royal residence, a military stronghold, and a symbol of British power. Today, it stands as a testament to Dublin's rich and complex history.

Our journey continues past the majestic Christ Church Cathedral, a stunning example of medieval architecture and a place of worship for over 1,000 years. Marvel at its grandeur and soak in the spiritual ambiance as we pass by this iconic landmark.

Finally, our adventure concludes at St. Patrick's Cathedral, Ireland's largest church and a true masterpiece of Gothic architecture. Built on the site where St. Patrick is said to have baptized converts to Christianity, the cathedral is steeped in history and legend, making it the perfect finale to our Dublin tour.

Best Free tours in Dublin

- **Sandeman's New Dublin Free Tour:** Sandeman's offers a highly rated free walking tour of Dublin led by knowledgeable local guides. The tour covers major landmarks such as Trinity College, Temple Bar, Dublin Castle, and more. While tipping is appreciated, it is not required.
- **Dublin City Free Walking Tour:** This tour takes you through Dublin's historic streets, providing insights into the city's rich history and culture. You'll visit attractions like O'Connell Street, the General Post Office, and the Ha'penny Bridge. The guides are passionate about sharing their love for Dublin, and tipping is optional.
- **Dublin Free Historical Walking Tours:** Led by experienced guides, these tours delve into Dublin's fascinating history, from Viking times to the present day. Highlights include Dublin's medieval quarter, Georgian Dublin, and the famous Dublin Writers Museum. While tips are welcome, there is no obligation to tip.
- **1916 Rising and War of Independence Walking Tour:** This tour focuses on Dublin's revolutionary past, exploring key sites associated with the 1916 Easter Rising and the War of Independence. Led by knowledgeable historians, the tour provides valuable insights into Ireland's struggle for independence. While tipping is appreciated, it is not mandatory.
- **Street Art Walking Tour:** Discover Dublin's vibrant street art scene on this guided walking tour, which showcases colorful murals and graffiti created by local and international artists. The tour provides an alternative perspective on the city's culture and creativity. Tipping is not expected but appreciated if you enjoyed the tour.

Interesting facts

Did you know that Dublin's famous St. Patrick's Cathedral is not actually the oldest church in the city? While St. Patrick's Cathedral is undoubtedly one of Dublin's most iconic landmarks, it's not the oldest. That honor belongs to Christ Church Cathedral, which predates St. Patrick's by several decades. Christ Church Cathedral, also known as the Cathedral of the Holy Trinity, has a history dating back over 1,000 years, making it one of the oldest buildings in Dublin.

Dublin is home to one of the world's oldest pubs, the Brazen Head. Tucked away on Lower Bridge Street, the Brazen Head has been serving thirsty patrons since 1198. With its cozy atmosphere, traditional Irish music sessions, and hearty pub grub, the Brazen Head is a must-visit for anyone looking to experience Dublin's rich pub culture and history.

Dublin's famous Temple Bar neighborhood wasn't always a trendy cultural hotspot. In fact, it was once a run-down and neglected area of the city. In the 1980s, Temple Bar underwent a major revitalization project, transforming it into the vibrant cultural quarter it is today. Now, Temple Bar is known for its bustling streets, lively pubs, art galleries, and street performers, attracting visitors from around the world.

Dublin is home to the world's first purpose-built parliament building. The Irish Houses of Parliament, also known as the Irish Parliament House or the Bank of Ireland building, was constructed in the late 18th century. Designed by architect Edward Lovett Pearce, the building served as the seat of the Irish Parliament until the Act of Union in 1800, which saw the Irish Parliament abolished and Ireland formally integrated into the United Kingdom.

Dublin's Phoenix Park is one of the largest enclosed parks in Europe, even larger than London's Hyde Park. Spanning over 1,700 acres, Phoenix Park is home to a diverse range of wildlife, historic monuments, and recreational facilities. Visitors can explore the park's picturesque landscapes, visit the Dublin Zoo, or take a stroll to see the residence of the President of Ireland, Áras an Uachtaráin.

These are just a few of the many fascinating facts that make Dublin such a unique and intriguing city. Whether you're exploring its ancient landmarks, vibrant neighborhoods, or lively pub scene, Dublin never fails to surprise and delight visitors with its rich history and culture.

Top Eats in Dublin

Restaurant	What to Try	Starting Price	Tips
Brother Hubbard	Moroccan Eggs	€10	Opt for brunch menu for affordable options
Bunsen	Classic Cheeseburger	€8	Go for the "Little Bunsen" option for smaller budget
Govinda's	Vegetarian Buffet	€8	Affordable buffet-style dining
Yamamori	Ramen or Sushi	€12	Lunch specials offer good value
Leo Burdock's	Fish and Chips	€10	Share portions to save money

Finding Michelin-starred restaurants in Dublin that offer a balance of culinary excellence and affordability can be a delightful endeavor. While these dining establishments are known for their exquisite cuisine and exceptional service, some manage to provide a Michelin-star experience without breaking the bank. Here are a few options to consider:

Chapter One, located on Parnell Square in the heart of Dublin, is renowned for its inventive and sophisticated Irish cuisine. Despite its prestigious Michelin star, Chapter One offers a lunch menu with prices starting around €35 per person, making it one of the more affordable Michelin-starred dining experiences in the city. Diners can expect meticulously prepared dishes using locally sourced ingredients, presented with creativity and flair.

Lunchtime at Liath, situated in the vibrant neighborhood of Blackrock, offers another opportunity to enjoy Michelin-starred cuisine at a reasonable price point. With a focus on seasonal and sustainable ingredients, Liath's lunch menu starts at around €55 per person, providing an accessible entry point to its innovative tasting menus. Diners can look forward to an array of beautifully crafted dishes that showcase the best of modern Irish cooking.

Meanwhile, Heron & Grey, located in the charming suburb of Blackrock, offers a unique dining experience with its ever-evolving tasting menus. Despite its Michelin star, Heron & Grey maintains an affordable pricing structure, with tasting menu prices starting at approximately €85 per person. Guests can indulge in a culinary journey that highlights the restaurant's commitment to innovation, flavor, and presentation.

Lastly, L'Ecrivain, nestled in the bustling city center, is another Michelin-starred gem that offers an accessible dining experience. With a focus on French-inspired cuisine crafted with Irish ingredients, L'Ecrivain's lunch menu starts at around €40 per person, making it an excellent choice for those seeking a taste of luxury without breaking the bank. Diners can expect impeccable service, elegant surroundings, and a menu that celebrates the best of both worlds.

In conclusion, while Michelin-starred dining in Dublin is often associated with high prices, these restaurants prove that exceptional culinary experiences can be enjoyed at more affordable price points. Whether you're savoring innovative Irish cuisine at Chapter One, exploring modern tasting menus at Liath and Heron & Grey, or indulging in French-inspired dishes at L'Ecrivain, these establishments offer an opportunity to dine like royalty without emptying your wallet.

Best Free Audio Guides and Apps for Dublin

Guide/App	Covers	Download	Cost
Dublin Discovery Trails	Various walking routes and landmarks	App Store/Google Play Store	Free
Dublin Culture Trail	Cultural sites, museums, and galleries	Website	Free
Dublin City Audio Guide	Historic landmarks and hidden gems	Website	Free

Creative Alternatives to Experience Paid Attractions for Free

- **Dublin Castle:** While the interior of Dublin Castle typically requires a paid admission, visitors can still admire the exterior of this historic landmark for free. Take a leisurely stroll around the castle grounds, marvel at its impressive architecture, and snap some photos of its iconic towers and turrets.
- **Guinness Storehouse:** While entry to the Guinness Storehouse usually comes with a fee, you can still experience the Guinness brand by visiting the nearby St. James's Gate Brewery. Take a self-guided walk around the brewery's exterior, learn about the history of Guinness from the informative plaques, and soak in the atmosphere of this iconic Dublin institution.
- **Kilmainham Gaol:** While guided tours of Kilmainham Gaol typically require a paid admission, visitors can still catch a glimpse of this historic prison from the outside. Take a walk around the perimeter of the gaol, read the informative signs, and imagine the stories of its former inmates from a distance.
- **Dublin Zoo:** While entry to Dublin Zoo usually requires a ticket, visitors can still enjoy the lush surroundings of Phoenix Park for free. Take a leisurely walk or bike ride through the park, spot deer grazing in the meadows, and enjoy picnicking by the tranquil ponds.
- **Trinity College and the Book of Kells:** While admission to the Book of Kells exhibition typically comes with a fee, visitors can still explore the exterior of Trinity

College for free. Take a walk around the campus, admire the historic buildings and manicured lawns, and soak in the atmosphere of this prestigious university.
- **National Museum of Ireland:** While entry to special exhibitions at the National Museum of Ireland may require a ticket, visitors can still explore the museum's permanent collections for free. Discover treasures from Ireland's past, including ancient artifacts, medieval treasures, and decorative arts.
- **National Gallery of Ireland:** While entry to special exhibitions at the National Gallery of Ireland may require a ticket, visitors can still admire the gallery's extensive collection of art for free. Marvel at works by famous Irish and international artists, including paintings, sculptures, and decorative arts.
- **Dublinia:** While admission to Dublinia usually comes with a fee, visitors can still explore the medieval quarter of Dublin for free. Wander through the cobbled streets of Temple Bar, admire the historic buildings, and soak in the atmosphere of this vibrant neighborhood.
- **Dublin Writers Museum:** While admission to the Dublin Writers Museum typically requires a ticket, visitors can still explore the literary history of Dublin for free. Take a walk around the city center, visit landmarks associated with famous writers such as James Joyce and Oscar Wilde, and imagine the stories that have unfolded on Dublin's streets.
- **Christ Church Cathedral:** While entry to Christ Church Cathedral usually requires a fee, visitors can still admire the exterior of this historic church for free. Take a walk around the cathedral grounds, marvel at its stunning architecture, and snap some photos of its impressive facade.

Luxurious Yet Affordable Experiences in Dublin

Here are indulgent experiences that won't break the bank:

- **Day Passes to Luxury Hotels**: The Marker Hotel, located in the trendy Docklands area, offers day passes to its award-winning spa and rooftop terrace for €40, providing access to facilities such as a sauna, steam room, and infinity pool with stunning views of the city skyline.
- **Afternoon Tea at The Westbury:** Treat yourself to a luxurious afternoon tea experience at The Westbury Hotel, starting at around €45 per person. Indulge in a selection of delicate sandwiches, freshly baked scones, and decadent pastries, all served in the elegant surroundings of The Gallery.
- **Dublin Bay Cruise:** Embark on a scenic cruise of Dublin Bay with Dublin Bay Cruises, starting at around €22 per person. Relax on deck as you sail past iconic landmarks such as Howth Head and Dun Laoghaire Harbour, taking in panoramic views of the city skyline and coastline.
- **Cocktail Masterclass at The Blind Pig:** Join a cocktail masterclass at The Blind Pig speakeasy, starting at around €35 per person. Learn the art of mixology from expert bartenders as you craft your own signature cocktails using premium spirits and fresh ingredients.
- **Dublin Whiskey Museum Tour:** Discover the fascinating history of Irish whiskey with a guided tour of the Dublin Whiskey Museum, starting at around €20 per

person. Learn about the origins of whiskey production in Ireland, sample a selection of fine whiskies, and enjoy interactive exhibits.
- **Dublin City Bike Tour:** Explore Dublin's highlights on two wheels with a guided bike tour, starting at around €25 per person. Pedal past iconic landmarks such as Trinity College, Dublin Castle, and St. Patrick's Cathedral, learning about the city's history and culture along the way.
- **Traditional Irish Music Session:** Immerse yourself in the vibrant atmosphere of a traditional Irish music session at a local pub, with no cover charge. Enjoy live music performances featuring fiddles, tin whistles, and bodhráns, and join in the craic with locals and fellow visitors alike.
- **Dublin Literary Pub Crawl:** Embark on a literary pub crawl through Dublin's historic streets, starting at around €15 per person. Follow in the footsteps of famous writers such as James Joyce and Oscar Wilde as you visit iconic pubs and hear entertaining stories and anecdotes.
- **Stroll through Dublin's Parks:** Spend a leisurely afternoon exploring Dublin's picturesque parks and gardens, such as St. Stephen's Green and Phoenix Park, with no entry fee. Enjoy a scenic walk amidst lush greenery, tranquil ponds, and colorful flowerbeds, escaping the hustle and bustle of the city.
- **Gourmet Food Market at Temple Bar:** Indulge your senses at the Temple Bar Food Market, held every Saturday, with no entry fee. Sample a variety of artisanal cheeses, freshly baked breads, gourmet chocolates, and other culinary delights from local producers.
- **Dublin Street Art Tour:** Discover Dublin's vibrant street art scene with a self-guided walking tour, with no cost. Wander through colorful neighborhoods such as Temple Bar and Smithfield, admiring striking murals and urban artworks by local and international artists.
- **Dublin's Historic Churches:** Explore Dublin's historic churches and cathedrals, such as Christ Church Cathedral and St. Patrick's Cathedral, with no admission fee. Marvel at their impressive architecture, intricate stained glass windows, and ornate interiors, soaking in the spiritual atmosphere.
- **Dublin Flea Market:** Browse for unique treasures and vintage finds at the Dublin Flea Market, held on the last Sunday of every month, with no entry fee. Discover an eclectic mix of clothing, jewelry, antiques, and crafts, while enjoying live music and delicious street food.
- **Dublin Bay Paddleboarding:** Experience Dublin from a different perspective with a paddleboarding session on Dublin Bay, starting at around €25 per person. Glide across the water, admiring views of the city skyline and coastline, while getting a workout and soaking up the sunshine.
- **Dublin Ghost Tour:** Embark on a spine-chilling ghost tour of Dublin's haunted sites and spooky landmarks, starting at around €15 per person. Follow your guide through dark alleyways and hidden courtyards, hearing tales of paranormal activity and supernatural encounters.
- **Dublin Food Walking Tour:** Embark on a culinary journey through Dublin's vibrant food scene with a guided walking tour, starting at around €40 per person. Sample a variety of Irish delicacies and international cuisines, while learning about the city's gastronomic history and culture.
- **Dublin Castle Gardens:** Escape the hustle and bustle of the city with a tranquil stroll through the gardens of Dublin Castle, with no entry fee. Discover hidden pathways, manicured lawns, and colorful flowerbeds, while admiring views of the castle's historic architecture.
- **Dublin's Historic Libraries:** Step back in time with a visit to Dublin's historic libraries, such as Marsh's Library and the Royal Irish Academy Library, with no

admission fee. Explore their rich collections of rare books, manuscripts, and artifacts, while soaking in the ambience of these literary treasures.
- **Dublin's Street Performers:** Experience the vibrant street performance scene in Dublin's city center, with no cost. Watch talented musicians, dancers, and entertainers showcase their skills on bustling streets and busy squares, adding to the city's lively atmosphere.
- **Dublin's Georgian Squares:** Take a leisurely stroll through Dublin's elegant Georgian squares, such as Merrion Square and Fitzwilliam Square, with no entry fee. Admire the grandeur of the historic townhouses, lush greenery, and iconic monuments, while imagining life in 18th-century Dublin.
- **Dublin's Coastal Walks:** Explore Dublin's stunning coastline with a scenic coastal walk along Dublin Bay, with no cost. Follow the scenic cliff paths from Howth to Sutton, or stroll along the sandy shores of Sandymount Strand, enjoying panoramic views of the Irish Sea and beyond.
- **Spa Deals**: The Buff Day Spa, located in the heart of Dublin city center, offers a range of affordable spa packages starting from €50, including massages, facials, and body treatments.
- **Afternoon Teas**: Indulge in a quintessentially luxurious experience with afternoon tea at one of Dublin's upscale hotels or tea rooms. The Westbury Hotel, located on Grafton Street, offers a sumptuous afternoon tea experience in its elegant Gallery lounge, featuring a selection of sandwiches, pastries, and freshly baked scones for €45 per person.
- **Oyster Happy Hours**: The Cliff Townhouse, located on St. Stephen's Green, offers oyster happy hour from 5-7pm daily, with freshly shucked oysters priced at €1 each, allowing you to indulge in a gourmet treat without breaking the bank.
- **Pint Happy Hours**: The Horseshoe Bar, located in the historic Shelbourne Hotel, offers happy hour specials on select drinks from 5-7pm daily, providing a taste of luxury at a fraction of the cost.
- **Cheaper Places to Drink than Temple Bar**: Avoid the tourist crowds and high prices of Temple Bar by seeking out hidden gems and local haunts in Dublin's lesser-known neighborhoods. Places like The Bernard Shaw in Portobello or The Black Sheep in Capel Street offer a relaxed atmosphere and affordable drink prices, making them popular spots among Dubliners.
- **Best Thrift Shops**: Discover unique finds and designer bargains at Dublin's thrift shops and vintage stores. Siopaella, with locations in Temple Bar and on Wicklow Street, offers a curated selection of pre-loved designer clothing and accessories at discounted prices, allowing you to score luxury items for a fraction of the retail cost.
- **Visit Dublin's Markets**: Explore Dublin's vibrant markets, where you can browse artisan crafts, locally produced goods, and delicious food offerings. Markets such as the Temple Bar Food Market, the Dublin Flea Market, and the Honest2Goodness Market in Glasnevin are great places to discover unique treasures and support local vendors without spending a fortune.
- **Trinity College Dublin**: Trinity College frequently hosts free public lectures and events open to the community. Keep an eye on their events calendar for talks on a wide range of topics, from literature and history to science and technology. Additionally, Trinity College's Chapel hosts free lunchtime concerts featuring performances by talented musicians and ensembles.
- **The National Library of Ireland**: The National Library of Ireland often hosts free lectures, workshops, and exhibitions exploring various aspects of Irish culture, history, and literature. Check their website or social media channels for upcoming events, which may include author talks, poetry readings, and panel discussions.

- **Dublin City Council Libraries**: Dublin's public libraries regularly host free lectures, workshops, and cultural events for all ages. From author readings and book clubs to language classes and heritage talks, there's something for everyone to enjoy. Visit the Dublin City Libraries website for information on upcoming events at branches across the city.
- **Irish Traditional Music Archive (ITMA)**: The ITMA, located in Temple Bar, occasionally hosts free concerts and performances showcasing traditional Irish music and song. Check their website for details on upcoming events, which may include lunchtime recitals, evening concerts, and special performances by renowned musicians.

Dublin Whiskey Tour

- **Teeling Distillery Tour** (Starting Price: €15)
  - Begin your whiskey adventure at the Teeling Distillery in Dublin. Take a guided tour of the distillery to learn about the whiskey-making process, from grain to glass. Enjoy a tasting session of Teeling's award-winning whiskeys, including their Small Batch and Single Malt expressions.
- **Getting There**: Take the Luas tram or a Dublin Bus to the Teeling Distillery on Newmarket Square.
- **The Dingle Whiskey Bar** (Budget-Friendly Luxury)
  - After the distillery tour, head to The Dingle Whiskey Bar for a luxurious but budget-friendly whiskey tasting experience. With an extensive selection of Irish whiskeys to choose from, including rare and limited editions, you can sample a variety of expressions without breaking the bank.
- **Getting There**: The Dingle Whiskey Bar is located in the heart of Dublin's Temple Bar district, easily accessible on foot or by Dublin Bus.
- **Dublin Liberties Distillery Tour** (Starting Price: €20)
  - Continue your whiskey journey with a visit to the Dublin Liberties Distillery. Take a guided tour of the distillery to discover the history and heritage of Irish whiskey production. Enjoy tastings of their premium whiskeys, such as The Dubliner and The Dead Rabbit.
- **Getting There**: Take a short walk or a Dublin Bus to the Dublin Liberties Distillery on Mill Street.
- **Dine at The Old Jameson Distillery**
  - Conclude your day with dinner at The Old Jameson Distillery, where you can enjoy hearty Irish cuisine in a historic setting. Pair your meal with a glass of Jameson whiskey for the perfect ending to your whiskey-filled day.
- **Getting There**: The Old Jameson Distillery is located in Smithfield, easily accessible by Luas tram or Dublin Bus.

Throughout your itinerary, utilize Dublin's efficient public transportation system, including buses, trams (Luas), and trains (DART), to get between destinations. Consider purchasing a Leap Card for discounted fares and unlimited travel on Dublin Bus, Luas, and DART services for a set period.

Top 20 Attractions with Starting Prices and Money-Saving Tips:

- **Guinness Storehouse**:
  - Starting Price: €20
  - Money-Saving Tip: Book tickets online in advance for discounted rates and skip-the-line access.
- **Dublin Castle**:
  - Starting Price: €8
  - Money-Saving Tip: Visit during special events or festivals for free entry to certain parts of the castle.
- **Trinity College and the Book of Kells**:
  - Starting Price: €14
  - Money-Saving Tip: Visit in the morning or late afternoon to avoid crowds, and book combined tickets for the Long Room and Book of Kells.
- **Temple Bar District**:
  - Starting Price: Free (prices vary for food and drinks)
  - Money-Saving Tip: Enjoy the atmosphere without breaking the bank by opting for lunch specials or happy hour deals.
- **National Museum of Ireland - Archaeology**:
  - Starting Price: Free (donations appreciated)
  - Money-Saving Tip: Take advantage of free admission and explore Ireland's ancient history and treasures.
- **Dublin Zoo**:
  - Starting Price: €17.50
  - Money-Saving Tip: Visit during off-peak hours or book tickets online for discounted rates.
- **St. Patrick's Cathedral**:
  - Starting Price: €8
  - Money-Saving Tip: Attend a service or concert at the cathedral for a unique and affordable experience.
- **Dublin's Literary Pub Crawl**:
  - Starting Price: €15
  - Money-Saving Tip: Look for discounts or special offers online, or opt for a self-guided literary tour.
- **Dublin City Bike Tour**:
  - Starting Price: €25
  - Money-Saving Tip: Rent a bike from a local shop and explore the city's landmarks at your own pace.
- **Dublin's Viking Splash Tour**:
  - Starting Price: €25
  - Money-Saving Tip: Look for group discounts or book tickets online in advance for reduced rates.
- **Dublinia and the Viking World Exhibition**:
  - Starting Price: €10
  - Money-Saving Tip: Check for combination tickets with other attractions for discounted rates.
- **Dublin Bay Cruise**:
  - Starting Price: €22
  - Money-Saving Tip: Look for special offers or group discounts, and bring your own snacks and drinks for the cruise.
- **Kilmainham Gaol**:
  - Starting Price: €8

- Money-Saving Tip: Book tickets in advance and visit during off-peak hours for a quieter experience.
- **Phoenix Park**:
  - Starting Price: Free
  - Money-Saving Tip: Pack a picnic and spend the day exploring the park's vast green spaces, walking trails, and Dublin Zoo.
- **Dublin's Little Museum**:
  - Starting Price: €10
  - Money-Saving Tip: Look for discounted tickets or free admission days, and explore Dublin's history and culture.
- **Grafton Street Shopping**:
  - Starting Price: Free (prices vary for shopping)
  - Money-Saving Tip: Browse the shops and street performers, and look for sales or discounts at major retailers.
- **Irish Whiskey Museum**:
  - Starting Price: €20
  - Money-Saving Tip: Book tickets online for discounted rates and learn about Ireland's whiskey heritage.
- **Dublin's Street Art and Murals**:
  - Starting Price: Free
  - Money-Saving Tip: Take a self-guided walking tour to discover Dublin's vibrant street art scene at no cost.
- **National Gallery of Ireland**:
  - Starting Price: Free (donations appreciated)
  - Money-Saving Tip: Attend free guided tours or workshops, and explore the gallery's extensive collection of art.
- **Dublin's Docklands Area**:
  - Starting Price: Free (prices vary for attractions)
  - Money-Saving Tip: Take a leisurely stroll along the River Liffey and enjoy the views of modern architecture and historical landmarks.

Recap

Dublin is a city full of possibilities for luxury on a budget travelers, offering a wealth of free and affordable experiences waiting to be discovered

1. Explore Dublin's Historical Gems for Free: While some of Dublin's iconic landmarks may charge admission fees, many historical sites can be enjoyed for free. Take advantage of complimentary entry to attractions like Dublin Castle's exterior and St. Patrick's Cathedral's grounds. Opt for self-guided tours or free audio guides to delve into their rich histories without breaking the bank.

2. Embrace the Literary Legacy on a Budget: Dublin's literary heritage is legendary, and exploring it needn't cost a fortune. Visit the Dublin Writers Museum for discounted admission during off-peak hours or consider exploring Trinity College's campus and its atmospheric libraries for free. Keep an eye out for budget-friendly literary events and walking tours, which offer insights into the city's vibrant literary scene.

3. Enjoy Affordable Cultural Experiences: Dublin boasts a vibrant arts and culture scene, with many affordable and even free events throughout the year. Check out free entry days at the National Museum of Ireland and the National Gallery of Ireland, or catch a discounted matinee performance at one of the city's theaters. Keep tabs on local listings for budget-friendly concerts, exhibitions, and festivals.

4. Savor Culinary Delights on a Budget: Dining out in Dublin doesn't have to break the bank, especially if you know where to look. Opt for lunch specials and early bird menus at upscale restaurants like The Westbury or The Morrison, where you can sample gourmet cuisine at a fraction of the price. Alternatively, explore Dublin's diverse food markets for wallet-friendly treats and local delicacies.

5. Navigate the City Like a Local: Dublin's compact size makes it easy to explore on foot or by bike, saving you money on transportation. Take advantage of Dublinbikes, the city's bike-sharing scheme, for affordable and eco-friendly travel around the city center. Use public transportation smartly by purchasing a Leap Card for discounted fares on buses, trams, and trains.

6. Discover Dublin's Green Spaces for Free: Escape the hustle and bustle of the city without spending a cent by exploring Dublin's lush parks and gardens. Pack a picnic and spend a leisurely afternoon in Phoenix Park, where you can spot deer and enjoy stunning views of Dublin's skyline. Alternatively, stroll through the tranquil surroundings of St. Stephen's Green or the Iveagh Gardens for a peaceful retreat from city life.

7. Immerse Yourself in Dublin's Live Music Scene: Dublin is renowned for its vibrant live music scene, and catching a performance needn't cost a fortune. Seek out free traditional Irish music sessions at local pubs like The Cobblestone or O'Donoghue's, where you can enjoy authentic tunes and a lively atmosphere without spending a penny. Check out listings for free gigs and open mic nights for more budget-friendly entertainment options.

Here's a chart highlighting some of the best free live music and live comedy venues in Dublin:

Venue	Type	Location	Description
The Cobblestone	Live Music	Smithfield	Traditional Irish music sessions nightly
O'Donoghue's	Live Music	Merrion Row	Traditional Irish music sessions nightly
The Porterhouse	Live Music	Various locations	Live music performances, mainly folk and blues
The Workman's Club	Live Music	Temple Bar	Free gigs and live music events
Whelan's	Live Music	Wexford Street	Free gigs and live music events
The International Bar	Live Comedy	Wicklow Street	Free comedy nights every week
The Comedy Crunch	Live Comedy	Stag's Head Pub	Free comedy show every Sunday evening
The Ha'penny Comedy Club	Live Comedy	The Ha'penny Bridge Inn	Free comedy nights every week
The Woolshed Baa & Grill	Live Comedy	Parnell Street	Free comedy nights every week
Anseo	Live Comedy	Camden Street Lower	Free comedy nights every week

8. Hunt for Bargains at Dublin's Markets: Dublin's markets offer a treasure trove of affordable goodies, from locally produced foods to handmade crafts and vintage finds. Explore the stalls at the Temple Bar Food Market or the Dublin Flea Market for delicious treats and unique souvenirs at reasonable prices. Haggle with vendors for the best deals and don't be afraid to explore off-the-beaten-path markets for hidden gems.

County Dublin

Visiting the towns of County Dublin provides a diverse array of experiences and attractions, catering to various interests and preferences. With rich history, stunning natural beauty, vibrant cultural scenes, ample shopping and dining options, as well as numerous community events and festivals, exploring County Dublin promises a fulfilling and enjoyable experience for all, easily accessible via public transportation or car from Dublin city center and surrounding areas. County Dublin, encompassing Dublin city and its surrounding areas, is home to several sizable towns. Some of the biggest towns in County Dublin include:

- Swords: Located in north County Dublin, Swords is the county's largest town by population. It has grown rapidly in recent years and offers a range of amenities, including shopping centers, parks, and cultural attractions.
- Blanchardstown: Situated in west County Dublin, Blanchardstown is another significant town known for its large shopping center, Blanchardstown Centre. It is a hub for retail, entertainment, and business activities.
- Dún Laoghaire: Positioned on the coast in south County Dublin, Dún Laoghaire is a bustling town renowned for its scenic harbor, Victorian architecture, and maritime heritage. It serves as a popular destination for tourists and locals alike.
- Tallaght: Located in southwest County Dublin, Tallaght is a major suburb with a diverse community and a range of amenities, including shopping centers, sports facilities, and parks. It is one of the largest residential areas in the county.
- Malahide: Found in north County Dublin, Malahide is an affluent coastal town known for its picturesque marina, historic castle, and vibrant village atmosphere. It attracts visitors with its scenic beauty and range of leisure activities.

Swords

Swords is conveniently located just a short distance from Dublin city center, making it easily accessible by various modes of transportation. Visitors can reach Swords by:

- **Car:** Swords is accessible via the M1 motorway, which connects Dublin to Belfast. The town is approximately a 20-minute drive from Dublin city center, depending on traffic conditions.
- **Public Transportation:** Dublin Bus operates several bus routes that serve Swords, including the 41, 41B, 41C, and 41X. The town is also served by the Swords Express, a dedicated bus service that connects Swords to Dublin city center. Additionally, the Swords Express operates a direct service to Dublin Airport, making it a convenient option for travelers.

Hotel/ Guesthouse	Starting Price (per night)	Key Amenities

Carnegie Court Hotel	€70 - €100	Stylish rooms, onsite restaurant, bar, free Wi-Fi, complimentary breakfast option, convenient location near Swords Castle and Dublin Airport.
Roganstown Hotel & Country Club	€80 - €120	Elegant rooms, golf course, spa facilities, fitness center, onsite restaurant, bar, free Wi-Fi, beautiful countryside setting, easy access to Dublin Airport and local attractions.
Forty Four Main Street	€60 - €90	Boutique guesthouse with individually decorated rooms, onsite restaurant, bar, free Wi-Fi, continental breakfast included, charming atmosphere, located in the heart of Swords close to shops, restaurants, and attractions.
Glenmore House	€50 - €80	Family-run guesthouse offering cozy rooms, onsite bar, free Wi-Fi, complimentary breakfast, friendly hospitality, convenient location near Dublin Airport and major transport links.
Travelodge Dublin Airport North Swords	€40 - €70	Budget-friendly hotel with clean and comfortable rooms, free parking, 24-hour reception, onsite café, free Wi-Fi, easy access to Dublin Airport and nearby attractions.

Top Attractions in Swords:

Swords boasts a range of attractions that cater to history buffs, nature enthusiasts, and families alike. Some of the top attractions to explore in Swords include:

- **Swords Castle:** Dating back to the 13th century, Swords Castle is a historic landmark that offers insight into the town's medieval past. Visitors can explore the castle grounds, including the restored Great Hall and the picturesque courtyard.
- **Swords Round Tower:** Located adjacent to Swords Castle, the Round Tower is one of only two remaining medieval round towers in County Dublin. Climb to the top for panoramic views of the surrounding area.
- **Swords Pavilions Shopping Centre:** For those looking to indulge in some retail therapy, Swords Pavilions is a must-visit destination. With over 90 stores, including major brands, fashion boutiques, and eateries, the shopping center offers something for every shopper.
- **Swords Millennium Park:** Spanning 23 acres, Swords Millennium Park is a green oasis in the heart of the town. The park features walking trails, playgrounds, sports facilities, and picnic areas, making it a popular destination for families and outdoor enthusiasts.
- **Airfield Estate:** Just a short drive from Swords, Airfield Estate is a working farm and heritage center that offers a range of activities and attractions for visitors of all ages. Explore the farmyard, gardens, and interactive exhibitions, or enjoy a meal at the on-site café.

Dining in Swords:

Swords boasts a diverse culinary scene, with a wide range of restaurants, cafes, and eateries to suit every palate and budget. Some popular dining options in Swords include:

- **The Old Schoolhouse Restaurant:** Housed in a historic building, The Old Schoolhouse Restaurant offers a menu of Irish and international cuisine, made with locally sourced ingredients.

- **Wrights Cafe Bar:** Located in Swords Pavilions Shopping Centre, Wrights Cafe Bar is a popular spot for casual dining and drinks. Enjoy classic pub fare, cocktails, and live music in a relaxed atmosphere.
- **Gourmet Food Parlour:** Known for its fresh and flavorful dishes, Gourmet Food Parlour offers a diverse menu of breakfast, lunch, and dinner options, as well as a selection of artisanal coffees and teas.
- **Masterson's Steakhouse & Wine Bar:** If you're in the mood for a hearty meal, head to Masterson's Steakhouse & Wine Bar for prime cuts of Irish beef, seafood dishes, and an extensive wine list.
- **Swords Garden Chinese Restaurant:** For those craving Asian cuisine, Swords Garden Chinese Restaurant offers a menu of authentic Chinese dishes, including dim sum, noodles, and stir-fries.

Entertainment and Nightlife:

Swords offers plenty of options for entertainment and nightlife, with a variety of bars, pubs, and entertainment venues to choose from. Some popular spots include:

- **The Old Boro:** Known for its friendly atmosphere and live music events, The Old Boro is a traditional Irish pub that offers a wide selection of beers, spirits, and pub grub.
- **Wright Venue:** Located just outside Swords, Wright Venue is one of Dublin's premier nightclubs, featuring multiple dance floors, VIP areas, and regular DJ performances.
- **Empire Swords:** Empire Swords is a popular sports bar and live music venue that offers a lively atmosphere, big-screen TVs for watching sports events, and regular live music performances.
- **The Hopsack:** For those looking for a more relaxed evening, The Hopsack is a cozy pub that offers craft beers, artisanal cocktails, and a welcoming atmosphere.
- **Stroll Through Swords Castle Grounds:**
    - Enjoy a leisurely walk through the picturesque Swords Castle grounds, soaking in the historic atmosphere and architectural beauty. (Free)
- **Picnic at Ward River Valley Park:**
    - Pack a picnic and head to Ward River Valley Park for a serene outdoor dining experience amidst lush greenery and scenic walking trails. (Free)
- **Explore Swords Village:**
    - Take a leisurely stroll through Swords Village, exploring its charming streets lined with boutique shops, cafes, and historic landmarks like the Round Tower. (Free)
- **Visit Swords Library:**
    - Spend a relaxing afternoon at Swords Library, browsing through its extensive collection of books, magazines, and multimedia resources. (Free)
- **Attend a Community Event at Swords Castle:**
    - Keep an eye out for community events and cultural activities held at Swords Castle, such as open-air concerts, theater performances, and art exhibitions. (Free or low-cost)
- **Hike the Estuary Walkway:**
    - Embark on a scenic hike along the Estuary Walkway, following the path of the Broadmeadow River as it winds through tranquil countryside and urban landscapes. (Free)
- **Enjoy a Sunset at Balheary Reservoir:**

- Take in breathtaking views of the sunset over Balheary Reservoir, a hidden gem offering serene surroundings and peaceful moments of reflection. (Free)
- **Visit Swords Courthouse:**
  - Explore the historic Swords Courthouse, admiring its elegant architecture and learning about its fascinating past through self-guided tours or guided visits. (Free)
- **Cycle Along the Royal Canal Greenway:**
  - Rent a bike or bring your own and cycle along the scenic Royal Canal Greenway, enjoying panoramic views of the waterway and surrounding countryside. (Inexpensive bike rental options available)
- **Relax at Swords Pavilions Shopping Centre:**
  - Treat yourself to a day of leisurely shopping and dining at Swords Pavilions Shopping Centre, indulging in window shopping, people-watching, and sampling local cuisine at affordable prices. (Free to browse, costs vary for shopping and dining)
-

Day Trips from Swords:

Swords is ideally situated for exploring the surrounding area, with several attractions and destinations within easy reach. Some popular day trips from Swords include:

- **Malahide Castle:** Just a short drive from Swords, Malahide Castle is a stunning medieval fortress set amidst beautiful gardens and grounds. Explore the castle's interiors, wander through the gardens, and enjoy a guided tour of the estate.
- **Newbridge House and Farm:** Located in nearby Donabate, Newbridge House and Farm is a historic estate that offers guided tours, interactive exhibits, and family-friendly activities, including animal encounters and nature trails.
- **Howth:** Situated on the rugged coastline of County Dublin, Howth is a charming fishing village known for its scenic walks, fresh seafood restaurants, and bustling harbor. Take a stroll along the pier, hike to the summit of Howth Head, or

Blanchardstown

Blanchardstown, situated in west County Dublin, is a bustling suburban town known for its vibrant atmosphere, excellent shopping facilities, and array of recreational activities. This guide will provide a detailed overview of Blanchardstown, highlighting its top attractions, dining options, shopping districts, and more.

Getting to Blanchardstown:

Blanchardstown is easily accessible from Dublin city center and surrounding areas by various means of transportation:

- **Car:** Blanchardstown is conveniently located near the M50 motorway, providing easy access by car from Dublin city center and neighboring towns.

- **Public Transportation:** Dublin Bus operates several bus routes serving Blanchardstown, including the 39, 39a, 40, and 76. The town is also served by the Blanchardstown Centre bus interchange, offering connections to other parts of Dublin.

Hotel/ Guesthouse	Starting Price (per night)	Key Amenities
Carlton Hotel Blanchardstown	€70 - €100	Stylish rooms, onsite restaurant, bar, fitness center, free Wi-Fi, complimentary breakfast option, convenient location near Blanchardstown Shopping Centre and National Aquatic Centre.
Crowne Plaza Dublin Blanchardstown	€80 - €120	Contemporary rooms, onsite restaurant, bar, fitness center, swimming pool, free Wi-Fi, complimentary breakfast option, easy access to Blanchardstown Shopping Centre, Phoenix Park, and Dublin city center.
Castleknock Hotel	€90 - €130	Modern rooms, onsite restaurant, bar, fitness center, swimming pool, spa facilities, free Wi-Fi, complimentary breakfast option, picturesque countryside setting, convenient location near Phoenix Park and Dublin city center.
Ibis Hotel Dublin West	€60 - €90	Comfortable rooms, onsite restaurant, bar, free parking, free Wi-Fi, budget-friendly accommodation, convenient location near Blanchardstown Shopping Centre, National Aquatic Centre, and Dublin city center.
Travelodge Dublin Phoenix Park	€50 - €80	Budget-friendly hotel with clean and comfortable rooms, free parking, 24-hour reception, onsite café, free Wi-Fi, easy access to Phoenix Park, Dublin Zoo, and nearby attractio

Top Attractions in Blanchardstown:

Blanchardstown offers a range of attractions and activities to suit visitors of all ages and interests. Some of the top attractions in Blanchardstown include:

- **Enjoy a Stroll in Millennium Park:**
    - Take a relaxing walk through Millennium Park, a beautifully landscaped green space with scenic walking trails, tranquil ponds, and lush gardens. (Free)
- **Picnic at Tolka Valley Park:**
    - Pack a picnic basket and head to Tolka Valley Park for a leisurely outdoor meal surrounded by nature's beauty, including woodlands, meadows, and wildlife habitats. (Free)
- **Explore Blanchardstown Village:**
    - Wander through Blanchardstown Village and soak up its charming atmosphere, dotted with quaint shops, cafes, and historic landmarks like the old village church. (Free)
- **Visit Draíocht Arts Centre:**
    - Discover contemporary art and cultural exhibitions at Draíocht Arts Centre, offering free admission to its galleries and occasional events. (Free)

- **Attend a Workshop at Blanchardstown Library:**
  - Participate in a workshop or seminar at Blanchardstown Library, where you can learn new skills, engage in creative activities, and meet like-minded individuals. (Free or low-cost)
- **Take a Walk by the Royal Canal:**
  - Enjoy a scenic stroll along the Royal Canal, marveling at the tranquil waterway, lush greenery, and historic canal locks along the route. (Free)
- **Relax at Corduff Park:**
  - Unwind and soak up the sun at Corduff Park, a peaceful green space with playgrounds, sports facilities, and open fields perfect for picnics or outdoor games. (Free)
- **Explore the National Aquatic Centre:**
  - While admission to the National Aquatic Centre may not be free, you can still enjoy the ambiance and energy of the facility by spectating swimming events or leisurely walking around the complex. (Free to watch)

Dining in Blanchardstown:

Blanchardstown boasts a diverse culinary scene, with a plethora of restaurants, cafes, and eateries offering a wide range of cuisines. Some popular dining options in Blanchardstown include:

- **The Blanchardstown Brasserie:** Located within the Crowne Plaza Dublin - Blanchardstown, The Blanchardstown Brasserie offers a menu of modern Irish cuisine with a focus on locally sourced ingredients.
- **Eddie Rocket's:** A popular American-style diner chain, Eddie Rocket's serves up classic burgers, fries, and milkshakes in a retro-themed setting, perfect for casual dining with family and friends.
- **The Bell Pub:** A traditional Irish pub, The Bell Pub offers a cozy atmosphere and a menu of pub grub favorites, including fish and chips, steak, and hearty Irish stews.
- **The Blue Elephant:** For those craving Thai cuisine, The Blue Elephant serves up authentic Thai dishes made with fresh ingredients and traditional flavors, offering a taste of Southeast Asia in Blanchardstown.
- **Hogs & Heifers:** Known for its BBQ ribs, burgers, and craft beers, Hogs & Heifers is a popular spot for meat lovers looking to indulge in hearty comfort food.

Entertainment and Nightlife:

Blanchardstown offers plenty of options for entertainment and nightlife, with a variety of bars, pubs, and entertainment venues to choose from. Some popular spots include:

- **The Bell Pub:** In addition to its restaurant, The Bell Pub offers a lively atmosphere in the evenings, with regular live music performances and pub quizzes.
- **The Carpenter:** A popular sports bar, The Carpenter features multiple big-screen TVs for watching sports events, as well as a selection of beers, cocktails, and pub snacks.
- **The Vineyard:** Known for its extensive wine list and relaxed ambiance, The Vineyard is a cozy wine bar offering a wide selection of wines, as well as charcuterie boards and cheese platters.

- **Blanchardstown Leisureplex:** Blanchardstown Leisureplex offers a range of entertainment options, including bowling, laser tag, and arcade games, making it a popular destination for family-friendly fun.

Day Trips from Blanchardstown:

Blanchardstown serves as an excellent base for exploring the surrounding area, with several attractions and destinations within easy reach. Some popular day trips from Blanchardstown include:

- **Phoenix Park:** Located just a short drive from Blanchardstown, Phoenix Park is one of Europe's largest urban parks, offering picturesque walking trails, historic landmarks, and abundant wildlife.
- **Dublin Zoo:** Situated within Phoenix Park, Dublin Zoo is a must-visit destination for animal lovers, with over 400 species of animals from around the world.
- **Newbridge House and Farm:** Located in nearby Donabate, Newbridge House and Farm is a historic estate that offers guided tours, interactive exhibits, and family-friendly activities, including animal encounters and nature trails.

Dún Laoghaire

Dún Laoghaire, nestled along the scenic coastline of south County Dublin, is a picturesque seaside town renowned for its maritime heritage, Victorian architecture, and vibrant cultural scene. This guide will provide an in-depth overview of Dún Laoghaire, highlighting its top attractions, dining options, shopping districts, and more.

Getting to Dún Laoghaire:

Dún Laoghaire is easily accessible from Dublin city center and surrounding areas by various modes of transportation:

- **DART:** The DART (Dublin Area Rapid Transit) is a commuter rail service that connects Dún Laoghaire with Dublin city center and other coastal towns along Dublin Bay. The DART station is centrally located in Dún Laoghaire, making it a convenient option for travelers.
- **Bus:** Dublin Bus operates several bus routes serving Dún Laoghaire, including the 7, 7a, 45a, and 111. The town is also served by the Aircoach, a dedicated bus service that provides direct connections to Dublin Airport and other destinations.
- **Car:** Dún Laoghaire is accessible by car via the N11 and M50 motorways, with ample parking available in the town center and surrounding areas.

Hotel/ Guesthouse	Starting Price (per night)	Key Amenities
Royal Marine Hotel	€80 - €120	Elegant rooms, onsite restaurants, bars, fitness center, swimming pool, spa facilities, stunning sea views, free Wi-Fi, complimentary breakfast option, convenient location near Dún Laoghaire Pier and town center.
Haddington House	€70 - €100	Boutique hotel with stylish rooms, onsite restaurant, bar, terrace overlooking the sea, free Wi-Fi, continental breakfast included, charming atmosphere, convenient location near Dún Laoghaire Harbor, East Pier, and town center.
Fitzpatrick Castle Hotel	€90 - €130	Historic castle hotel with modern rooms, onsite restaurant, bar, fitness center, swimming pool, spa facilities, free Wi-Fi, complimentary breakfast option, picturesque location overlooking Dublin Bay, convenient access to Dún Laoghaire town center, Dalkey, and Killiney Hill.
The Royal Hotel & Merrill Leisure Club	€60 - €90	Comfortable rooms, onsite restaurant, bar, leisure club with swimming pool and gym, free Wi-Fi, complimentary breakfast option, budget-friendly accommodation, convenient location near Dún Laoghaire town center, seafront, and amenities.
Rochestown Lodge Hotel & Spa	€50 - €80	Modern rooms, onsite restaurant, bar, fitness center, swimming pool, spa facilities, free Wi-Fi, complimentary breakfast option, budget-friendly accommodation, convenient location near Dún Laoghaire town center, seafront, and amenities.

Top Attractions in Dún Laoghaire:

- **Enjoy a Promenade along Dún Laoghaire Pier:**
    - Take a leisurely stroll along Dún Laoghaire Pier, enjoying panoramic views of Dublin Bay and the surrounding coastline. (Free)

- **Picnic at People's Park:**
    - Pack a picnic and relax in People's Park, a beautifully landscaped park with colorful flower beds, mature trees, and a charming Victorian-style tearoom. (Free)
- **Explore Dún Laoghaire Harbour:**
    - Wander around Dún Laoghaire Harbour, admiring the array of yachts and boats, browsing the shops and cafes along the waterfront, and soaking up the maritime atmosphere. (Free)
- **Visit the National Maritime Museum:**
    - Explore the history of Ireland's maritime heritage at the National Maritime Museum, which offers free admission to its exhibits and occasional guided tours. (Free)
- **Attend a Workshop at LexIcon Library:**
    - Participate in a workshop or seminar at LexIcon Library, Dún Laoghaire's modern library and cultural center, offering free events and activities for all ages. (Free or low-cost)
- **Take a Dip in the Forty Foot:**
    - Brave the chilly waters and take a refreshing dip in the famous Forty Foot, a historic bathing spot favored by locals and visitors alike. (Free)
- **Hike the Cliff Path Loop:**
    - Embark on a scenic hike along the Cliff Path Loop, which offers stunning views of Dublin Bay, the coastline, and the iconic Dún Laoghaire Martello Towers. (Free)
- **Relax at Sandycove Beach:**
    - Spend a day soaking up the sun at Sandycove Beach, a tranquil cove with clear waters, sandy shores, and rocky outcrops perfect for sunbathing or swimming. (Free)
- **Explore the James Joyce Tower and Museum:**
    - Visit the James Joyce Tower and Museum, a historic landmark that offers free admission to its exhibits, including memorabilia related to the famous author's life and works. (Free)
- **Indulge in Ice Cream at Teddy's:**
    - Treat yourself to a cone of delicious ice cream from Teddy's, a beloved local institution known for its creamy scoops and scenic location overlooking Dún Laoghaire Harbour. (Inexpensive)
-

Dining in Dún Laoghaire:

Dún Laoghaire boasts a diverse culinary scene, with a wide range of restaurants, cafes, and eateries offering delicious cuisine from around the world. Some popular dining options in Dún Laoghaire include:

- **The Cookbook Cafe:** Located in the Pavilion Theatre, The Cookbook Cafe offers a menu of seasonal dishes made with locally sourced ingredients, as well as a selection of fine wines and craft beers.
- **Hartley's Restaurant:** Situated on Harbour Road, Hartley's Restaurant specializes in seafood and Irish cuisine, with a focus on fresh, locally sourced ingredients and inventive flavor combinations.

- **Fallon & Byrne:** A gourmet food emporium and restaurant, Fallon & Byrne offers a range of dining options, including a brasserie, wine bar, and rooftop terrace, as well as a deli and bakery selling artisanal produce.
- **Teddy's Ice Cream:** A Dún Laoghaire institution, Teddy's Ice Cream has been serving up delicious ice cream cones and sundaes for over 60 years, making it a favorite spot for locals and visitors alike.
- **Mao:** For those craving Asian cuisine, Mao offers a menu of healthy and flavorful dishes inspired by the cuisines of Asia, including Thailand, Vietnam, and Japan.

Entertainment and Nightlife:

Dún Laoghaire offers plenty of options for entertainment and nightlife, with a range of bars, pubs, and entertainment venues to suit every taste and preference. Some popular spots include:

- **The Purty Kitchen:** A historic pub and live music venue, The Purty Kitchen hosts regular music sessions, comedy nights, and events, making it a popular spot for locals and visitors alike.
- **The Forty Foot:** Situated on the East Pier, The Forty Foot is a traditional Irish pub offering stunning views of Dublin Bay, as well as a selection of craft beers, cocktails, and pub grub.
- **The Lighthouse Cinema:** Dún Laoghaire's Lighthouse Cinema is a boutique cinema that screens a diverse range of films, including arthouse, independent, and classic movies, providing a unique cinematic experience for film enthusiasts.

Day Trips from Dún Laoghaire:

Dún Laoghaire serves as an excellent base for exploring the surrounding area, with several attractions and destinations within easy reach. Some popular day trips from Dún Laoghaire include:

- **Killiney Hill:** Located just a short drive from Dún Laoghaire, Killiney Hill offers panoramic views of Dublin Bay and the Wicklow Mountains, as well as walking trails, picnic areas, and historic landmarks.
- **Dalkey:** Situated adjacent to Killiney Hill, the charming village of Dalkey is known for its picturesque streets, historic buildings, and scenic coastal walks, as well as its selection of cafes, restaurants, and artisanal shops.
- **Powerscourt Estate:** Located in County Wicklow, Powerscourt Estate is a historic estate that features a stunning mansion, formal gardens, and waterfall, as well as a range of activities and attractions for visitors to enjoy.

Tallaght

Tallaght, situated in southwest County Dublin, is a vibrant suburban town known for its rich history, diverse community, and array of amenities. This guide will provide an in-depth overview of Tallaght, highlighting its top attractions, dining options, shopping districts, and more.

Getting to Tallaght:

Tallaght is conveniently located within easy reach of Dublin city center and surrounding areas, with various transportation options available:

- **Luas:** The Luas Red Line provides direct tram service to Tallaght from Dublin city center. The Tallaght Luas stop is centrally located, making it a convenient option for commuters and visitors.
- **Bus:** Dublin Bus operates several bus routes serving Tallaght, including the 27, 49, 54a, and 77. The town is also served by the Aircoach, a dedicated bus service that provides connections to Dublin Airport and other destinations.
- **Car:** Tallaght is accessible by car via the M50 motorway, with ample parking available in the town center and surrounding areas.

Hotel/ Guesthouse	Starting Price (per night)	Key Amenities
Maldron Hotel Tallaght	€70 - €100	Modern rooms, onsite restaurant, bar, fitness center, swimming pool, free Wi-Fi, complimentary breakfast option, convenient location near The Square Shopping Centre, Tallaght Stadium, and Tallaght Hospital.
Glashaus Hotel	€80 - €120	Stylish rooms, onsite restaurant, bar, free Wi-Fi, complimentary breakfast option, convenient location near Tallaght Stadium, The Square Shopping Centre, and public transportation links.
Plaza Hotel Tallaght	€90 - €130	Contemporary rooms, onsite restaurant, bar, fitness center, swimming pool, free Wi-Fi, complimentary breakfast option, spacious conference and event facilities, convenient location near Tallaght Stadium, The Square Shopping Centre, and public transportation links.
Abberley Court Hotel	€60 - €90	Comfortable rooms, onsite restaurant, bar, free Wi-Fi, complimentary breakfast option, budget-friendly accommodation, convenient location near Tallaght Stadium, The Square Shopping Centre, and public transportation links.
Kingswood Hotel Citywest	€50 - €80	Modern rooms, onsite restaurant, bar, fitness center, free parking, free Wi-Fi, budget-friendly accommodation, convenient location near Citywest Convention Centre, Citywest Business Campus, and public transportation links.

Top Attractions in Tallaght:

Tallaght offers a range of attractions and landmarks that showcase its cultural heritage and natural beauty. Some of the top attractions in Tallaght include:

- **Tallaght Stadium:** Home to Shamrock Rovers Football Club, Tallaght Stadium is a modern sports venue that hosts soccer matches, concerts, and other events throughout the year.
- **Tallaght Library:** Situated in the heart of Tallaght, Tallaght Library is a hub of cultural activity, offering a range of resources, events, and exhibitions for visitors of all ages.
- **Tallaght Adventure World:** A popular destination for families, Tallaght Adventure World features indoor and outdoor activities, including go-karting, laser tag, and an adventure playground.

- **The Square Tallaght:** As one of Ireland's largest shopping centers, The Square Tallaght is a shopper's paradise, offering a diverse selection of shops, restaurants, and entertainment options.
- **Tymon Park:** Located on the outskirts of Tallaght, Tymon Park is a picturesque green space that features walking trails, sports facilities, and picnic areas, making it an ideal spot for outdoor recreation and relaxation.

Dining in Tallaght:

Tallaght boasts a diverse culinary scene, with a wide range of restaurants, cafes, and eateries offering cuisine from around the world. Some popular dining options in Tallaght include:

- **The Olive Tree Restaurant:** Located in the Plaza Hotel Tallaght, The Olive Tree Restaurant offers a menu of Mediterranean-inspired dishes, as well as a selection of fine wines and cocktails.
- **KC Peaches:** A popular cafe chain, KC Peaches serves up fresh and healthy dishes made with locally sourced ingredients, including salads, sandwiches, and smoothies.
- **The Dragon Inn:** For those craving Chinese cuisine, The Dragon Inn offers a menu of traditional and contemporary dishes, including dim sum, noodles, and stir-fries.
- **The Blazin' Grill:** Known for its flame-grilled steaks and burgers, The Blazin' Grill offers a menu of hearty comfort food favorites, as well as a selection of craft beers and cocktails.
- **The Eagle House:** Situated in Tallaght Village, The Eagle House is a traditional Irish pub that offers a cozy atmosphere, live music performances, and a menu of pub grub classics.

Entertainment and Nightlife:

Tallaght offers plenty of options for entertainment and nightlife, with a variety of bars, pubs, and entertainment venues to choose from. Some popular spots include:

- **The Square Bar:** Located in The Square Tallaght, The Square Bar offers a lively atmosphere, live music performances, and a selection of beers, wines, and cocktails.
- **Molloys Pub:** A traditional Irish pub, Molloys Pub offers a cozy ambiance, friendly service, and a menu of pub grub favorites, as well as a selection of craft beers and spirits.
- **Cuckoo's Nest:** Situated in Tallaght Village, Cuckoo's Nest is a popular spot for live music, DJ nights, and karaoke, offering a vibrant atmosphere and late-night entertainment.
- **The Old Mill Bar:** Known for its historic charm and character, The Old Mill Bar is housed in a converted mill building and offers a menu of traditional Irish dishes, as well as a selection of beers and whiskeys.

Day Trips from Tallaght:

Tallaght serves as an excellent base for exploring the surrounding area, with several attractions and destinations within easy reach. Some popular day trips from Tallaght include:

- **Hellfire Club:** Located in the Dublin Mountains, the Hellfire Club is a historic ruin that offers panoramic views of Dublin city and the surrounding countryside, as well as walking trails and picnic areas.

Malahide

Malahide, located just north of Dublin, is a picturesque coastal town renowned for its scenic beauty, historic landmarks, and vibrant atmosphere. Nestled along the shores of the Irish Sea, Malahide offers visitors a tranquil retreat from the bustling city life while still providing easy access to Dublin's attractions.

With a history dating back over a thousand years, Malahide boasts a rich heritage that is evident in its well-preserved medieval castle, charming village center, and scenic coastal walks. The focal point of the town is Malahide Castle, a magnificent fortress surrounded by sprawling gardens, woodlands, and a picturesque lake. Visitors can explore the castle's interior, wander through the tranquil gardens, or enjoy a leisurely picnic on the grounds.

Beyond its historic landmarks, Malahide is also known for its vibrant dining scene, with an array of restaurants, cafes, and pubs offering everything from traditional Irish fare to international cuisine. Whether enjoying freshly caught seafood overlooking the harbor or savoring a pint of Guinness in a cozy pub, visitors are sure to find something to tantalize their taste buds.

For outdoor enthusiasts, Malahide offers plenty of opportunities to explore its natural beauty, from scenic coastal walks along the Velvet Strand to birdwatching in the nearby Malahide Estuary. The town's marina is also a popular spot for sailing and water sports, while nearby Malahide Golf Club offers a challenging course set amidst stunning coastal scenery.

Luxury but Affordable Accommodation in Malahide

Accommodation	Pros	Cons	Starting Price
Grand Hotel Malahide	Seafront location, modern amenities	Can be noisy during peak season	€120 per night
Marine Court Hotel	Central location, friendly staff	Limited on-site amenities	€100 per night
White Sands Hotel	Scenic views, beach access	Some rooms may be outdated	€90 per night

Creative Alternatives to Experience Paid Attractions for Free in Malahide

- **Malahide Castle Gardens**: While admission to the castle itself may require a fee, visitors can explore the expansive gardens and woodland walks surrounding the castle for free.
- **Malahide Beach**: Spend a relaxing day soaking up the sun on the sandy shores of Malahide Beach, taking in panoramic views of Dublin Bay and Lambay Island.
- **Malahide Marina**: Take a leisurely stroll along the marina promenade, admiring the luxury yachts and sailboats moored in the harbor, all without spending a penny.

Best Free Audio Guides and Apps for Malahide

Guide/App	Covers	Download	Cost
Malahide Heritage Trail	Historic sites, local landmarks	Website	Free
Malahide Coastal Walk	Scenic coastal routes, wildlife spotting	App Store/Google Play Store	Free
Malahide Castle Audio Guide	Castle history, gardens tour	Website	Free

Luxurious Yet Affordable Experiences in Malahide

- **Malahide Castle Gardens**: Spend a leisurely afternoon exploring the lush gardens and woodland walks surrounding Malahide Castle, where admission is free.
- **Malahide Marina**: Take a scenic stroll along the marina promenade, soaking up views of the harbor and luxury yachts without spending a dime.
- **Velvet Strand**: Relax on the sandy shores of Velvet Strand beach, enjoying panoramic views of Dublin Bay and the Irish Sea, all for free.

Howth

Howth, a charming coastal village nestled on the outskirts of Dublin, offers a delightful escape from the hustle and bustle of city life. Perched on the scenic Howth Peninsula, this picturesque village boasts stunning vistas of the Irish Sea, rugged cliffs, and lush greenery, making it a haven for nature lovers and outdoor enthusiasts alike.

Steeped in maritime history, Howth has long been a thriving fishing village, and its bustling harbor remains a focal point of activity. Visitors can watch as fishing boats unload their daily catch or embark on a scenic boat tour to explore the surrounding coastline and nearby islands.

Howth is also renowned for its culinary delights, with an array of seafood restaurants, quaint cafes, and traditional pubs lining its charming streets. Whether indulging in freshly caught fish and chips or savoring a pint of Guinness overlooking the harbor, visitors are sure to delight in the village's gastronomic offerings.

For outdoor enthusiasts, Howth offers a myriad of activities, from scenic hikes along the cliff paths to leisurely strolls through its lush parks and gardens. The Howth Head Loop Trail offers breathtaking views of Dublin Bay and beyond, while the tranquil grounds of Howth Castle provide a peaceful retreat from the hustle and bustle of everyday life.

Luxury but Affordable Accommodation in Howth

Accommodation	Pros	Cons	Starting Price
King Sitric	Seaside location, charming rooms	Limited availability in peak season	€120 per night
Marine Hotel	Stunning sea views, spa facilities	Some rooms may be outdated	€100 per night
Deer Park Hotel	Scenic setting, golf course nearby	Remote location, car recommended	€90 per night

Top Cheap Eats in Howth

Restaurant	What to Try	Starting Price	Tips
The Doghouse	Gourmet Hot Dogs	€5	Opt for lunch specials for budget-friendly options
Howth Market	Various Street Food	€5-10	Explore the market stalls for affordable eats
The Brass Monkey	Seafood Chowder	€8	Lunch menu offers good value for money
O'Connell's	Traditional Irish Fare	€10	Enjoy hearty pub grub at reasonable prices
Octopussy's Seafood Tapas	Seafood Tapas	€12	Share dishes to sample a variety of flavors

Creative Alternatives to Experience Paid Attractions for Free in Howth

- **Howth Castle**: Explore the exterior and gardens for free or attend special events and open days hosted by the castle.
- **Howth Cliff Walk**: Enjoy panoramic views of the coastline and Dublin Bay on a leisurely stroll along the cliff paths, free of charge.
- **Howth Harbour**: Watch the fishing boats come and go, soak up the atmosphere of the bustling harbor, and enjoy the scenic views, all without spending a dime.

Best Free Audio Guides and Apps for Howth

Guide/App	Covers	Download	Cost
Howth Audio Guide	Coastal walks, historic sites, local lore	App Store/Google Play Store	Free
Howth Heritage Trail	Heritage sites, maritime history	Website	Free
Howth Nature Trail	Natural landmarks, wildlife spotting	Website	Free

Luxurious Yet Affordable Experiences in Howth

- **Howth Castle Gardens**: Wander through the tranquil gardens surrounding the castle, admiring the lush greenery and scenic views, free of charge.
- **Howth Market**: Indulge in artisanal treats and locally sourced produce at this bustling market, where you can sample gourmet delights without breaking the bank.
- **Howth Lighthouse**: Take a leisurely stroll along the pier to admire the iconic lighthouse and soak up the coastal views, all for free.

Galway

Galway City, located on the west coast of Ireland, situated at the mouth of Galway Bay and overlooking the Atlantic Ocean, Galway is often referred to as the "City of the Tribes," a nod to the 14 merchant families who once dominated its commerce and politics.

Steeped in history, Galway's medieval streets are adorned with historic landmarks such as Lynch's Castle and the Spanish Arch, offering visitors a glimpse into its storied past. The city's colorful buildings, bustling markets, and lively street performers create a lively and welcoming atmosphere that captivates visitors from around the world.

Galway's cultural scene is second to none, with an array of theaters, galleries, and music venues showcasing the best of Irish and international talent. The annual Galway International Arts Festival, held in July, attracts artists and performers from across the globe, while the city's traditional pubs are renowned for their live music sessions and lively atmosphere.

In addition to its cultural attractions, Galway is a paradise for foodies, with an abundance of restaurants, cafes, and food markets serving up delicious fare made from locally sourced ingredients. From fresh seafood caught off the nearby coast to hearty Irish stews and international cuisine, Galway offers a culinary experience to suit every palate.

Luxury but Affordable Accommodation in Galway City

Hotel/ Guesthouse	Starting Price (per night)	Key Amenities
The Galmont Hotel & Spa	€90 - €120	Elegant rooms, onsite restaurants, bars, fitness center, swimming pool, spa facilities, stunning views of Lough Atalia, free Wi-Fi, complimentary breakfast option, convenient location near Eyre Square and Galway city center.
The Connacht Hotel	€70 - €100	Modern rooms, onsite restaurant, bar, fitness center, swimming pool, leisure club, children's play area, free Wi-Fi, complimentary breakfast option, ample parking, convenient location near Galway city center and Salthill Promenade.
The Hardiman	€100 - €150	Historic hotel with stylish rooms, onsite restaurant, bar, fitness center, spa facilities, elegant decor, free Wi-Fi, complimentary breakfast option, central location on Eyre Square, within walking distance of Galway's shops, restaurants, and attractions.
Jurys Inn Galway	€80 - €120	Comfortable rooms, onsite restaurant, bar, free Wi-Fi, budget-friendly accommodation, convenient location near Galway city center

Top Cheap Eats in Galway City

Restaurant	What to Try	Starting Price	Tips
McDonagh's Fish & Chips	Fish and Chips	€10	Enjoy fresh seafood with stunning harbor views
The Pie Maker	Gourmet Pies	€8	Opt for the lunch menu for discounted prices
Kai	Modern Irish Cuisine	€12	Early bird menus offer great value for money
The Dough Bros	Wood-Fired Pizza	€10	Lunchtime deals offer good value for money
The Secret Garden	Vegetarian and Vegan Options	€12	Enjoy a tranquil atmosphere and delicious food

Creative Alternatives to Experience Paid Attractions for Free in Galway City

- **Spanish Arch**: Take a leisurely stroll along the promenade near the Spanish Arch, enjoying views of the River Corrib and Galway Bay, all without spending a penny.
- **Lynch's Castle**: Admire the exterior of Lynch's Castle, a medieval landmark in the heart of Galway, and learn about its history from informational plaques located nearby, for free.
- **Galway City Museum**: While admission fees may apply to certain exhibitions, visitors can explore the exterior of the Galway City Museum and enjoy views of the Claddagh and Galway Bay from its riverside location, without paying admission fees.

Best Free Audio Guides and Apps for Galway City

Guide/App	Covers	Cost

Galway Audio Guide	Historic sites, local landmarks	Free
Galway Walking Tours	Guided walking routes, points of interest	Free
Galway Food Trail	Culinary highlights, artisanal producers	Free

Luxurious Yet Affordable Experiences in Galway City

- **Galway Bay Cruise**: Take a leisurely cruise along Galway Bay, enjoying panoramic views of the city skyline and coastline, for a nominal fee.
- **Connemara Day Trip**: Embark on a guided day trip to Connemara, exploring its rugged landscapes, picturesque villages, and ancient monuments, all for a modest cost.
- **Traditional Music Session**: Immerse yourself in the lively atmosphere of a traditional Irish music session at one of Galway's cozy pubs, enjoying toe-tapping tunes and warm hospitality without breaking the bank.
- **Walk along the Salthill Promenade:** Enjoy a leisurely stroll along the scenic Salthill Promenade, overlooking Galway Bay and the Atlantic Ocean. (Free)
- **Visit the Spanish Arch:** Explore the historic Spanish Arch, a 16th-century stone archway overlooking the River Corrib. (Free)
- **Galway City Museum:** Discover the history and culture of Galway City at the Galway City Museum, featuring exhibits on archaeology, history, and maritime heritage. (Free admission)
- **Traditional Music Session:** Experience the lively atmosphere of a traditional Irish music session at a local pub in Galway City. (Cost: Price of drinks)
- **Galway Market:** Browse the stalls at the Galway Market, offering a diverse selection of artisan crafts, locally produced foods, and handmade goods. (Free to visit)
- **Kayaking on the River Corrib:** Rent a kayak and explore the scenic beauty of the River Corrib, paddling past landmarks such as the Claddagh and the Cathedral. (Starting Price: €20 per person)
- **Galway City Walking Tour:** Join a guided walking tour of Galway City, exploring its medieval streets, historic landmarks, and vibrant street art. (Starting Price: €10 per person)
- **Galway Arts Centre:** Visit the Galway Arts Centre to admire contemporary art exhibitions, live performances, and cultural events. (Free admission to exhibitions)
- **Eyre Square:** Relax in Eyre Square, a bustling public park in the heart of Galway City, surrounded by shops, cafes, and historic monuments. (Free)
- **Galway Cathedral:** Marvel at the stunning architecture of Galway Cathedral, with its soaring spires and intricate stained glass windows. (Free admission)
- **Galway City Tourist Train:** Hop aboard the Galway City Tourist Train for a fun and informative sightseeing tour of the city's top attractions. (Starting Price: €10 per person)
- **Galway Hooker Brewery Tour:** Take a guided tour of the Galway Hooker Brewery to learn about the brewing process and sample craft beers. (Starting Price: €15 per person)
- **Galway City Gastronomy Tour:** Embark on a gastronomic journey through Galway City, sampling delicious local specialties and culinary delights. (Starting Price: €25 per person)
- **Galway Whiskey Trail:** Follow the Galway Whiskey Trail to visit whiskey bars and distilleries, tasting a variety of Irish whiskeys along the way. (Cost: Price of drinks)

- **Galway Bay Boat Cruise:** Take a scenic boat cruise on Galway Bay, admiring panoramic views of the coastline and the Cliffs of Moher in the distance. (Starting Price: €20 per person)
- **Galway City Bike Tour:** Explore Galway City on two wheels with a guided bike tour, pedaling past landmarks like the Long Walk and the National University of Ireland. (Starting Price: €15 per person)
- **Galway Atlantaquaria:** Dive into the underwater world at Galway Atlantaquaria, Ireland's largest aquarium, featuring marine life exhibits and interactive displays. (Starting Price: €10 per person)
- **Galway Ghost Tour:** Join a spine-chilling ghost tour of Galway City, uncovering tales of haunted buildings, mysterious legends, and paranormal activity. (Starting Price: €15 per person)
- **Galway City Escape Room:** Test your wits and teamwork skills at a Galway City escape room, solving puzzles and unraveling mysteries to escape before time runs out. (Starting Price: €20 per person)
- **Galway Film Fleadh:** Immerse yourself in the world of cinema at the Galway Film Fleadh, Ireland's leading film festival, featuring screenings, workshops, and special events. (Starting Price: Ticket prices vary)
-

Clifden

Clifden serves as the vibrant gateway to the stunning landscapes of Connemara. Surrounded by majestic mountains, pristine beaches, and scenic countryside, Clifden offers visitors a perfect blend of natural beauty, outdoor adventures, and traditional Irish charm.

Founded in the early 19th century by John D'Arcy, Clifden is a quaint and picturesque town known for its colorful buildings, bustling streets, and welcoming atmosphere. The town's central square, known as Market Square, is a hub of activity, with lively markets, artisanal shops, and cozy cafes offering a taste of local life.

Clifden's rich history is evident in its architectural landmarks, such as the neo-Gothic Clifden Castle and the charming Clifden Courthouse, which now serves as the town's heritage center. Visitors can learn about Clifden's maritime past at the Station House Museum, housed in the former railway station, and explore the ruins of the nearby Kylemore Abbey, a stunning 19th-century mansion set amidst lush gardens and woodland.

Beyond its historical attractions, Clifden is a paradise for outdoor enthusiasts, with an array of activities to enjoy amidst its breathtaking landscapes. From hiking and biking along the Connemara National Park trails to horseback riding along the scenic coastline and water sports on the wild Atlantic waves, there's no shortage of adventures to be had in this coastal gem.

Luxury but Affordable Accommodation in Clifden

Accommodation	Pros	Cons	Starting Price
Abbeyglen Castle Hotel	Scenic views, historic charm	Slightly out of town center	€130 per night
Clifden Station House Hotel	Central location, leisure facilities	Limited parking	€120 per night
Foyles Hotel	Family-friendly, modern amenities	Some rooms may be small	€100 per night

Top Cheap Eats in Clifden

Restaurant	What to Try	Starting Price	Tips
The Walsh's Bakery	Gourmet Sandwiches	€8	Opt for the lunch menu for discounted prices
Guys Bar & Snug	Traditional Irish Fare	€12	Lunch specials offer good value for money
Veldon's Seafarer	Seafood Chowder	€9	Ideal for a quick and affordable lunch
Off the Square	Wood-Fired Pizza	€10	Lunchtime deals offer good value for money
The Twisted Mackerel	Pub Grub	€10	Generous portions make it a good value meal

Creative Alternatives to Experience Paid Attractions for Free in Clifden

- **Clifden Castle**: While guided tours of the castle may require a fee, visitors can explore the exterior of this historic landmark and enjoy panoramic views of the surrounding countryside, all without spending a penny.
- **Connemara National Park**: Spend a day exploring the stunning landscapes of Connemara National Park, taking in the breathtaking views of mountains, lakes, and woodlands, all for free.
- **Sky Road Drive**: Take a scenic drive along the famous Sky Road route, enjoying panoramic views of the Connemara coastline and offshore islands, all for free.

Best Free Audio Guides and Apps for Clifden

Guide/App	Covers	Cost
Clifden Audio Guide	Historic sites, local landmarks	Free
Connemara National Park App	Hiking trails, wildlife	Free
Sky Road Driving Guide	Scenic drives, points of interest	Free

Luxurious Yet Affordable Experiences in Clifden

- **Connemara Pony Trek**: Embark on a guided pony trek through the scenic countryside surrounding Clifden, taking in panoramic views of mountains, lakes, and coastline, all for a modest cost.
- **Kylemore Abbey Gardens**: Explore the beautifully landscaped gardens surrounding Kylemore Abbey, taking in the colorful floral displays and tranquil lakeside views, all for a nominal fee.
- **Traditional Music Session**: Immerse yourself in the lively atmosphere of a traditional Irish music session at one of Clifden's cozy pubs, enjoying toe-tapping tunes and warm hospitality without breaking the bank.
- **Sky Road**: Take a scenic drive along the famous Sky Road, offering breathtaking panoramic views of Clifden Bay and the surrounding coastline. The road is accessible free of charge, providing an unforgettable journey through Connemara's stunning landscapes.
- **Clifden Beaches**: Spend a leisurely day lounging on the pristine beaches near Clifden, such as Mannin Bay or Dog's Bay. Enjoy the serene coastal scenery and perhaps dip your toes in the refreshing Atlantic waters, all at no cost.
- **Alcock and Brown Landing Site**: Discover the aviation history of Clifden by visiting the Alcock and Brown Landing Site, where the pioneering aviators completed the first non-stop transatlantic flight in 1919. The site is marked by a monument and offers stunning views of the surrounding countryside, with no admission fee.
- **Clifden Market**: Browse the stalls at Clifden Market, held regularly in the town center, where you can find locally crafted goods, artisanal products, and unique souvenirs. Entry to the market is free, allowing you to peruse at your leisure.
- **Traditional Music Sessions**: Immerse yourself in the vibrant culture of Clifden by attending a traditional music session at one of the local pubs. Many establishments host live music performances free of charge, providing an authentic Irish experience.
- **Connemara Giant Connemara Ponies**: Visit the Connemara Giant Connemara Ponies farm, where you can meet these iconic Irish ponies and learn about their history and heritage. Guided tours are available at affordable rates, offering an educational and memorable experience for all ages.
- **Connemara Heritage and History Centre**: Delve into the rich history and heritage of Connemara at the Connemara Heritage and History Centre, where exhibits

showcase the region's cultural legacy. Entry prices are reasonable, allowing you to explore the exhibits and learn about Connemara's fascinating past.
- **Connemara Greenway**: Cycle or walk along the Connemara Greenway, a scenic trail that winds its way through Connemara's picturesque landscapes. Enjoy stunning views of mountains, lakes, and coastline along the way, with access to the Greenway free of charge.
-

County Kerry

County Kerry, located in the southwest of Ireland, is renowned for its breathtaking scenery, rugged coastline, and rich cultural heritage. One of the most iconic landmarks in County Kerry is the Ring of Kerry, a scenic drive that winds its way along the coastline, offering panoramic views of the Atlantic Ocean, lush green countryside, and charming coastal villages. This 179-kilometer route takes travelers through some of Kerry's most picturesque landscapes, including the towering peaks of the MacGillycuddy's Reeks, the sparkling waters of Killarney's lakes, and the dramatic cliffs of the Skellig Coast.

History seeps through the very soil of County Kerry, with ancient sites and archaeological wonders dotting the landscape. One of the most famous historical sites in the county is the Skellig Michael, a UNESCO World Heritage Site located off the coast of the Iveragh Peninsula. This remote island is home to an ancient monastic settlement dating back to the 6th century, where monks lived in solitude and prayer amidst the rugged beauty of the Atlantic.

In addition to its natural beauty and historical sites, County Kerry is also renowned for its vibrant cultural heritage. Traditional music, dance, and storytelling are deeply ingrained in the fabric of Kerry's communities, with lively sessions held in pubs and village halls throughout the county. Visitors can experience the magic of Irish music and dance at festivals such as the Fleadh Cheoil Chiarraí, which celebrates Kerry's rich musical heritage with concerts, workshops, and lively sessions.

Kerry's history is also intertwined with tales of rebellion and resistance, particularly during the struggle for Irish independence in the early 20th century. The county played a significant role in the War of Independence and the Irish Civil War, with key events taking place in towns such as Tralee, Killarney, and Listowel. Today, visitors can learn about Kerry's revolutionary past at museums and heritage centers across the county, including the Kerry County Museum in Tralee.

For outdoor enthusiasts, County Kerry offers a wealth of opportunities for adventure and exploration. The Killarney National Park, Ireland's oldest national park, is a haven for hikers, cyclists, and nature lovers, with miles of trails winding through ancient woodlands, shimmering lakes, and cascading waterfalls. The Dingle Peninsula, with its rugged cliffs and sandy beaches, is a paradise for surfers, kayakers, and wildlife enthusiasts, while the Gap of Dunloe offers stunning views of the MacGillycuddy's Reeks and the Black Valley.

Top Attractions:
- **Ring of Kerry**: A scenic driving route that offers panoramic views of mountains, lakes, and coastal cliffs.
- **Killarney National Park**: Ireland's oldest national park, home to the Lakes of Killarney, Muckross House, and Torc Waterfall.
- **Dingle Peninsula**: A stunning coastal area with picturesque villages, ancient ruins, and dramatic cliffs.
- **Gap of Dunloe**: A narrow mountain pass that can be explored by foot, bike, or traditional horse-drawn carriage.

- **Skellig Islands**: Located off the coast of Kerry, these UNESCO World Heritage sites are home to ancient monastic ruins and abundant birdlife.
- **Slea Head Drive**: A scenic coastal drive that offers views of rugged cliffs, sandy beaches, and historic sites.
- **Ross Castle**: A 15th-century fortress located on the shores of Lough Leane, near Killarney.
- **Skellig Ring**: A less crowded alternative to the Ring of Kerry, offering stunning views of the Skellig Islands.
- **Carrantuohill**: Ireland's highest peak, offering challenging hiking trails and breathtaking views from the summit.
- **Inch Beach**: A beautiful stretch of sandy beach popular for swimming, surfing, and long walks.

Money-Saving Tips:

- **Transportation**: Explore the area by public bus, bike rental, or carpooling to save on transportation costs.
- **Killarney National Park:** Explore the stunning landscapes of Killarney National Park with its picturesque lakes, mountains, and woodland trails. Free entry.
- **Ross Castle:** Visit the 15th-century Ross Castle, located on the shores of Lough Leane. Guided tours available from €5.00.
- **Gap of Dunloe:** Take a scenic hike or horse-drawn carriage ride through the breathtaking Gap of Dunloe. Carriage rides start from €25.00 per person.
- **Muckross House and Gardens:** Tour the elegant Muckross House and its beautiful gardens, set against the backdrop of the Lakes of Killarney. Guided tours from €9.00.
- **Torc Waterfall:** Admire the cascading waters of Torc Waterfall, located in the heart of Killarney National Park. Free entry.
- **Dingle Peninsula:** Drive the scenic Slea Head Drive along the rugged Dingle Peninsula, stopping at picturesque villages and historic sites. Free, except for fuel costs.
- **Inch Beach:** Relax on the pristine shores of Inch Beach, known for its wide expanse of golden sand and stunning Atlantic views. Free entry.
- **Ring of Kerry:** Embark on a self-guided drive along the famous Ring of Kerry, passing through charming towns, coastal cliffs, and scenic vistas. Free, except for fuel costs.
- **Skellig Islands:** Take a boat trip to the UNESCO World Heritage-listed Skellig Islands, home to ancient monastic ruins and seabird colonies. Boat tours start from €50.00 per person.
- **Killarney Jaunting Cars:** Enjoy a traditional jaunting car ride through Killarney National Park, accompanied by a knowledgeable jarvey. Rides from €25.00 per person.
- **Carrantuohill:** Hike to the summit of Carrantuohill, Ireland's highest peak, for breathtaking views of the surrounding mountains and valleys. Free, except for transportation costs.
- **Killarney Brewing Company:** Take a guided tour of Killarney Brewing Company and sample their range of craft beers. Tours from €10.00 including tastings.
- **Glenbeigh Horse Riding:** Experience horse riding along the beaches and trails of Glenbeigh, with options for riders of all levels. Trail rides from €35.00 per person.
- **Kenmare Lace and Design Centre:** Learn about the intricate art of Kenmare lace-making at the Kenmare Lace and Design Centre. Entry from €3.00.

- **Ballycarbery Castle:** Explore the atmospheric ruins of Ballycarbery Castle, overlooking the scenic estuary of the River Fertha. Free entry.
- **Valentia Island:** Visit Valentia Island and discover its rugged coastline, historic sites, and panoramic views. Free, except for transportation costs.
- **Killarney Golf & Fishing Club:** Tee off at Killarney Golf & Fishing Club, renowned for its championship courses set amidst stunning natural scenery. Green fees from €40.00.
- **Kenmare Bay Cruise:** Take a scenic cruise on Kenmare Bay, passing by picturesque villages, islands, and wildlife habitats. Cruises from €15.00 per person.
- **Ladies View:** Enjoy panoramic views of the Lakes of Killarney from Ladies View, named after Queen Victoria's ladies-in-waiting who admired the scenery. Free entry.
- **Kerry Cliffs:** Marvel at the dramatic Kerry Cliffs, towering 300 meters above the Atlantic Ocean, offering breathtaking views of the Skellig Islands. Entry from €4.00.
-

Sample Itinerary:

- Day 1: Explore Killarney National Park, including Muckross House and Torc Waterfall.
- Day 2: Drive the Ring of Kerry, stopping at viewpoints, beaches, and quaint villages along the way.
- Day 3: Visit the Dingle Peninsula, including Slea Head Drive, Dunquin Pier, and the town of Dingle.
- Day 4: Take a boat tour to the Skellig Islands (weather permitting) or explore the Gap of Dunloe.
- Day 5: Hike in the MacGillycuddy's Reeks mountains or relax on Inch Beach.
- Day 6: Visit Ross Castle and enjoy a leisurely walk or bike ride around Killarney town.
- Day 7: Depart from Kerry, taking in any final sights along the way.

Killarney: The Jewel of County Kerry

Situated on the shores of Lough Leane and surrounded by the rugged peaks of the MacGillycuddy's Reeks, Killarney serves as the gateway to Killarney National Park, Ireland's oldest national park and a UNESCO Biosphere Reserve.

Killarney's history dates back over a thousand years, with ancient landmarks such as Ross Castle and Muckross Abbey bearing testament to its storied past. The town's charming streets are lined with colorful buildings, traditional pubs, and quaint shops, creating a warm and inviting atmosphere that captivates visitors from around the world.

One of Killarney's most iconic attractions is the Ring of Kerry, a scenic driving route that winds its way through some of Ireland's most spectacular landscapes, including rugged coastlines, pristine lakes, and rolling hillsides. Visitors can also explore the Gap of

Dunloe, a narrow mountain pass carved by glaciers, and take a boat trip to the idyllic islands of Innisfallen and Ross Island.

In addition to its natural beauty, Killarney is known for its vibrant cultural scene, with traditional music sessions, lively festivals, and theatrical performances taking place throughout the year. The town's bustling markets and artisanal food producers showcase the best of local produce and crafts, while its world-class golf courses and luxury spas offer relaxation and indulgence for visitors seeking a taste of luxury.

Luxury but Affordable Accommodation in Killarney

Accommodation	Pros	Cons	Starting Price
The Brehon	Spa facilities, scenic views	Slightly out of town center	€130 per night
Killarney Plaza Hotel	Central location, modern amenities	Limited parking	€120 per night
Scotts Hotel	Historic charm, family-friendly	Some rooms may be small	€100 per night

Top Cheap Eats in Killarney

Restaurant	What to Try	Starting Price	Tips
Murphy's Bar & Grill	Traditional Irish	€12	Lunch specials offer good value for ...
Hannigan's Bar & Restaurant	Gourmet Sandwiches	€8	Opt for the lunch menu for discounted prices
Quinlan's Seafood Bar	Seafood Chowder	€9	Generous portions make it a good value meal
The Shire	Wood-Fired Pizza	€10	Lunchtime deals offer good value for money
Treyvaud's	International Cuisine	€12	Early bird menus offer great value for money

Creative Alternatives to Experience Paid Attractions for Free in Killarney

- **Ross Castle**: While guided tours of the castle may require a fee, visitors can explore the exterior of this historic landmark and enjoy panoramic views of Lough Leane and the surrounding countryside for free.
- **Muckross House Gardens**: Take a leisurely stroll through the beautifully landscaped gardens surrounding Muckross House, admiring the colorful floral displays and tranquil lakeside views, without paying admission fees.
- **Torc Waterfall**: Embark on a scenic hike to Torc Waterfall, one of Killarney's most famous natural landmarks, and enjoy the breathtaking cascade of water flowing amidst lush greenery, all for free.

Best Free Audio Guides and Apps for Killarney

Guide/App	Covers	Download	Cost
Killarney Audio Guide	Historic sites, local landmarks	Website	Free
Killarney National Park App	Hiking trails, wildlife	App Store/Google Play Store	Free
Killarney Town Trail	Cultural landmarks, architectural highlights	Website	Free

Luxurious Yet Affordable Experiences in Killarney

- **Killarney National Park**: Spend a day exploring the pristine landscapes of Killarney National Park, taking in the breathtaking views of lakes, mountains, and woodlands, all for free.
- **Traditional Music Session**: Immerse yourself in the vibrant culture of Killarney by attending a traditional music session at one of the town's cozy pubs, enjoying lively tunes and warm hospitality without breaking the bank.
- **Scenic Drive along the Ring of Kerry**: Take a self-guided drive along the iconic Ring of Kerry route, stopping at scenic viewpoints and attractions along the way, and soak up the stunning vistas of Ireland's southwest coast, all at your own pace and for a nominal cost.
- **Jaunting Car Tour of Killarney National Park**: Take a traditional jaunting car tour through Killarney National Park, where you'll be transported back in time as you journey through ancient woodlands, past shimmering lakes, and majestic mountains. Prices start at around €20 per person for a one-hour tour.
- **Muckross House and Gardens**: Explore the grandeur of Muckross House, a magnificent Victorian mansion set amidst beautifully landscaped gardens. Guided tours of the house and gardens are available for approximately €10 per person, offering a glimpse into Ireland's aristocratic past.
- **Boat Trip to Innisfallen Island**: Embark on a boat trip to Innisfallen Island, located on the picturesque Lough Leane. Here, you can explore the ruins of an ancient monastery and enjoy stunning views of the surrounding landscape. Boat trips typically cost around €15 per person.
- **Traditional Irish Music Session**: Immerse yourself in the lively atmosphere of a traditional Irish music session at one of Killarney's charming pubs. Enjoy the toe-tapping rhythms of fiddles, flutes, and bodhráns, all while sipping on a pint of Guinness. Admission is usually free, but it's customary to buy a drink or two to support the musicians.
- **Torc Waterfall Hike**: Lace up your hiking boots and embark on a scenic trek to Torc Waterfall, one of Killarney's most iconic natural attractions. The hike is free, and the waterfall can be accessed via a short walking trail from the nearby car park.
- **Ross Castle Guided Tour**: Step back in time with a guided tour of Ross Castle, a 15th-century fortress located on the shores of Lough Leane. Learn about the castle's fascinating history and the legendary O'Donoghue clan who once ruled here. Guided tours are priced at around €5 per person.
- **Killarney Brewing Company Tour**: Discover the art of craft beer brewing with a tour of the Killarney Brewing Company. Learn about the brewing process, sample a selection of locally brewed beers, and enjoy a behind-the-scenes look at this thriving brewery. Tours start at approximately €12 per person.
- **Cycle the Gap of Dunloe**: Rent a bike and cycle the scenic Gap of Dunloe, a narrow mountain pass flanked by rugged cliffs and sparkling lakes. Enjoy breathtaking views of the surrounding landscape as you pedal through this stunning natural wonder. Bike rentals start at around €15 per day.
- **Killarney Falconry Experience**: Get up close and personal with birds of prey with a falconry experience in Killarney. Learn the art of falconry from expert handlers and

enjoy the thrill of flying majestic birds such as hawks and owls. Experiences typically start at €25 per person for a one-hour session.
- **Traditional Irish Afternoon Tea**: Treat yourself to a decadent afternoon tea experience at one of Killarney's elegant hotels or tearooms. Indulge in a selection of finger sandwiches, scones with clotted cream and jam, and an assortment of sweet treats, all accompanied by a pot of fine Irish tea. Prices vary depending on the venue, but you can expect to pay around €20-€25 per person.
-

Dingle

Perched on the edge of the Atlantic Ocean, Dingle is surrounded by dramatic cliffs, pristine beaches, and rolling green hills, making it a paradise for outdoor enthusiasts and nature lovers. The town itself is a colorful maze of narrow streets lined with traditional pubs, artisanal shops, and cozy cafes, creating a vibrant and inviting atmosphere that captures the essence of Irish charm.

Dingle's rich heritage is evident in its ancient landmarks, such as the iconic Gallarus Oratory, an ancient stone church dating back over a thousand years, and the imposing ruins of Dunbeg Fort, a prehistoric cliffside fortress. Visitors can also explore the town's maritime history at the Dingle Oceanworld Aquarium and learn about the area's Gaelic past at the Blasket Islands Centre.

In addition to its historical attractions, Dingle is famous for its lively music scene, with traditional Irish music sessions taking place in pubs and venues throughout the town. The annual Dingle Film Festival attracts filmmakers and cinephiles from around the world, while the Dingle Food Festival showcases the best of local cuisine and artisanal produce.

Luxury but Affordable Accommodation in Dingle

Accommodation	Pros	Cons	Starting Price
Dingle Skellig Hotel	Seafront location, spa facilities	Slightly out of town center	€130 per night
Dingle Bay Hotel	Central location, modern amenities	Limited parking	€120 per night
Pax Guest House	Historic charm, family-friendly	Some rooms may be small	€100 per night

Top Cheap Eats in Dingle

Restaurant	What to Try	Starting Price	Tips
Murphy's Ice Cream	Gourmet Ice Cream	€4	Indulge in unique flavors made from local ingredients
The Fish Box	Fish and Chips	€10	Enjoy fresh seafood with stunning harbor views
Reel Dingle Fish	Seafood Chowder	€9	Ideal for a quick and affordable lunch
The Little Cheese Shop	Gourmet Sandwiches	€8	Opt for the lunch menu for discounted prices
John Benny's Pub	Traditional Irish Fare	€12	Lunch specials offer good value for money

Creative Alternatives to Experience Paid Attractions for Free in Dingle

- **Gallarus Oratory**: While guided tours of the oratory may require a fee, visitors can admire the exterior of this ancient stone church and marvel at its architectural beauty from the outside, all without spending a penny.
- **Dunbeg Fort**: Take a leisurely walk along the cliffside path near Dunbeg Fort, enjoying panoramic views of the rugged coastline and Atlantic Ocean, without paying admission fees.
- **Dingle Peninsula Drive**: Embark on a scenic drive around the Dingle Peninsula, stopping at viewpoints and attractions along the way, and soak up the stunning vistas of Ireland's southwest coast, all for free.

Best Free Audio Guides and Apps for Dingle

Guide/App	Covers	Download	Cost

Dingle Audio Guide	Historic sites, local landmarks	Website	Free
Dingle Peninsula App	Scenic drives, points of interest	App Store/Google Play Store	Free
Dingle Food Trail	Culinary highlights, artisanal producers	Website	Free

Luxurious Yet Affordable Experiences in Dingle

- **Coastal Walks**: Take a leisurely stroll along the scenic coastline of the Dingle Peninsula, enjoying panoramic views of the Atlantic Ocean and rugged cliffs, all for free.
- **Traditional Music Session**: Immerse yourself in the lively atmosphere of a traditional Irish music session at one of Dingle's cozy pubs, enjoying toe-tapping tunes and warm hospitality without breaking the bank.
- **Dingle Distillery Tour**: Embark on a guided tour of the Dingle Distillery, where you can learn about the art of whiskey-making and sample some of the finest spirits produced in Ireland, all for a nominal fee.
- **Dolphin Boat Tour with Dingle Dolphin Tours:**
    - Starting Price: €20-€25 per person
    - Specifics: Embark on a thrilling boat tour to see Fungie, the resident bottlenose dolphin of Dingle Bay, and enjoy panoramic views of the rugged coastline.
- **Hike along the Dingle Peninsula:**
    - Starting Price: Free
    - Specifics: Explore the breathtaking scenery of the Dingle Peninsula on foot, with numerous hiking trails offering stunning coastal vistas and scenic overlooks.
- **Visit Dingle Distillery:**
    - Starting Price: €15 per person for a guided tour
    - Specifics: Discover the art of whiskey distillation at Dingle Distillery, where you can take a guided tour and sample their award-winning spirits.
- **Explore Dingle Town:**
    - Starting Price: Free
    - Specifics: Wander through the charming streets of Dingle Town, lined with colorful shops, cozy pubs, and artisanal galleries showcasing local crafts.
- **Enjoy a Seafood Feast:**
    - Starting Price: €20-€30 per person
    - Specifics: Indulge in a delicious seafood meal at one of Dingle's renowned seafood restaurants, where you can savor fresh fish, shellfish, and other local delicacies.
- **Dingle Oceanworld Aquarium:**
    - Starting Price: €14 per adult
    - Specifics: Immerse yourself in the wonders of the ocean at Dingle Oceanworld Aquarium, home to a diverse array of marine life including sharks, turtles, and penguins.
- **Take a Scenic Drive along Slea Head:**
    - Starting Price: Free
    - Specifics: Hit the open road and embark on a scenic drive along the Slea Head Drive, one of Ireland's most stunning coastal routes, offering panoramic views of the Atlantic Ocean.
- **Dingle Peninsula Boat Trip:**
    - Starting Price: €20-€30 per person

- Specifics: Join a boat trip around the Dingle Peninsula, where you can admire the rugged cliffs, hidden coves, and ancient ruins from the sea.
- **Visit Dunquin Pier:**
  - Starting Price: Free
  - Specifics: Take a leisurely stroll to Dunquin Pier, a picturesque spot overlooking the Blasket Islands, and enjoy breathtaking views of the Atlantic Ocean.
- **Dingle Whiskey Bar:**
  - Starting Price: Varies
  - Specifics: Unwind with a whiskey tasting experience at one of Dingle's cozy whiskey bars, where you can sample a wide selection of Irish spirits in a relaxed atmosphere.
- **Explore Inch Beach:**
  - Starting Price: Free
  - Specifics: Spend a day at Inch Beach, a stunning stretch of golden sand that's perfect for sunbathing, swimming, and beachcombing.
- **Dingle Peninsula Bike Tour:**
  - Starting Price: €20-€30 per person for bike rental
  - Specifics: Cycle along the scenic roads of the Dingle Peninsula on a guided bike tour, stopping to admire the breathtaking views and historic landmarks along the way.
- **Dingle Artisan Food Market:**
  - Starting Price: Varies
  - Specifics: Browse the stalls of Dingle's weekly artisan food market, where you can sample and purchase a wide range of locally produced cheeses, baked goods, and gourmet treats.
- **Visit Gallarus Oratory:**
  - Starting Price: €5 per adult
  - Specifics: Explore the ancient stone church of Gallarus Oratory, a remarkable example of early Christian architecture dating back to the 7th century.
- **Kayak or Stand-Up Paddleboard Rental:**
  - Starting Price: €20-€30 per person
  - Specifics: Take to the water and rent a kayak or stand-up paddleboard to explore Dingle Bay and its secluded coves at your own pace.
- **Attend a Traditional Music Session:**
  - Starting Price: Free
  - Specifics: Experience the lively atmosphere of a traditional music session at one of Dingle's cozy pubs, where local musicians gather to play Irish tunes.
- **Dingle Peninsula Horseback Riding:**
  - Starting Price: €30-€40 per person for a guided ride
  - Specifics: Explore the rugged terrain of the Dingle Peninsula on horseback, with guided rides available for riders of all levels.
- **Visit the Blasket Islands Visitor Center:**
  - Starting Price: €5 per adult
  - Specifics: Learn about the history and culture of the Blasket Islands at the visitor center in Dunquin, with exhibits showcasing the islands' unique heritage.
- **Dingle Brewing Company Tour:**
  - Starting Price: €10 per person for a guided tour

- Specifics: Discover the art of craft brewing at Dingle Brewing Company, where you can take a guided tour of the brewery and sample their range of handcrafted beers.
- **Dingle Peninsula Photography Tour:**
  - Starting Price: €20-€30 per person
  - Specifics: Join a guided photography tour of the Dingle Peninsula, where you can capture stunning landscapes, dramatic seascapes, and colorful villages with the help of a professional photographer.

Kenmare

The town's name, "Kenmare" or "An Neidín" in Irish, translates to "little nest," reflecting its cozy and inviting atmosphere. Kenmare's charming streets are lined with colorful shops, traditional pubs, and artisanal cafes, creating a vibrant yet relaxed ambiance that captures the essence of Irish charm.

Kenmare's history dates back over 300 years, with landmarks such as Kenmare Stone Circle and Cromwell's Bridge bearing testament to its ancient past. Visitors can explore the town's rich heritage at the Kenmare Heritage Centre, which offers fascinating insights into the area's Gaelic roots and Anglo-Norman influences.

In addition to its historical attractions, Kenmare is a haven for outdoor enthusiasts, with an array of activities to enjoy amidst its stunning natural landscapes. From scenic hikes along the Kerry Way and kayaking adventures on Kenmare Bay to leisurely drives along the breathtaking Ring of Beara, there's something for everyone to enjoy in this tranquil corner of Ireland.

Luxury but Affordable Accommodation in Kenmare

Accommodation	Pros	Cons	Starting Price
Brook Lane Hotel	Central location, modern amenities	Limited parking	€130 per night
Kenmare Bay Hotel & Resort	Scenic views, leisure facilities	Slightly out of town center	€120 per night
O'Donnabhain's Guesthouse	Historic charm, family-friendly	Some rooms may be small	€100 per night

Top Cheap Eats in Kenmare

Restaurant	What to Try	Starting Price	Tips
Jam Cafe	Gourmet Sandwiches	€8	Opt for the lunch menu for discounted prices
Davitt's Restaurant	Traditional Irish Fare	€12	Lunch specials offer good value for money
PF McCarthy's	Pub Grub	€10	Generous portions make it a good value meal
Kenmare Ice Cream	Gourmet Ice Cream	€4	Indulge in unique flavors made from local ingredients
No. 35 Restaurant	International Cuisine	€12	Early bird menus offer great value for money

Creative Alternatives to Experience Paid Attractions for Free in Kenmare

- **Kenmare Stone Circle**: While guided tours of the stone circle may require a fee, visitors can admire this ancient monument and learn about its significance from informational plaques located nearby, all without spending a penny.
- **Kenmare Heritage Centre**: Explore the exterior of the Kenmare Heritage Centre and enjoy views of the historic buildings in the town center, all without paying admission fees.
- **Kenmare Bay**: Take a leisurely stroll along the waterfront, admiring views of Kenmare Bay and the surrounding countryside, all for free.

Best Free Audio Guides and Apps for Kenmare

Guide/App	Covers	Download	Cost
Kenmare Audio Guide	Historic sites, local landmarks	Website	Free
Kenmare Walking Tours	Guided walking routes, points of interest	App Store/Google Play Store	Free
Ring of Beara App	Scenic drives, attractions	App Store/Google Play Store	Free

Luxuriuos Yet Affordable Experiences in Kenmare

- **Kayak or Stand-Up Paddleboard on Kenmare Bay:**
    - Starting Price: €20-€30 per person
    - Specifics: Rent a kayak or stand-up paddleboard and explore the serene waters of Kenmare Bay, with stunning views of the surrounding mountains and coastline.
- **Explore Kenmare Town:**
    - Starting Price: Free
    - Specifics: Wander through the picturesque streets of Kenmare Town, lined with colorful shops, artisan boutiques, and cozy cafes. Don't miss the opportunity to browse for unique souvenirs or enjoy a leisurely stroll along the waterfront.
- **Sample Local Cuisine at Kenmare Restaurants:**
    - Starting Price: €20-€30 per person for a meal
    - Specifics: Indulge in a delicious meal featuring locally sourced ingredients at one of Kenmare's acclaimed restaurants or gastropubs. From fresh seafood to traditional Irish dishes, there's something to satisfy every palate.
- **Take a Scenic Drive along the Ring of Beara:**
    - Starting Price: Free
    - Specifics: Embark on a breathtaking drive along the scenic Ring of Beara, a lesser-known but equally stunning coastal route that offers panoramic views of the Atlantic Ocean and rugged landscapes.
- **Visit the Kenmare Lace and Design Centre:**
    - Starting Price: €5 per adult
    - Specifics: Discover the intricate art of Kenmare lace-making at the Kenmare Lace and Design Centre, where you can learn about the history of this traditional craft and admire exquisite lace creations.
- **Explore the Kenmare Stone Circle:**
    - Starting Price: Free
    - Specifics: Step back in time at the Kenmare Stone Circle, an ancient archaeological site consisting of 15 standing stones dating back to the

Bronze Age. Take a peaceful walk among the stones and soak in the mystical atmosphere.
- **Taste Whiskey at Kenmare Distillery:**
    - Starting Price: €15 per person for a tour and tasting
    - Specifics: Delve into the world of Irish whiskey at Kenmare Distillery, where you can take a guided tour of the distillery and sample a selection of their handcrafted spirits.
-

County Cork

A land of rugged coastlines, vibrant cities, and rolling countryside, located in the southwestern corner of Ireland. Stretching from the wild Atlantic coast to the lush green hills of inland villages, County Cork is a treasure trove of natural beauty, rich history, and unique cultural experiences. Let's embark on a journey to uncover the many delights that await in this enchanting corner of Ireland.

At the heart of County Cork lies its vibrant capital, Cork City, known affectionately as the "Rebel County." This dynamic city boasts a unique blend of old-world charm and modern sophistication, with its lively streets, historic landmarks, and thriving cultural scene. Wander along the picturesque River Lee, explore the bustling English Market, and soak up the atmosphere in lively pubs and traditional music venues. Don't miss iconic landmarks such as Cork City Gaol, St. Fin Barre's Cathedral, and the charming narrow streets of Shandon.

Venturing beyond the city limits, County Cork offers a diverse array of landscapes and attractions to explore. Along its rugged coastline, you'll find stunning beaches, dramatic cliffs, and picturesque fishing villages. The stunning Beara Peninsula, with its winding coastal roads and panoramic views, is a paradise for hikers, cyclists, and nature lovers. Further west, the rugged beauty of Mizen Head, Ireland's southernmost point, captivates visitors with its dramatic cliffs and historic lighthouse.

Inland, County Cork's rolling countryside is dotted with quaint villages, historic castles, and lush green farmland. The charming village of Blarney is famous for its iconic Blarney Castle, home to the legendary Blarney Stone, said to bestow the "gift of gab" upon those who kiss it. Nearby, the historic town of Cobh, known as the "Titanic's last port of call," offers fascinating maritime history and breathtaking views across Cork Harbour.

For those seeking outdoor adventures, County Cork offers a wealth of opportunities to explore its natural wonders. Lace up your hiking boots and traverse the rugged trails of the Sheepshead Peninsula or cycle along the scenic routes of the Great Western Greenway. Anglers can cast their lines in pristine rivers and lakes, while water sports enthusiasts can take to the waves along the county's beautiful coastline.

County Cork is also a haven for foodies, with its rich culinary heritage and abundance of local produce. Indulge in fresh seafood from the Atlantic, artisan cheeses from local creameries, and hearty traditional dishes served in cozy pubs and acclaimed restaurants. Sample local delicacies such as Cork's famous "spiced beef," creamy chowder, and irresistible pastries from renowned bakeries.

Throughout County Cork, you'll encounter a warm welcome and genuine hospitality from its friendly inhabitants, who take pride in sharing their unique culture and heritage. From lively festivals celebrating music, food, and folklore to intimate village gatherings and traditional ceilidhs, there's always something happening in County Cork to delight and inspire visitors.

Top Attractions:
- **Blarney Castle**: Famous for the Blarney Stone, where visitors can kiss the stone to gain the gift of eloquence.

- **Cork City**: Explore Ireland's second-largest city, known for its lively atmosphere, historic landmarks, and culinary scene.
- **Kinsale**: A picturesque seaside town known for its colorful streets, gourmet restaurants, and historic forts.
- **Ring of Beara**: A scenic driving route offering breathtaking views of rugged coastline, mountains, and picturesque villages.
- **Cobh**: A historic port town famous as the last port of call for the Titanic and the departure point for millions of Irish emigrants.
- **Fota Wildlife Park**: A conservation park with over 90 species of animals in naturalistic habitats.
- **Mizen Head**: Ireland's most southwestern point, offering dramatic cliffs, a historic lighthouse, and scenic walking trails.
- **English Market, Cork**: A vibrant indoor food market dating back to 1788, offering a wide range of fresh produce, meats, and artisanal goods.
- **Gougane Barra**: A tranquil valley with a scenic lake, forest walks, and a picturesque church located on an island.
- **Sheep's Head Peninsula**: A hidden gem with scenic coastal walks, deserted beaches, and stunning views of Bantry Bay and the Atlantic Ocean.

Money-Saving Tips:

- **Blarney Castle**: Book tickets online in advance to save on admission fees and avoid waiting in line to kiss the Blarney Stone.
- **Accommodation**: Consider staying in guesthouses, B&Bs, or self-catering accommodations for a more budget-friendly option compared to hotels.
- **Culinary Experiences**: Explore local markets, bakeries, and cafes for affordable dining options, and consider picnics with locally sourced ingredients.
- **Transportation**: Renting a car can provide flexibility and access to remote areas, but public buses are available for budget-conscious travelers.
- **Free Attractions**: Take advantage of free attractions such as parks, beaches, and scenic viewpoints to experience the natural beauty of County Cork without spending money.

Sample Itinerary:

- Day 1: Explore Cork City, visiting the English Market, St. Fin Barre's Cathedral, and Cork City Gaol.
- Day 2: Visit Blarney Castle and Gardens, then explore the charming town of Kinsale for lunch and a stroll along the harbor.
- Day 3: Drive the Ring of Beara, stopping at picturesque villages like Castletownbere and Eyeries, and enjoy scenic walks along the coast.
- Day 4: Explore the historic port town of Cobh, visiting the Titanic Experience, Cobh Heritage Centre, and St. Colman's Cathedral.
- Day 5: Spend a day at Fota Wildlife Park, exploring the extensive grounds and learning about conservation efforts.
- Day 6: Drive to Mizen Head, stopping at Gougane Barra along the way for walks and scenic views.
- Day 7: Discover the Sheep's Head Peninsula, hiking along the Sheep's Head Way trail and enjoying the coastal scenery.

Luxury on a budget Cork experiences

- **Explore Blarney Castle and Gardens:**
  - Starting Price: €18.00
  - Description: Kiss the legendary Blarney Stone for the gift of eloquence, explore the beautiful gardens, and discover the history of Blarney Castle.
- **Indulge in Gourmet Food at the English Market:**
  - Starting Price: Varies
  - Description: Sample artisanal cheeses, fresh seafood, and gourmet delicacies at Cork's historic English Market.
- **Take a Scenic Drive along the Wild Atlantic Way:**
  - Starting Price: Free
  - Description: Enjoy breathtaking coastal views as you drive along the rugged cliffs and sandy beaches of the Wild Atlantic Way.
- **Visit Cobh Heritage Centre:**
  - Starting Price: €9.00
  - Description: Learn about Ireland's maritime history, including the story of the Titanic, at the interactive Cobh Heritage Centre.
- **Tour Jameson Distillery Midleton:**
  - Starting Price: €20.00
  - Description: Discover the art of whiskey-making on a guided tour of the Jameson Distillery in Midleton, followed by a tasting of their renowned Irish whiskey.
- **Explore Fota Wildlife Park:**
  - Starting Price: €16.00
  - Description: Encounter exotic animals from around the world in a naturalistic setting at Fota Wildlife Park.
- **Enjoy a Seafood Feast in Kinsale:**
  - Starting Price: Varies
  - Description: Indulge in fresh seafood dishes at one of Kinsale's renowned restaurants, known as the "Gourmet Capital of Ireland."
- **Visit Cork City Gaol:**
  - Starting Price: €10.00
  - Description: Step back in time with a guided tour of Cork City Gaol, a historic former prison offering insights into Ireland's penal history.
- **Relax at Inchydoney Beach:**
  - Starting Price: Free
  - Description: Unwind on the sandy shores of Inchydoney Beach, renowned for its picturesque coastline and surfing opportunities.
- **Explore the Ruins of Charles Fort:**
  - Starting Price: €5.00
  - Description: Wander through the impressive stone fortifications of Charles Fort, offering panoramic views of Kinsale Harbor.
- **Take a Boat Trip to Garnish Island:**
  - Starting Price: €12.00 (boat trip)
  - Description: Embark on a scenic boat trip to Garnish Island, home to lush gardens, exotic plants, and scenic walking trails.
- **Discover the History of Cork City on a Walking Tour:**
  - Starting Price: Free (self-guided) or €15.00 (guided)
  - Description: Explore Cork City's historic landmarks, charming streets, and hidden gems on a guided walking tour or self-guided exploration.
- **Savor Artisanal Cheese at the Old Butter Roads Food Trail:**

- Starting Price: Varies
- Description: Follow the Old Butter Roads Food Trail and sample delicious artisanal cheeses from local producers.
- **Cycle the Great Western Greenway:**
  - Starting Price: Free (bring your bike) or rental fees apply
  - Description: Cycle along the Great Western Greenway, a scenic route offering stunning views of County Cork's countryside and coastline.
- **Attend a Traditional Music Session in a Local Pub:**
  - Starting Price: Price of drinks
  - Description: Immerse yourself in Ireland's traditional music scene by attending a lively session at a local pub in Cork.
- **Hike to the Top of Hungry Hill:**
  - Starting Price: Free
  - Description: Challenge yourself with a hike to the summit of Hungry Hill, the highest peak in the Caha Mountains, offering panoramic views of Bantry Bay.
- **Visit the Jameson Experience in Midleton:**
  - Starting Price: €20.00
  - Description: Learn about the heritage of Jameson Irish whiskey on a guided tour of the Jameson Experience, followed by a tasting of their signature spirits.
- **Explore the Gardens of Bantry House:**
  - Starting Price: €10.00
  - Description: Wander through the exquisite gardens of Bantry House, featuring terraced lawns, vibrant flower beds, and scenic views of Bantry Bay.
- **Take a Boat Trip to Cape Clear Island:**
  - Starting Price: €12.00 (ferry)
  - Description: Escape to Cape Clear Island for a day of hiking, birdwatching, and exploring Ireland's southernmost inhabited island.
- **Relax with Afternoon Tea at a Luxury Hotel:**
  - Starting Price: Varies
  - Description: Treat yourself to a decadent afternoon tea experience at one of County Cork's luxury hotels, enjoying a selection of teas, sandwiches, and pastries in elegant surroundings.

Kinsale: Ireland's Gourmet Capital by the Sea

Kinsale, a picturesque fishing town nestled along the rugged coastline of County Cork, is celebrated as Ireland's Gourmet Capital, renowned for its culinary delights, historic charm, and breathtaking coastal landscapes. With its colorful buildings, narrow winding streets, and scenic harbor, Kinsale exudes a quaint and inviting atmosphere that captivates visitors from near and far.

Steeped in history, Kinsale boasts a rich maritime heritage that dates back centuries. The town's historic streets are lined with beautifully preserved buildings, many of which date back to the 17th and 18th centuries when Kinsale was a bustling port and trading center. Visitors can explore landmarks such as Desmond Castle and Charles Fort, which offer fascinating insights into the town's storied past.

Kinsale's culinary scene is second to none, with an array of award-winning restaurants, cozy cafes, and traditional pubs serving up mouthwatering dishes made from locally sourced ingredients. From freshly caught seafood and gourmet cuisine to hearty Irish stews and artisanal cheeses, Kinsale offers a culinary experience to suit every taste and budget.

Beyond its culinary delights, Kinsale is a haven for outdoor enthusiasts, with an abundance of activities to enjoy along its rugged coastline. Visitors can take scenic walks along the coastal cliffs, embark on boat tours of the nearby islands, or try their hand at water sports such as sailing, kayaking, and paddleboarding in the sheltered waters of Kinsale Harbor.

Luxury but Affordable Accommodation in Kinsale

Accommodation	Pros	Cons	Starting Price
Actons Hotel	Seafront location, modern amenities	Limited parking	€120 per night
Trident Hotel			

I apologize for the interruption. Let me continue with the accommodation options for Kinsale:

Luxury but Affordable Accommodation in Kinsale

Accommodati	Pros	Cons	Starting
Actons Hotel	Seafront location, modern amenities	Limited parking	€120 per night
Trident Hotel	Stunning harbor views, spa	Some rooms may be small	€100 per night
Perryville	Historic charm, gourmet breakfast	Limited availability in peak season	€90 per night

Top Cheap Eats in Kinsale

Restaurant	What to Try	Starting Price	Tips
Dino's	Fish and Chips	€10	Enjoy panoramic views of the harbor while dining
The Poet's Corner	Traditional Irish Fare	€12	Lunch specials offer good value for money
Lemon Leaf Café	Gourmet Sandwiches	€8	Opt for the lunch menu for discounted prices
Jim Edwards	Seafood Chowder	€9	Generous portions make it a good value meal
The Blue Haven	Pub Grub	€10	Lunch specials offer good value for money

Creative Alternatives to Experience Paid Attractions for Free in Kinsale

- **Kinsale Harbor**: Take a leisurely stroll along the waterfront, admiring the colorful boats and scenic views of the harbor, all without spending a penny.
- **Desmond Castle**: While guided tours of the castle may require a fee, visitors can explore the exterior of the historic building and learn about its history from informational plaques located around the site.
- **Charles Fort**: Enjoy panoramic views of Kinsale Harbor and the surrounding coastline from the exterior of Charles Fort, a 17th-century star-shaped fortress, without paying admission fees.

Best Free Audio Guides and Apps for Kinsale

Guide/App	Covers	Download	Cost
Kinsale Audio Guide	Historic sites, local landmarks	Website	Free
Kinsale Walking Tours	Guided walking routes, points of interest	App Store/Google Play	Free
Kinsale Heritage Trail	Cultural landmarks, architectural highlights	Website	Free

Luxurious Yet Affordable Experiences in Kinsale

- **Scenic Coastal Walks**: Take a leisurely stroll along the scenic coastal paths surrounding Kinsale, enjoying panoramic views of the rugged coastline and tranquil seascape, all for free.
- **Gourmet Picnic**: Pick up some locally sourced artisanal delights from one of Kinsale's specialty food shops and enjoy a gourmet picnic in one of the town's scenic parks or harborside promenades, without breaking the bank.
- **Artisanal Tasting Tour**: Embark on a self-guided tasting tour of Kinsale's artisanal producers, sampling locally crafted cheeses, chocolates, and beverages, all while soaking up the town's vibrant atmosphere, for a nominal cost.

County Clare

Renowned for its stunning coastal cliffs, expansive sandy beaches, and lush green landscapes, Clare captivates visitors with its dramatic scenery and timeless charm. From the majestic Cliffs of Moher to the otherworldly limestone landscape of the Burren, Clare offers endless opportunities for outdoor adventures and exploration. Steeped in history and tradition, the county is dotted with ancient ruins, medieval castles, and picturesque villages, providing a glimpse into Ireland's storied past. Clare is a destination that delights the senses and stirs the soul.

Top Attractions:
- **Cliffs of Moher Coastal Walk:**
    - Starting Price: Free
    - Specifics: Embark on a scenic coastal walk along the Cliffs of Moher, one of Ireland's most iconic natural landmarks. Enjoy breathtaking views of the Atlantic Ocean and rugged cliffs towering above the sea.
- **Visit the Burren National Park:**
    - Starting Price: Free
    - Specifics: Explore the unique limestone landscape of the Burren National Park, with its ancient archaeological sites, colorful wildflowers, and hidden caves. Take a guided walk or hike and marvel at the area's natural beauty.
- **Dolphin Watching in Kilrush:**
    - Starting Price: €20-€25 per person
    - Specifics: Join a boat tour from Kilrush to spot dolphins, seals, and other marine wildlife in the waters of the Shannon Estuary. Enjoy an unforgettable eco-friendly adventure in one of Ireland's most scenic coastal areas.
- **Explore the Burren Perfumery:**
    - Starting Price: Free entry; products available for purchase
    - Specifics: Discover the art of natural perfumery at the Burren Perfumery, where you can take a self-guided tour of the production facilities and sample a range of artisanal fragrances made with locally sourced ingredients.
- **Take a Guided Tour of Bunratty Castle and Folk Park:**
    - Starting Price: €15-€20 per adult
    - Specifics: Step back in time at Bunratty Castle and Folk Park, a medieval fortress and living history museum that offers guided tours of the castle, traditional Irish village, and surrounding grounds.
- **Explore the Cliffs of Moher Visitor Centre:**
    - Starting Price: €8-€10 per adult
    - Specifics: Learn about the geological and cultural significance of the Cliffs of Moher at the visitor center, which features interactive exhibits, audiovisual presentations, and stunning panoramic views of the cliffs.
- **Visit the Aillwee Cave and Birds of Prey Centre:**
    - Starting Price: €15-€20 per adult for combined ticket

- Specifics: Descend into the underground wonders of Aillwee Cave, a network of ancient limestone caverns filled with fascinating rock formations. Afterward, visit the Birds of Prey Centre to see majestic raptors in flight.
- **Take a Boat Trip to the Aran Islands:**
  - Starting Price: €25-€30 per person
  - Specifics: Embark on a scenic boat trip from Doolin or Kilronan to the Aran Islands, where you can explore ancient stone forts, rugged landscapes, and traditional Irish culture

Money-Saving Tips:

- **Cliffs of Moher Visitor Experience**: Consider visiting early in the morning or late in the evening to avoid crowds and admission fees.
- **Bunratty Castle and Folk Park**: Look for discounted tickets online or consider purchasing a combined ticket for multiple attractions.
- **Outdoor Activities**: Explore the Burren and coastal areas on foot or by bike to experience the natural beauty of County Clare for free.
- **Local Pubs**: Enjoy traditional Irish music sessions in local pubs for the price of a pint, or consider visiting during off-peak times for quieter sessions.
- **Picnics**: Pack a picnic with locally sourced ingredients from farmers' markets or shops to enjoy a meal with a view at one of County Clare's scenic spots.

Sample Itinerary:

- Day 1: Explore the Cliffs of Moher and nearby visitor center. Take a coastal walk or boat tour for different perspectives.
- Day 2: Visit Bunratty Castle and Folk Park, exploring the medieval castle, village, and traditional crafts demonstrations.
- Day 3: Discover the unique landscape of the Burren, exploring Aillwee Cave and hiking or cycling along marked trails.
- Day 4: Take a scenic drive along the Loop Head Peninsula, stopping at lighthouses, beaches, and scenic viewpoints.
- Day 5: Relax in Lahinch, enjoying the beach, surfing, or a round of golf. Explore the town's shops, cafes, and pubs.
- Day 6: Spend the day birdwatching or kayaking in the Shannon Estuary, or explore the historic town of Ennis.
- Day 7: Depart from County Clare, taking in any final sights or experiences before heading to your next destination.

Conclusion:

County Clare offers a diverse range of attractions and experiences for visitors to enjoy, from stunning natural landmarks to rich cultural heritage. By following this guide and implementing money-saving tips, you can make the most of your trip to this beautiful region of Ireland.

County Wicklow

Top Attractions:

- **Glendalough**: A picturesque valley with an ancient monastic settlement, scenic walking trails, and serene lakes.
- **Powerscourt Estate**: A grand country estate featuring formal gardens, waterfalls, and a historic house with stunning views of Sugarloaf Mountain.
- **Wicklow Mountains National Park**: Ireland's largest national park, offering rugged landscapes, mountain peaks, and diverse flora and fauna.
- **Sally Gap**: A scenic mountain pass with panoramic views of the Wicklow Mountains, Lough Tay (the Guinness Lake), and the surrounding countryside.
- **Avoca Village**: A charming village known for its handweaving mill, craft shops, and scenic riverside setting.
- **The Wicklow Way**: Ireland's oldest waymarked long-distance walking trail, offering challenging hikes and beautiful scenery.
- **Powerscourt Waterfall**: Ireland's highest waterfall, located in Powerscourt Estate, with picnic areas and walking trails.
- **Russborough House**: A stately home with impressive architecture, extensive gardens, and a renowned art collection.

- **Glendalough Chocolate Factory**: A family-owned chocolate factory offering tours, tastings, and a shop with artisan chocolates.
- **Mount Usher Gardens**: A beautifully landscaped garden with a diverse collection of plants, trees, and flowers.

Money-Saving Tips:

- **Glendalough:**
    - Nestled in a picturesque valley, Glendalough is renowned for its ancient monastic settlement founded by St. Kevin in the 6th century. Visitors can explore the well-preserved ruins of churches, round towers, and Celtic crosses, while scenic walking trails meander through lush woodlands and past serene lakes.
    - Starting Price: Free entry; guided tours available for a fee
- **Powerscourt Estate:**
    - Set against the backdrop of the Wicklow Mountains, Powerscourt Estate is a sprawling country estate renowned for its breathtaking beauty and historical significance. The estate features meticulously manicured formal gardens, including Italian and Japanese gardens, ornamental lakes, and the stunning Powerscourt Waterfall. Visitors can also explore the elegant Palladian-style house, which offers panoramic views of Sugarloaf Mountain.
    - Starting Price: €10-€15 per adult for gardens entry; additional fees for house tour
- **Wicklow Mountains National Park:**
    - Covering over 20,000 hectares of rugged terrain, the Wicklow Mountains National Park is a haven for outdoor enthusiasts and nature lovers. The park boasts a diverse landscape of sweeping moors, craggy peaks, deep glacial valleys, and pristine lakes. Visitors can enjoy hiking, mountain biking, birdwatching, and picnicking amidst stunning scenery.
    - Starting Price: Free entry; guided tours and activities available for a fee
- **Sally Gap:**
    - Offering some of the most breathtaking vistas in the Wicklow Mountains, Sally Gap is a scenic mountain pass that winds its way through heather-covered hills and blanket bog. Visitors can stop at designated viewpoints to admire panoramic views of Lough Tay, often referred to as the Guinness Lake due to its dark peaty waters, and the surrounding countryside.
    - Starting Price: Free; guided tours available for a fee
- **Avoca Village:**
    - Tucked away in the heart of Wicklow, Avoca Village is a charming enclave known for its rich heritage, artisanal crafts, and scenic riverside setting. Visitors can explore Avoca Handweavers, Ireland's oldest working mill, where traditional weaving techniques have been passed down for generations. The village also boasts a selection of craft shops, cafes, and galleries showcasing local artwork.
    - Starting Price: Free entry; shopping and dining prices vary
- **The Wicklow Way:**
    - Stretching over 130 kilometers, the Wicklow Way is Ireland's oldest waymarked long-distance walking trail, offering a diverse range of landscapes and terrain. From gentle strolls through lush valleys to challenging hikes along rugged mountain ridges, the trail provides ample

opportunities to immerse oneself in the natural beauty of the Wicklow Mountains.
    - Starting Price: Free; guided tours and equipment rental available for a fee
- **Powerscourt Waterfall:**
    - Tumbling from a height of 121 meters, Powerscourt Waterfall is Ireland's highest waterfall and a spectacular natural attraction within Powerscourt Estate. Visitors can marvel at the cascading waters, picnic amidst the tranquil surroundings, and explore scenic walking trails that wind through ancient woodlands.
    - Starting Price: €6-€8 per adult; discounted rates for families
- **Russborough House:**
    - A testament to Georgian grandeur, Russborough House is one of Ireland's finest stately homes, boasting elegant architecture, opulent interiors, and extensive landscaped gardens. Visitors can admire the impressive art collection, which includes works by renowned artists such as Gainsborough, Reynolds, and Vermeer, and explore the surrounding parkland dotted with ornamental lakes and follies.
    - Starting Price: €12-€15 per adult for house and garden entry; additional fees for guided tours
- **Glendalough Chocolate Factory:**
    - : A haven for chocolate lovers, the Glendalough Chocolate Factory is a family-owned artisanal chocolate maker that offers guided tours, tastings, and hands-on workshops. Visitors can learn about the chocolate-making process from bean to bar, sample a variety of decadent chocolates, and purchase sweet treats to take home.
    - Starting Price: €5-€10 per person for tours and tastings
- **Mount Usher Gardens:**
    - Nestled along the banks of the River Vartry, Mount Usher Gardens is a hidden gem renowned for its tranquil beauty and botanical diversity. Visitors can wander through lush woodland pathways, admire colorful flower borders, and relax amidst the serene surroundings of this enchanting garden paradise.
    - Starting Price: €7-€10 per adult for garden entry; discounted rates for seniors and students

Sample Itinerary:

- Day 1: Explore Glendalough, visiting the monastic site, hiking the trails, and enjoying a picnic by the lakes.
- Day 2: Visit Powerscourt Estate, exploring the gardens, waterfalls, and house, followed by a walk or drive around the Wicklow Mountains.
- Day 3: Take a scenic drive through Sally Gap, stopping for photos and short walks along the way, before exploring Avoca Village and the Chocolate Factory.
- Day 4: Discover the history and art at Russborough House, followed by a leisurely stroll through Mount Usher Gardens.
- Day 5: Enjoy outdoor activities such as hiking, cycling, or horseback riding along the Wicklow Way or in Wicklow Mountains National Park.
- Day 6: Relax with a scenic drive or walk along the coast, visiting nearby beaches or seaside towns like Bray or Greystones.
- Day 7: Depart from County Wicklow, taking in any final sights or experiences before heading to your next destination.

Wicklow Town

Wicklow Town, often referred to as the "Gateway to the Garden of Ireland," is a charming coastal town situated in County Wicklow, just south of Dublin. Steeped in history and surrounded by breathtaking natural beauty, Wicklow Town offers visitors a perfect blend of historic landmarks, scenic landscapes, and vibrant culture.

The town's origins date back to Viking times, and its rich maritime heritage is evident in its picturesque harbor, where colorful fishing boats bob on the gentle waves. Wicklow Gaol, a former prison turned museum, offers visitors a glimpse into Ireland's tumultuous past, with immersive exhibits and guided tours exploring the lives of prisoners and rebels throughout history.

Wicklow Town is also a gateway to the stunning Wicklow Mountains National Park, where visitors can explore rugged mountains, lush forests, and cascading waterfalls. The famous Wicklow Way, Ireland's oldest long-distance hiking trail, begins in the town and winds its way through the scenic landscapes of the national park, offering breathtaking views and unforgettable outdoor adventures.

In addition to its natural beauty, Wicklow Town boasts a vibrant arts and cultural scene, with numerous galleries, theaters, and music venues showcasing the talents of local artists and performers. The town's lively pubs and restaurants offer a taste of traditional Irish hospitality, with delicious seafood, hearty pub grub, and live music adding to the festive atmosphere.

Luxury but Affordable Accommodation in Wicklow Town

Accommodatio	Pros	Cons	Starting Price
The Grand Hotel	Central location, sea views	Limited on-site parking	€120 per night
The Bridge	Historic charm, friendly staff	Some rooms may be small	€100 per night
The Royal Hotel	Modern amenities, leisure facilities	Slightly out of town	€90 per night

Top Cheap Eats in Wicklow Town

Restaurant	What to Try	Starting Price	Tips
The Lighthouse	Fish and Chips	€10	Enjoy panoramic views of the harbor while dining

Phil Healy's	Traditional Irish Fare	€12	Lunch specials offer good value for money
The Mystic Celt	Pub Grub	€10	Generous portions make it a good value meal
The Coffee Shop	Soup and Sandwiches	€7	Ideal for a quick and affordable lunch
The Tap	Gourmet Burgers	€12	Opt for the lunch menu for discounted prices

Creative Alternatives to Experience Paid Attractions for Free in Wicklow Town

- **Wicklow Gaol**: While guided tours of the gaol may require a fee, visitors can explore the exterior of the historic building and learn about its history from informational plaques located around the site.
- **Wicklow Mountains National Park**: Embark on a hike along one of the park's many trails, such as the Wicklow Way, to experience the stunning natural beauty of the area without paying admission fees.
- **Wicklow Harbor**: Take a leisurely stroll along the waterfront, admiring the colorful fishing boats and enjoying views of the Irish Sea, all for free.

Best Free Audio Guides and Apps for Wicklow Town

Guide/App	Covers	Download	Cost
Wicklow Town Audio Guide	Historic sites, local landmarks	Website	Free
Wicklow Way App	Hiking trails, points of interest	App Store/Google Play Store	Free
Wicklow Arts Trail	Art galleries, cultural venues	Website	Free

Luxurious Yet Affordable Experiences in Wicklow Town

- **Wicklow Gaol Museum**: Explore the atmospheric interiors of Wicklow Gaol, delving into the town's fascinating history and heritage, all for a nominal fee.
- **Wicklow Mountains National Park**: Embark on a scenic hike through the pristine landscapes of the national park, enjoying panoramic views of mountains, lakes, and forests, without breaking the bank.
- **Wicklow Harbor**: Indulge in a leisurely seafood lunch at one of the waterfront restaurants, soaking up the ambiance and scenic views of the harbor, all at an affordable price.

Bray

Nestled along the stunning coastline of County Wicklow, Bray is a charming seaside town that effortlessly combines natural beauty with vibrant culture. As you arrive in Bray, the first thing that strikes you is the breathtaking view of the shimmering Irish Sea stretching out before you, framed by the majestic cliffs and lush green hillsides that characterize this picturesque coastal haven.

One of the highlights of any visit to Bray is a leisurely stroll along the iconic Bray Promenade. Lined with palm trees and dotted with charming Victorian-era bandstands, this picturesque seafront walkway offers stunning views of the rugged coastline and sparkling waters below. Take your time to soak in the salty sea air, listen to the sound of waves crashing against the shore, and admire the panoramic vistas that stretch out towards the horizon.

As you continue your exploration of Bray, you'll discover a wealth of attractions and activities to suit every taste and interest. History buffs will delight in the town's rich heritage, from the historic Victorian architecture of the Seafront to the ancient ruins of the nearby monastic settlement at Bray Head. Art enthusiasts will find plenty to admire in the town's vibrant arts scene, with galleries, studios, and public art installations showcasing the talents of local artists.

For outdoor enthusiasts, Bray offers a wealth of opportunities to connect with nature and enjoy the great outdoors. Lace up your hiking boots and embark on an adventure along the scenic Bray Head Cliff Walk, where you'll be rewarded with breathtaking views of the Irish Sea and Bray's dramatic coastline. Alternatively, pack a picnic and spend a leisurely afternoon exploring the tranquil surrounds of Kilruddery House & Gardens, where lush green lawns, ornamental gardens, and ancient woodlands provide the perfect backdrop for a relaxing day out.

Chart of Luxury but Affordable Accommodation in Bray:

Accommodation	Pros	Cons	Starting Price (per night)
The Martello Hotel	- Stunning sea views	- Some rooms may be small	€80
The Royal Hotel & Merrill	- Historic charm	- Limited on-site amenities	€90
The Esplanade Hotel	- Beachfront location	- Rooms can be noisy during peak season	€100
The Wilton Hotel	- Modern facilities	- Located slightly away from city center	€70

Top Cheap Eats in Bray:

Restaurant	Cuisine	Location	Must-Try Dish	Starting Price	Tips for Saving Money
The Happy Pear	Vegetarian	Harbour Road	Buddha Bowl	€10	Opt for takeaway
Box Burger	Burgers	Strand Road	Classic Cheeseburger	€12	Lunch specials
Platform Pizza	Pizza	Bray Promenade	Margherita Pizza	€9	Lunch deals
Coffee Delights	Café	Quinsborough Road	Full Irish Breakfast	€8	Breakfast specials
Quinlan's Seafood Bar	Seafood	Strand Road	Fish and Chips	€14	Early bird specials

- **Bray Promenade**: Take a leisurely stroll along the picturesque Bray Promenade, lined with colorful Victorian-era buildings and offering stunning views of Bray Head and the Irish Sea. Price: Free.
- **Bray Head Cliff Walk**: Embark on the Bray Head Cliff Walk, a scenic trail that winds along the rugged coastline, offering breathtaking vistas of the sea and surrounding countryside. Price: Free.
- **Bray to Greystones Cliff Walk**: For a longer adventure, tackle the Bray to Greystones Cliff Walk, a 7-kilometer trail that traverses steep cliffs and lush greenery, providing spectacular views of the coastline. Price: Free.
- **Killruddery House and Gardens**: Explore the historic Killruddery House and Gardens, a 17th-century estate featuring beautifully manicured gardens, ornate architecture, and scenic walking trails. Price: Gardens admission - €6.
- **Bray Seafront Amusements**: Indulge in some classic seaside fun at Bray Seafront Amusements, where you can enjoy arcade games, carnival rides, and traditional amusement park treats. Price: Varies depending on activities chosen.
- **Bray Heritage Centre**: Discover the rich history of Bray at the Bray Heritage Centre, where interactive exhibits and guided tours explore the town's maritime heritage, cultural significance, and famous residents. Price: Admission - €5.
- **Bray to Dublin by DART**: Hop on the Dublin Area Rapid Transit (DART) train and embark on a scenic journey from Bray to Dublin, enjoying panoramic views of Dublin Bay and the Dublin Mountains along the way. Price: Adult single ticket - €3.30.
- **Bray Bowl**: Have a fun-filled evening at Bray Bowl, a family-friendly bowling alley offering lanes, arcade games, and tasty snacks for an enjoyable and affordable outing. Price: Bowling - €6 per game.
- **Bray Head Hotel**: Treat yourself to a delicious meal at the Bray Head Hotel, where you can savor traditional Irish cuisine made with locally sourced ingredients in a cozy and welcoming atmosphere. Price: Main course - Starting from €12.
- **Bray Beach**: Unwind and relax on Bray Beach, a sandy stretch of shoreline where you can soak up the sun, take a refreshing dip in the sea, or simply enjoy a peaceful picnic with stunning ocean views. Price: Free.

Glendalough

Glendalough is a tranquil valley renowned for its natural beauty, rich history, and spiritual significance. Meaning "Valley of the Two Lakes" in Irish, Glendalough is home to an ancient monastic settlement founded by St. Kevin in the 6th century, making it one of Ireland's most important historical sites.

The focal point of Glendalough is its picturesque Upper and Lower Lakes, which are surrounded by dense forests, rugged cliffs, and cascading waterfalls. Visitors can embark on scenic hikes along the valley's network of trails, taking in panoramic views of the lakes and surrounding mountains along the way.

The Glendalough Monastic Site, nestled at the heart of the valley, is a treasure trove of ancient ruins, including a round tower, cathedral, and several churches and monastic buildings. The site's atmospheric surroundings and spiritual significance make it a popular pilgrimage destination for visitors seeking solace and reflection.

Beyond its historical landmarks, Glendalough offers plenty of opportunities for outdoor recreation, from fishing and kayaking on the lakes to rock climbing and mountain biking in the surrounding mountains. The nearby Wicklow Way, Ireland's oldest long-distance hiking trail, passes through Glendalough, offering visitors the chance to explore the stunning landscapes of the Wicklow Mountains National Park.

Luxury but Affordable Accommodation near Glendalough

Accommodation	Pros	Cons	Starting Price
Tudor Lodge	Scenic location, cozy rooms	Limited dining options nearby	€100 per night
Lynham's Hotel	Modern amenities, friendly staff	Slightly out of town center	€90 per night
Glendalough Hotel	Historic charm, on-site dining	Some rooms may be small	€80 per night

Top Cheap Eats near Glendalough

Restaurant	What to Try	Starting Price	Tips
Wicklow Heather	Irish Stew	€10	Lunch specials offer good value for money
Glendalough Green	Vegetarian Fare	€8	Ideal for a quick and affordable lunch
Lynham's Bar & Grill	Pub Grub	€12	Generous portions make it a good value meal
The Wicklow Way Café	Soup and Sandwiches	€7	Grab a picnic lunch to enjoy in the great outdoors

Creative Alternatives to Experience Paid Attractions for Free in Glendalough

- **Glendalough Upper Lake**: Enjoy a leisurely stroll along the shores of Upper Lake, taking in panoramic views of the surrounding mountains and forests, all without spending a penny.
- **Glendalough Monastic Site**: While guided tours of the monastic site may require a fee, visitors can explore the ruins and scenic surroundings independently for free.
- **Wicklow Mountains National Park**: Embark on a hike along one of the park's many trails, such as the Glendalough Spinc Loop, to experience the breathtaking beauty of the Wicklow Mountains without paying admission fees.

Best Free Audio Guides and Apps for Glendalough

Guide/App	Covers	Download	Cost
Glendalough Audio Guide	Monastic site, history, legends	Website	Free
Wicklow Mountains National Park Guide	Hiking trails, wildlife	App Store/Google Play Store	Free
Glendalough Walking Tours	Scenic routes, local landmarks	Website	Free

Luxurious Yet Affordable Experiences near Glendalough

- **Upper Lake Hike**: Take a leisurely hike around Upper Lake, immersing yourself in the serene beauty of the surrounding mountains and forests, all for free.
- **Monastic Ruins Exploration**: Wander through the ancient ruins of Glendalough's monastic settlement, marveling at the centuries-old architecture and tranquil atmosphere without spending a penny.
- **Picnic by Lower Lake**: Pack a picnic lunch and enjoy a scenic meal by the shores of Lower Lake, soaking up the peaceful ambiance and breathtaking views of the valley, all at no cost.

Mayo

Nestled on the rugged west coast of Ireland, Mayo is a captivating county renowned for its stunning landscapes, rich history, and warm hospitality. Stretching from the wild Atlantic shores to the majestic peaks of the Nephin Mountains, Mayo offers a diverse range of experiences for visitors to enjoy. Whether you're exploring ancient ruins, hiking along coastal cliffs, or indulging in traditional Irish music and cuisine, Mayo promises an unforgettable journey into the heart of Ireland's wild and untamed beauty.

History and Heritage:

Mayo is steeped in history, with evidence of human habitation dating back thousands of years. The county is dotted with ancient monuments, including megalithic tombs, stone circles, and ring forts, bearing witness to the lives of Ireland's earliest inhabitants. Mayo's history is also intertwined with Ireland's rich cultural heritage, from the arrival of the Celts and the spread of Christianity to the struggles of the Great Famine and the fight for Irish independence. Visitors can delve into Mayo's past at museums, heritage centers, and historic sites such as Westport House, Ballintubber Abbey, and the National Museum of Ireland - Country Life.

Natural Beauty:

From rugged coastlines to rolling green hills, Mayo's natural beauty is truly awe-inspiring. The county is home to some of Ireland's most iconic landscapes, including Achill Island, the largest island off the coast of Ireland, renowned for its towering sea cliffs and sandy beaches. The Great Western Greenway, Ireland's longest off-road cycling and walking trail, winds its way through Mayo's picturesque countryside, offering stunning views of Clew Bay and the surrounding mountains. For outdoor enthusiasts, Mayo provides ample opportunities for hiking, surfing, fishing, and birdwatching amidst its unspoiled wilderness.

Cultural Experiences:

Mayo's vibrant cultural scene is alive with music, dance, and storytelling, reflecting the county's rich artistic heritage. Traditional Irish music sessions can be found in pubs and music venues throughout Mayo, where visitors can join locals in a lively celebration of Ireland's musical traditions. The county also hosts a variety of festivals and events, from the Westport Arts Festival to the Féile Chois Cuain traditional music festival, showcasing the best of Mayo's cultural talent and creativity.

Hospitality and Warmth:

One of Mayo's greatest charms is its warm hospitality and friendly locals, who welcome visitors with open arms and a genuine sense of warmth. Whether you're enjoying a pint of Guinness in a cozy pub, savoring a hearty meal of locally sourced produce, or chatting with fishermen in a seaside village, you'll find that Mayo's people are always eager to share their stories, traditions, and love for their homeland.

As you embark on your journey through Mayo, prepare to be captivated by the county's natural beauty, rich history, and vibrant culture, as you uncover the hidden gems and timeless treasures that make Mayo a truly special place to explore.

Mayo, located on the west coast of Ireland, is home to several vibrant towns and breathtaking natural attractions. Here are some of the main towns and their highlights in Mayo:

- **Castlebar:**
  - County town of Mayo, bustling with shops, restaurants, and cultural attractions.
  - Visit the National Museum of Ireland - Country Life, showcasing rural Irish life.
  - Explore the grounds of the historic Castlebar House and Gardens.
  - Enjoy outdoor activities at Lough Lannagh, including walking trails and water sports.
- **Westport:**
  - Picturesque town known for its Georgian architecture and vibrant atmosphere.
  - Climb Croagh Patrick, Ireland's holy mountain, for stunning views of Clew Bay.
  - Explore Westport House and Gardens, a historic estate with adventure activities.
  - Enjoy traditional music sessions and lively pubs in the town center.
- **Ballina:**
  - Gateway to the Wild Atlantic Way, situated on the River Moy.
  - Visit the Jackie Clarke Collection, a vast archive of Irish historical documents.
  - Explore Belleek Woods and the scenic paths along the River Moy.
  - Attend the annual Salmon Festival, celebrating Ballina's fishing heritage.
- **Achill Island:**
  - Ireland's largest island, renowned for its rugged coastline and stunning beaches.
  - Visit Keem Bay, a secluded beach nestled between cliffs.
  - Explore the Deserted Village at Slievemore, an abandoned 19th-century settlement.
  - Enjoy water sports such as surfing, kayaking, and windsurfing.
- **Westport Quay:**
  - Picturesque harbor area with shops, cafes, and seafood restaurants.
  - Walk or cycle along the Great Western Greenway, a scenic trail that passes through the Quay.
  - Take a boat trip to Clare Island or Inishturk for island exploration.
  - Visit the Westport House Pirate Adventure Park for family fun.
- **Newport:**
  - Quaint town situated along the Newport River and the Great Western Greenway.
  - Explore Burrishoole Abbey, a medieval monastic site with scenic surroundings.
  - Cycle or walk the Greenway trail, passing through Newport and offering stunning views of Clew Bay.
  - Enjoy fishing or boating on nearby Lough Beltra and Lough Feeagh.

- **Claremorris:**
  - Market town known for its vibrant community and traditional Irish culture.
  - Visit Clare Lake Park for scenic walks, picnics, and wildlife watching.
  - Explore the ruins of Balla Abbey, a medieval Cistercian monastery.
  - Attend cultural events and festivals, including music sessions and theater performances.

here's a chart showcasing luxury but affordable accommodation options in Mayo:

Accommodation Name	Location	Pros	Cons	Starting Price (per night)
Ashford Castle	Cong	- Historic castle setting	- May be more expensive than other options	€200
Westport Plaza Hotel	Westport	- Central location in Westport town center	- Limited availability during peak seasons	€100
Mount Falcon Estate	Ballina	- Stunning estate with fishing and golf	- Remote location may require transportation	€150
Knockranny House Hotel	Westport	- Panoramic views of Clew Bay	- Limited onsite amenities	€120
The Lodge at Ashford	Cong	- Boutique luxury with modern amenities	- May book up quickly during busy periods	€180

These accommodations offer a blend of luxury amenities and affordability, making them ideal choices for travelers seeking a memorable stay in Mayo without breaking the bank.

Restaurant Name	Location	What to Try	Starting Price (per dish)	Money-Saving Tips
The Big Green Egg	Westport	Gourmet burgers	€10 - €15	Look for daily specials or combo deals for better value
The Tavern Bar & Grill	Ballina	Fish and chips	€8 - €12	Check for early bird specials or lunchtime discounts
An Port Mór	Westport	Seafood chowder	€6 - €10	Consider sharing dishes or ordering smaller portions
The Market Kitchen	Castlebar	Homemade soup and sandwiches	€5 - €8	Opt for takeaway options to enjoy your meal outdoors
The Old Arch Bar	Claremorris	Traditional Irish stew	€8 - €12	Take advantage of midweek deals or happy hour promotions
Jalan Jalan	Ballina	Malaysian noodles	€9 - €13	Look for lunch specials or combo meals for better value
Cinnamon Alley	Westport	Artisan pizzas	€10 - €15	Share pizzas or opt for a half-and-half option to try more

Cafe Rua	Castlebar	Gourmet sandwiches	€6 - €10	Consider ordering a side salad instead of a full meal
McHale's Bar & Grill	Ballina	BBQ ribs	€10 - €14	Keep an eye out for seasonal promotions or special events
The Pantry Cafe	Westport	Homemade quiche	€7 - €10	Ask for tap water instead of bottled water to save money
The Courthouse	Kinvara	Irish breakfast	€6 - €10	Take advantage of early bird specials or set menu options
The Talbot Hotel	Belmullet	Traditional fish and chips	€8 - €12	Look for lunch specials or weekday discounts
The Croagh Patrick Cafe	Murrisk	Soup and sandwich combo	€7 - €10	Bring your own reusable cup for discounted takeaway coffee
Jackie Clarke Collection Cafe	Ballina	Homemade cakes and pastries	€3 - €5	Check for loyalty programs or discount vouchers
The Pantry Cafe	Newport	Freshly baked scones	€2 - €4	Share desserts or opt for smaller portions
Healy's Cafe	Castlebar	Vegetarian falafel wrap	€6 - €9	Skip extras like sides or drinks to save money
The Loft Bar & Grill	Westport	Pulled pork sandwich	€9 - €12	Take advantage of early bird specials or lunchtime deals
Linenhall Street Cafe	Castlebar	Soup and sandwich combo	€7 - €10	Look for student discounts or special offers
The Pantry Cafe	Ballina	Homemade soup	€4 - €7	Ask for a discount if purchasing multiple items
Puddleduck Cafe	Westport	Vegetarian curry	€8 - €12	Consider opting for takeout instead of dining in

These cheap eats offer delicious and budget-friendly options for dining in Mayo, with various cuisines and dishes to suit every taste. Remember to keep an eye out for special promotions, discounts, and combo deals to get the best value for your money.

Creative Alternatives to Experience Main Paid Attractions for Free:

- **Visit During Off-Peak Hours:** Some attractions may offer free or discounted admission during off-peak hours or specific days of the week. Research the attraction's schedule and plan your visit accordingly.
- **Utilize Membership Benefits:** If you have a membership to a museum, zoo, or other attraction in your home country, check if it offers reciprocal benefits with attractions in the destination you're visiting. This could grant you free or discounted entry.
- **Attend Free Events or Tours:** Many attractions host free events, guided tours, or open house days where admission is waived. Keep an eye out for these opportunities and plan your visit accordingly.
- **Take Advantage of City Passes:** Some destinations offer city passes that provide discounted or free entry to multiple attractions for a fixed price. Compare the cost of the pass to individual attraction tickets to see if it's worth purchasing.

- **Volunteer or Work Exchange Programs:** Some attractions offer volunteer or work exchange programs where participants contribute their time in exchange for free admission. Look into these opportunities if you're interested in a more immersive experience.
- **Explore Outdoor Spaces:** Instead of paying for indoor attractions, explore outdoor spaces such as parks, gardens, and beaches, which are often free to visit and offer scenic views and recreational activities.
- **Research Free Days:** Some attractions offer designated free days or evenings throughout the year. Plan your visit accordingly to take advantage of these opportunities.
- **Use Student or Senior Discounts:** If you're a student or senior, inquire about discounted admission rates at attractions. Bring valid identification to take advantage of these discounts.
- **Attend Cultural Festivals:** Many destinations host cultural festivals and events that showcase local heritage, traditions, and arts. Attend these festivals for a taste of the destination's culture without paying admission fees.
- **Explore Free Exhibitions:** Some museums and galleries offer free admission to certain exhibitions or permanent collections. Check their websites for information on free exhibitions and plan your visit accordingly.

20 Luxurious Yet Affordable Experiences in Mayo:

- **Scenic Coastal Walks:** Enjoy breathtaking views of the Atlantic Ocean and rugged coastline with free coastal walks along the Wild Atlantic Way.
- **Picnic at Achill Island:** Pack a gourmet picnic and spend the day relaxing on the sandy beaches of Achill Island, surrounded by stunning scenery.
- **Historic Castle Tours:** Explore the ruins of medieval castles such as Rockfleet Castle or Kildavnet Tower, which offer free or low-cost admission.
- **Traditional Music Sessions:** Immerse yourself in the rich musical heritage of Mayo by attending free traditional music sessions at local pubs and venues.
- **Visit Ancient Megalithic Sites:** Discover Mayo's ancient past by visiting megalithic sites such as Carrowmore Megalithic Cemetery or the Ceide Fields, which offer free guided tours.
- **Sample Local Cuisine:** Indulge in delicious local cuisine at affordable prices by dining at cozy pubs and cafes that offer traditional Irish dishes made with fresh, locally sourced ingredients.
- **Explore Hidden Beaches:** Escape the crowds and discover hidden gems along Mayo's coastline, where you can enjoy secluded beaches and coves for free.
- **Artisan Craft Markets:** Browse artisan craft markets and fairs held in towns and villages throughout Mayo, where you can find unique handmade souvenirs and gifts at affordable prices.
- **Cultural Workshops:** Participate in free or low-cost cultural workshops and demonstrations, such as traditional Irish dancing, storytelling, or craft-making, offered by local community centers and organizations.
- **Wildlife Watching:** Observe native wildlife in their natural habitats by taking a free birdwatching or seal-watching tour along Mayo's coastline or visiting nature reserves such as Ballycroy National Park.
- **Explore Historic Villages:** Wander through picturesque villages such as Westport, Cong, and Ballina, where you can admire charming architecture, browse quaint shops, and soak up the local atmosphere for free.

- **Visit Local Museums:** Discover Mayo's history and heritage by visiting free local museums and heritage centers, such as the National Museum of Ireland – Country Life or the Jackie Clarke Collection in Ballina.
- **Gardens and Parks:** Spend a leisurely afternoon exploring lush gardens and parks such as Belleek Woods in Ballina or Westport House and Gardens, which offer free or low-cost entry.
- **Photography Tours:** Capture the beauty of Mayo's landscapes and landmarks on a self-guided photography tour, exploring scenic viewpoints, historic sites, and hidden gems throughout the county.
- **Cultural Festivals:** Attend free cultural festivals and events held throughout Mayo, celebrating music, literature, art, and folklore, where you can experience the vibrant spirit of the local community.
- **Stargazing:** Experience the magic of Mayo's night sky by stargazing at designated dark sky sites such as Ballycroy National Park or attending free astronomy events organized by local astronomy clubs.
- **Heritage Walks:** Join free guided heritage walks offered by local tourism organizations and discover Mayo's fascinating history and folklore, exploring ancient ruins, historic landmarks, and hidden treasures.
- **Beach Bonfires:** Gather with friends and family for a memorable beach bonfire at one of Mayo's designated fire-friendly beaches, where you can enjoy a cozy evening under the stars for free.
- **Visit Working Farms:** Learn about traditional farming practices and rural life in Mayo by visiting working farms that offer free tours and demonstrations, where you can meet farm animals and sample local produce.
- **Sunset Kayaking:** Embark on a sunset kayaking adventure along Mayo's coastline, where you can paddle through calm waters and witness the spectacular colors of the setting sun reflecting off the sea. Many local outfitters offer affordable kayak rentals and guided tours for a memorable and budget-friendly experience.

Westport

Founded in the 18th century by the Browne family, Westport is known for its Georgian architecture, tree-lined streets, and colorful shop fronts, creating a postcard-perfect setting that enchants visitors from near and far. The town's historic significance is evident in landmarks such as Westport House, a stately home with stunning gardens and a rich history dating back over 300 years.

Westport's natural beauty is unrivaled, with lush green countryside, rugged coastline, and pristine beaches just waiting to be explored. The nearby Connemara National Park and Achill Island offer outdoor enthusiasts a paradise for hiking, cycling, and water sports, while the Great Western Greenway provides scenic walking and cycling trails along the old Westport to Achill railway line.

In addition to its outdoor attractions, Westport is a cultural hotspot, with a thriving arts scene, lively music festivals, and traditional Irish music sessions taking place in pubs and venues throughout the town. The annual Westport Arts Festival and Westport Music Festival showcase the best of local and international talent, while the town's artisanal food markets and craft shops offer a taste of authentic Irish craftsmanship and cuisine.

Luxury but Affordable Accommodation in Westport

Accommodation	Pros	Cons	Starting Price
Knockranny House Hotel	Scenic views, spa facilities	Slightly out of town center	€130 per night
Westport Plaza Hotel	Central location, modern amenities	Limited parking	€120 per night
Clew Bay Hotel	Historic charm, family-friendly	Some rooms may be small	€100 per night

Top Cheap Eats in Westport

Restaurant	What to Try	Starting Price	Tips
The Pantry & Corkscrew	Gourmet Sandwiches	€8	Opt for the lunch menu for discounted prices
The Creel	Seafood Chowder	€9	Ideal for a quick and affordable lunch

Cronin's Sheebeen	Pub Grub	€10	Generous portions make it a good value meal
An Port Mór	Traditional Irish Fare	€12	Lunch specials offer good value for money
Sage Restaurant	Modern Irish Cuisine	€12	Early bird menus offer great value for money

Creative Alternatives to Experience Paid Attractions for Free in Westport

- **Westport House Gardens**: While admission fees may apply to enter the house, visitors can explore the beautiful gardens surrounding Westport House, taking in the colorful floral displays and tranquil lakeside views, all for free.
- **Great Western Greenway**: Enjoy a scenic walk or cycle along the Great Western Greenway, a 42-kilometer trail that follows the route of the old Westport to Achill railway line, offering breathtaking views of Clew Bay and the surrounding countryside, for free.
- **Westport Quay**: Take a leisurely stroll along the waterfront at Westport Quay, admiring views of Clew Bay and the iconic Croagh Patrick mountain, all without spending a penny.

Best Free Audio Guides and Apps for Westport

Guide/App	Covers	Cost
Westport Audio Guide	Historic sites, local landmarks	Free
Westport Walking Tours	Guided walking routes, points of interest	Free
Croagh Patrick App	Hiking trails, points of interest	Free

Luxurious Yet Affordable Experiences in Westport

- **Croagh Patrick Hike**: Embark on a self-guided hike up Croagh Patrick, Ireland's holy mountain, and enjoy breathtaking views of Clew Bay and the surrounding countryside, all for free.
- **Connemara Day Trip**: Join a guided day trip to Connemara, exploring its rugged landscapes, picturesque villages, and ancient monuments, all for a modest cost.
- **Traditional Music Session**: Immerse yourself in the lively atmosphere of a traditional Irish music session at one of Westport's cozy pubs, enjoying toe-tapping tunes and warm hospitality without breaking the bank.

As you walk through the streets of Mayo, take a moment to appreciate the architectural diversity that tells the stories of the county's rich history and heritage. Here are some interesting things to notice:

- **Medieval Castles and Towers:** Keep an eye out for remnants of Mayo's medieval past, such as the imposing ruins of Rockfleet Castle or the picturesque Kildavnet Tower on Achill Island. These ancient structures are steeped in history and offer glimpses into Mayo's tumultuous past.
- **Georgian Townhouses:** Admire the elegant Georgian townhouses that line the streets of towns like Westport and Ballina, with their distinctive features such as sash windows, decorative doorways, and intricate wrought iron railings. These grand residences reflect Mayo's prosperity during the Georgian era and showcase the architectural tastes of the time.
- **Thatched Cottages:** Look for traditional thatched cottages scattered throughout Mayo's rural villages, with their charming whitewashed walls and intricately woven roofs. These quaint dwellings offer a glimpse into Ireland's rural heritage and provide a nostalgic reminder of simpler times.
- **Victorian Landmarks:** Marvel at Mayo's Victorian landmarks, such as the ornate Westport House and the majestic Ballina Railway Station. These architectural gems are symbols of Mayo's industrial and cultural heritage and serve as reminders of the county's vibrant past.
- **Religious Buildings:** Explore Mayo's rich religious heritage through its churches, chapels, and monastic sites. From the ancient ruins of Moyne Abbey to the grandeur of St. Patrick's Church in Newport, these sacred buildings reflect Mayo's deep spiritual traditions and offer moments of peace and contemplation.
- **Quaint Bridges and Waterways:** Cross over charming stone bridges that span tranquil rivers and streams, such as the iconic Newport Bridge or the picturesque bridges of Westport Quay. These scenic waterways are integral to Mayo's landscape and provide a tranquil backdrop for leisurely strolls.

To explore the sights of Mayo via bus, you can board the Route 52 bus, which travels from Ballina in the north to Westport in the south, passing through towns such as Crossmolina, Castlebar, and Newport along the way. The cost of a single journey on this route varies depending on the distance traveled, but fares typically range from €2.50 to €10.

Imagine boarding the Route 52 bus at the main stop in Ballina. As you embark on your journey, you'll pass by the bustling streets of Ballina's town center, with its vibrant shops, cafes, and historic landmarks such as St. Muredach's Cathedral.

Continuing south, you'll traverse the scenic countryside of Mayo, passing by rolling green hills, picturesque villages, and ancient ruins. Keep an eye out for sights such as the majestic Nephin Mountains, the tranquil shores of Lough Conn, and the quaint village of Foxford, famous for its woollen mills and fishing heritage.

As you approach Castlebar, Mayo's county town, you'll be greeted by the imposing facade of the County Courthouse and the bustling activity of the town center. Take a moment to explore Castlebar's charming streets, lined with shops, restaurants, and historic buildings such as the Linenhall Arts Centre.

From Castlebar, the bus continues its journey southward, passing through the scenic countryside of Newport before reaching its final destination in the bustling town of Westport. Here, you can disembark and explore the charming streets of Westport's town center, with its colorful shops, lively pubs, and stunning views of Clew Bay and Croagh Patrick.

Throughout your bus journey, you'll have the opportunity to soak in the sights and sounds of Mayo's diverse landscapes and communities, offering a memorable and uplifting experience that celebrates the county's rich history, heritage, and natural beauty.

Waterford

Ireland's Oldest City is situated on the banks of the River Suir in the sunny southeast of Ireland, is renowned as the country's oldest city, boasting a history that spans over a thousand years. Founded by the Vikings in the 9th century, Waterford has evolved into a vibrant urban center that seamlessly blends its rich heritage with modern amenities and cultural attractions.

The city's historic heart is adorned with medieval architecture, narrow winding streets, and picturesque quaysides, offering visitors a glimpse into its storied past. The iconic Waterford Crystal factory, established in 1783, is one of the city's most famous landmarks, where visitors can witness master craftsmen at work and explore a dazzling array of exquisite crystal creations.

Waterford is also home to a wealth of cultural attractions, including the award-winning Waterford Museum of Treasures, which showcases the city's illustrious history through a fascinating collection of artifacts and exhibits. The stunning Waterford Greenway, Ireland's longest off-road cycling and walking trail, winds its way through the picturesque countryside, offering breathtaking views of the River Suir and surrounding landscapes.

In addition to its historic landmarks and cultural offerings, Waterford boasts a lively culinary scene, with an array of restaurants, cafes, and artisanal food producers showcasing the best of Irish cuisine. From fresh seafood harvested from the nearby coast to traditional Irish pub fare and international delicacies, Waterford offers something to tantalize every palate.

Luxury but Affordable Accommodation in Waterford City

Accommodation	Pros	Cons	Starting Price
Granville Hotel	Central location, historic charm	Limited on-site parking	€120 per night
Tower Hotel	Riverside location, modern amenities	Some rooms may be small	€100 per night
Dooley's Hotel	Friendly staff, family-friendly	Slightly out of city center	€90 per night

Top Cheap Eats in Waterford City

Restaurant	What to Try	Starting Price	Tips
The Reg	Traditional Irish Fare	€12	Lunch specials offer good value for money
The Bodega	Gourmet Sandwiches	€8	Opt for the lunch menu for discounted prices
Momo Restaurant	Wood-Fired Pizza	€10	Generous portions make it a good value meal

Revolution Gastro Bar	Tapas	€12	Share plates to sample a variety of flavors
Burzza	Gourmet Burgers	€10	Lunchtime deals offer good value for money

Creative Alternatives to Experience Paid Attractions for Free in Waterford City

- **Waterford Museum of Treasures**: While admission fees may apply to certain exhibits, visitors can explore the exterior of the museum and learn about the city's history from informational plaques located around the building.
- **Waterford Greenway**: Enjoy a leisurely stroll or cycle along the scenic Waterford Greenway, taking in panoramic views of the River Suir and surrounding countryside, all without spending a penny.
- **Waterford Quays**: Take a relaxing walk along the quayside, admiring the historic architecture and bustling activity of the riverfront, all for free.

Luxurious Yet Affordable Experiences in Waterford City

- **Waterford Greenway**: Embark on a leisurely cycle or walk along the Waterford Greenway, a scenic trail that stretches for 46 kilometers along an old railway line, offering panoramic views of the lush countryside, historic viaducts, and charming villages. Price: Free.
- **Waterford Crystal Factory Tour**: Discover the world-renowned craftsmanship of Waterford Crystal with a guided factory tour at the House of Waterford Crystal. Witness skilled artisans at work, learn about the glass-making process, and marvel at exquisite crystal creations. Price: Adult tour ticket - €13.
- **Reginald's Tower**: Step back in time at Reginald's Tower, a historic landmark that dates back to Viking times and now houses a fascinating museum showcasing Waterford's maritime history and archaeological treasures. Price: Adult admission - €4.
- **The People's Park**: Relax and unwind in the serene surroundings of The People's Park, a beautifully landscaped green space featuring manicured gardens, a picturesque bandstand, and scenic river views. Price: Free.
- **Waterford Museum of Treasures**: Immerse yourself in the history and heritage of Waterford at the award-winning Waterford Museum of Treasures, home to a vast collection of artifacts, artworks, and interactive exhibits spanning over 1,000 years of history. Price: Adult admission - €10.
- **Bishop's Palace**: Explore the elegant Georgian interiors of the Bishop's Palace, a historic museum that offers insight into Waterford's social, political, and cultural past through a stunning collection of period furnishings, decorative arts, and multimedia displays. Price: Adult admission - €7.
- **City Sightseeing Tour**: Hop aboard a City Sightseeing Tour bus and embark on a guided journey through Waterford City, where you'll discover iconic landmarks, hidden gems, and fascinating anecdotes about the city's heritage and architecture. Price: Adult ticket - €12.
- **Waterford Heritage Walking Tours**: Join a guided walking tour of Waterford City with Waterford Heritage Tours and delve into its storied past, from its Viking origins to its medieval heyday and beyond. Price: Adult tour ticket - €10.
- **Theatre Royal**: Enjoy a night of entertainment at the historic Theatre Royal, where you can catch a variety of live performances including plays, musicals, concerts,

and comedy shows, all at affordable prices. Price: Ticket prices vary depending on the performance.

Limerick

Limerick's history dates back over a thousand years, with evidence of human settlement dating to ancient times. The city's name is derived from the Irish word "Luimneach," meaning "bare ground," a reference to the fertile soil along the River Shannon. Throughout its history, Limerick has been shaped by Viking invasions, Norman conquests, and battles for power and control. Today, remnants of this rich past can be seen in the city's historic landmarks, including King John's Castle, St. Mary's Cathedral, and the Treaty Stone, which commemorates the end of the Williamite War in Ireland.

Cultural Capital:

Limerick is renowned as a cultural hub, with a thriving arts scene that celebrates music, literature, and the performing arts. The city has produced notable literary figures such as Frank McCourt, author of "Angela's Ashes," and renowned poets like Michael Hartnett and Desmond O'Grady. Visitors can immerse themselves in Limerick's cultural heritage by attending music concerts, theater performances, and literary events held in venues like the Lime Tree Theatre and the Belltable Arts Centre. The Limerick City Gallery of Art showcases works by local and international artists, while the Hunt Museum houses a diverse collection of art and artifacts spanning centuries of history.

Main Towns and Their Highlights:

- **Limerick City:** The heart of the region, Limerick City boasts a mix of medieval and modern architecture, including King John's Castle, St. Mary's Cathedral, and the iconic Thomond Bridge. Visitors can explore the bustling streets of the city center, shop at the Milk Market, and enjoy traditional music sessions in lively pubs.
- **Adare:** Known as Ireland's prettiest village, Adare is famed for its thatched cottages, historic churches, and scenic parks. Visitors can stroll along the Adare Heritage Trail, visit Adare Manor, and explore the picturesque streets lined with boutiques and craft shops.
- **Newcastle West:** Located in the heart of County Limerick, Newcastle West is a charming market town with a rich history and vibrant community. Highlights include the Desmond Castle, the Newcastle West Courthouse, and the Desmond Hall Heritage Centre.

- **Limerick City:** As the largest city in the county, Limerick City is brimming with historical landmarks, cultural attractions, and lively entertainment venues. Highlights include King John's Castle, St. Mary's Cathedral, the Treaty Stone, and the Hunt Museum, which houses a diverse collection of art and artifacts.
- **Adare:** Known as one of Ireland's prettiest villages, Adare is famous for its picturesque thatched cottages, historic churches, and charming streetscapes.

Visitors can explore Adare Manor, stroll through the beautiful Adare Park, and admire the architectural beauty of Adare's medieval buildings.
- **Newcastle West:** Situated in the heart of County Limerick, Newcastle West is a bustling market town with a rich history and vibrant community. Highlights include Desmond Castle, the Newcastle West Courthouse, and the Desmond Hall Heritage Centre, which offers insights into the town's past.
- **Castleconnell:** Nestled along the banks of the River Shannon, Castleconnell is a scenic village renowned for its outdoor recreational opportunities. Visitors can enjoy fishing, kayaking, and hiking along the picturesque riverside trails, or explore nearby attractions such as Castleconnell Castle and the O'Brien Bridge.
- **Kilmallock:** Located in the southern part of the county, Kilmallock is a medieval town steeped in history and architectural heritage. Highlights include the impressive remains of Kilmallock's city walls, the historic Collegiate Church of St. Peter and St. Paul, and the picturesque Ballyhoura Mountains, which offer scenic hiking and biking trails.

Luxury but Affordable Accommodation in Limerick:

Accommodation Name	Location	Pros	Cons	Starting Price (per night)
Savoy Hotel	Limerick City	Central location, luxurious amenities	Higher prices during peak seasons	€120
Limerick Strand Hotel	Limerick City	Riverside location, spa facilities	Limited parking availability	€100
Absolute Hotel	Limerick City	Modern design, rooftop bar	Smaller rooms compared to other options	€90
Clayton Hotel Limerick	Limerick City	Views of River Shannon, leisure center	Some rooms may be dated	€80
George Boutique Hotel	Limerick City	Boutique style, city center location	Limited onsite dining options	€70

These accommodations offer a blend of luxury amenities and affordability, making them ideal choices for travelers seeking a comfortable stay in Limerick without breaking the bank.

Here are 20 ways to enjoy luxury in Limerick on a budget or for free:

- **Visit King John's Castle**: Explore this iconic landmark and immerse yourself in Limerick's medieval history. While there is an admission fee for the full castle experience, you can still admire the exterior and enjoy the views of the River Shannon for free.
- **Stroll along the Riverside Walks**: Take a leisurely walk along the banks of the River Shannon and soak up the picturesque views of the city. The Riverside Walks offer a tranquil escape from the hustle and bustle of urban life.
- **Admire the Architecture of Hunt Museum**: While entry to the museum requires a fee, you can still appreciate the beautiful architecture of the building from the

outside. The museum is housed in the historic 18th-century Custom House, making it a sight to behold.
- **Attend a Free Concert at the Milk Market**: The Milk Market often hosts free concerts and live music events, providing a perfect opportunity to enjoy some entertainment without spending a dime.
- **Explore People's Park**: Spend a leisurely afternoon in this charming Victorian park, admiring the floral displays, historic monuments, and peaceful surroundings. Pack a picnic and enjoy a luxurious outdoor dining experience.
- **Join a Walking Tour of the City**: Many local guides offer free walking tours of Limerick, providing insights into the city's history, culture, and landmarks. It's a great way to learn more about the city without breaking the bank.
- **Visit Limerick City Gallery of Art**: Entry to this contemporary art gallery is free, allowing you to admire works by both Irish and international artists. Spend an afternoon browsing the exhibitions and appreciating the creativity on display.
- **Enjoy Street Performances in the City Center**: Keep an eye out for street performers and buskers entertaining crowds in Limerick's city center. You can enjoy music, magic, and other performances for free while soaking up the vibrant atmosphere.
- **Take a Self-Guided Tour of St. Mary's Cathedral**: While guided tours of the cathedral may require a fee, you can still explore this historic landmark on your own. Marvel at the beautiful architecture and intricate details of this medieval masterpiece.
- **Attend a Literary Event at The Belltable**: The Belltable Arts Centre hosts various literary events, readings, and performances throughout the year. Keep an eye on their schedule for free or low-cost events celebrating Limerick's rich literary heritage.
- **Relax in a Traditional Irish Pub**: While buying drinks may incur costs, spending time in one of Limerick's cozy pubs is a luxurious experience in itself. Enjoy the warm hospitality, live music sessions, and lively atmosphere without feeling pressured to overspend.
- **Take a Day Trip to Adare**: Explore the picturesque village of Adare, known for its thatched cottages, historic churches, and beautiful parklands. While there may be some costs associated with transportation, you can enjoy a budget-friendly day out exploring the village and its surroundings.
- **Attend a Free Workshop or Lecture**: Keep an eye out for free workshops, lectures, and cultural events happening in Limerick. From art classes to historical talks, there are plenty of opportunities to engage with the local community and learn something new.
- **Explore the University of Limerick Campus**: Wander around the scenic campus of the University of Limerick and admire its modern architecture, landscaped gardens, and impressive facilities. It's a great way to experience a slice of academic luxury without spending a penny.
- **Visit the Treaty Stone**: Take a stroll to Thomond Bridge and see the Treaty Stone, where the Treaty of Limerick was signed in 1691. This historic monument is free to visit and offers insights into Limerick's past.
- **Attend a Free Event at the Lime Tree Theatre**: The Lime Tree Theatre hosts a variety of events, including concerts, plays, and performances. Keep an eye on their schedule for free or low-cost events that you can enjoy without breaking the bank.
- **Take in the Views from the Shannon Bridge**: Walk across the Shannon Bridge and enjoy panoramic views of the river and surrounding areas. It's a peaceful spot to watch the boats go by and admire the beauty of Limerick's waterways.

- **Experience the Limerick City Museum**: Entry to the Limerick City Museum is free, allowing you to learn about the city's history, heritage, and culture. Explore artifacts, exhibitions, and interactive displays showcasing Limerick's fascinating past.
- **Attend a Free Outdoor Festival or Event**: Throughout the year, Limerick hosts various outdoor festivals, markets, and events that are free to attend. From food festivals to cultural celebrations, there's always something happening in the city.
- **Relax on the Riverbank**: Find a quiet spot along the River Shannon, spread out a blanket, and enjoy a luxurious picnic by the water. Watch the swans glide by and listen to the soothing sounds of the river for the ultimate budget-friendly relaxation experience.

Kilkenny

Ireland's Medieval Gem

Kilkenny, often referred to as the Marble City, is a picturesque town located in the heart of Ireland's Ancient East. Renowned for its rich medieval heritage, vibrant arts scene, and scenic beauty, Kilkenny offers visitors a unique blend of history, culture, and charm.

At the heart of Kilkenny lies its magnificent medieval castle, a symbol of the town's historic significance. Built in the 12th century by the Norman invaders, Kilkenny Castle boasts a stunning architectural design, surrounded by beautifully landscaped gardens and parklands. Visitors can explore the castle's opulent interiors, stroll through its pristine gardens, or enjoy panoramic views of the city from its towering battlements.

Beyond its castle, Kilkenny is also home to a wealth of historic landmarks, including St. Canice's Cathedral, a magnificent Gothic cathedral dating back to the 13th century, and the medieval Smithwick's Brewery, where visitors can learn about the town's brewing heritage.

In addition to its rich history, Kilkenny is renowned for its vibrant arts scene, with numerous galleries, studios, and craft shops dotted throughout the town. The Kilkenny Arts Festival, held annually in August, attracts artists and performers from around the world, showcasing the best of contemporary and traditional Irish arts.

For outdoor enthusiasts, Kilkenny offers plenty of opportunities to explore its scenic surroundings, from leisurely walks along the banks of the River Nore to exhilarating hikes in the nearby countryside. The picturesque village of Bennettsbridge, famous for its craft workshops and artisanal products, is just a short drive away, making it an ideal day trip destination.

Luxury but Affordable Accommodation in Kilkenny

Accommodation	Pros	Cons	Starting Price
Pembroke Hotel	Central location, modern amenities	Limited on-site parking	€120 per night
Kilkenny Hibernian Hotel	Historic charm, friendly staff	Some rooms may be small	€100 per night
Springhill Court Hotel	Leisure facilities, family-friendly	Slightly out of town center	€90 per night

Top Cheap Eats in Kilkenny

Restaurant	What to Try	Starting Price	Tips
Kyteler's Inn	Traditional Irish Fare	€10	Enjoy live music in the evenings for added ambiance
Langton's	Pub Grub	€12	Lunch specials offer good value for money
Zuni Café	Soup and Sandwiches	€8	Ideal for a quick and affordable lunch
Matt the Miller's	Gourmet Burgers	€10	Opt for the lunch menu for discounted prices
Marble City Bar	Irish Stew	€9	Generous portions make it a good value meal

Creative Alternatives to Experience Paid Attractions for Free in Kilkenny

- **Kilkenny Castle Grounds**: While admission to the castle itself may require a fee, visitors can explore the extensive parklands and gardens surrounding the castle for free.
- **St. Canice's Cathedral**: Attend a service or concert at this historic cathedral to experience its stunning architecture and serene atmosphere without paying admission.
- **Smithwick's Brewery**: While tours of the brewery may require a fee, visitors can sample locally brewed beers at many of Kilkenny's pubs and bars, experiencing the town's brewing heritage firsthand.

Best Free Audio Guides and Apps for Kilkenny

Guide/App	Covers	Download	Cost
Kilkenny Heritage Trail	Historic sites, local landmarks	Website	Free
Kilkenny Arts Festival Guide	Festival events, performances	App Store/Google Play Store	Free
Kilkenny Castle Audio Guide	Castle history, gardens tour	Website	Free

Luxurious Yet Affordable Experiences in Kilkenny

- **St. Canice's Cathedral**: Attend a choral evensong or organ recital at this historic cathedral, experiencing its majestic architecture and tranquil atmosphere without spending a penny.
- **Kilkenny Arts Festival**: Immerse yourself in the vibrant arts scene of Kilkenny by attending free exhibitions, performances, and events during the annual arts festival held in August.
- **Wander through Kilkenny Castle Grounds**: Explore the beautiful grounds of Kilkenny Castle, stroll along the riverbank, and admire the majestic architecture of this iconic landmark. Entry to the castle grounds is free, offering a taste of luxury without the cost.
- **Visit St. Canice's Cathedral and Round Tower**: Climb the historic round tower for panoramic views of Kilkenny city and beyond. While there is a small fee to climb the tower, exploring the cathedral grounds and cemetery is free.

- **Take a Walk along the Medieval Mile**: Immerse yourself in Kilkenny's medieval past as you stroll along the Medieval Mile, home to historic landmarks such as St. Canice's Cathedral, Rothe House, and the Smithwick's Experience.
- **Explore Kilkenny Design Centre**: Browse the collections of Irish crafts, jewelry, and homewares at the Kilkenny Design Centre, housed in a historic 18th-century building. Entry to the center is free, allowing you to admire the craftsmanship of local artisans.
- **Attend a Free Event at Kilkenny Arts Festival**: Keep an eye out for free events, exhibitions, and performances during the annual Kilkenny Arts Festival, which celebrates the best of Irish and international arts and culture.
- **Picnic in Kilkenny Castle Park**: Pack a picnic and relax in the scenic surroundings of Kilkenny Castle Park. With its manicured lawns, picturesque gardens, and views of the castle, it's the perfect spot for a budget-friendly outdoor feast.
- **Visit Black Abbey**: Admire the stunning stained glass windows and medieval architecture of Black Abbey, one of Kilkenny's most beautiful historic churches. Entry to the abbey is free, allowing you to appreciate its spiritual and architectural significance.
- **Explore the National Craft Gallery**: Discover contemporary Irish craft and design at the National Craft Gallery, located in the historic Castle Yard. Entry to the gallery is free, offering a glimpse into Ireland's vibrant craft culture.
- **Take a Self-Guided Walking Tour**: Download a self-guided walking tour of Kilkenny city and explore at your own pace. Wander through narrow medieval streets, discover hidden gems, and learn about the city's rich history and heritage.
- **Attend a Free Concert at Kilkenny Castle**: Keep an eye out for free outdoor concerts and performances held in the grounds of Kilkenny Castle during the summer months. Relax on the grass and enjoy live music against the backdrop of this historic landmark.
- **Visit Dunmore Cave**: Explore the mysterious underground chambers of Dunmore Cave, located just outside Kilkenny city. While there is an admission fee, the cave's natural beauty and historical significance make it a worthwhile budget-friendly excursion.
- **Take a Brewery Tour at Sullivan's Brewing Company**: While there may be a fee for guided brewery tours, you can still visit Sullivan's Brewing Company and sample their craft beers in the taproom. Enjoy a taste of luxury without the cost of a full tour.
- **Attend a Free Workshop at Kilkenny's Craft Studios**: Join a free craft workshop or demonstration at Kilkenny's Craft Studios, where local artisans showcase their skills in pottery, glassblowing, textiles, and more.
- **Explore the Butler Gallery**: Discover contemporary art exhibitions at the Butler Gallery, located in the historic Evan's Home. Entry to the gallery is free, allowing you to immerse yourself in the world of Irish and international art.
- **Take a Scenic Drive along the River Nore**: Follow the meandering path of the River Nore and enjoy scenic views of Kilkenny's countryside and historic landmarks. Pack a picnic and stop at riverside parks for a budget-friendly day out.
- **Enjoy a Pint of Smithwick's in a Traditional Pub**: While buying drinks may incur costs, treating yourself to a pint of Smithwick's in a cozy traditional pub is a quintessential Kilkenny experience. Relax by the fire and soak up the atmosphere without overspending.
- **Attend a Free Literary Event**: Keep an eye out for free literary events, readings, and book launches held at Kilkenny's bookshops, libraries, and cultural venues. From poetry readings to author talks, there's always something happening for book lovers.

- **Explore the Gardens at Butler House**: Wander through the beautiful gardens of Butler House, located adjacent to Kilkenny Castle. Admire the manicured lawns, colorful flower beds, and tranquil water features for a peaceful and luxurious escape.
- **Join a Free Guided Tour of Rothe House**: Take a guided tour of Rothe House, a historic Tudor merchant's townhouse located on the Medieval Mile. While there may be a fee for entry, guided tours are often offered for free, providing insights into Kilkenny's rich history.
- **Watch the Sunset at Woodstock Gardens**: Head to Woodstock Gardens and Arboretum in nearby Inistioge to watch the sunset over the picturesque landscape. With its serene surroundings and panoramic views, it's a luxurious experience that won't cost a penny.

County Donegal

A region of stunning natural beauty, rich cultural heritage, and warm hospitality. Renowned for its wild and untamed landscapes, Donegal offers visitors a chance to explore some of the most breathtaking scenery in the country, from towering sea cliffs and pristine beaches to rolling hills and tranquil lakes.

The county's name, "Donegal" or "Dún na nGall" in Irish, translates to "fort of the foreigners," reflecting its ancient history as a stronghold of Gaelic chieftains and later as a refuge for Viking invaders. Today, Donegal is known for its traditional Irish language and culture, with a strong emphasis on music, dance, and storytelling.

One of Donegal's most iconic landmarks is the Slieve League Cliffs, some of the highest sea cliffs in Europe, offering panoramic views of the Atlantic Ocean and the rugged coastline below. Other natural attractions include Glenveagh National Park, with its pristine wilderness and majestic mountains, and the windswept beaches of Donegal's Wild Atlantic Way.

In addition to its natural beauty, Donegal is home to a wealth of historical and cultural sites, including ancient stone forts, medieval castles, and picturesque fishing villages. Visitors can explore the ruins of Donegal Castle, stroll through the quaint streets of Ardara, or learn about the county's maritime history at the Donegal Maritime Museum.

Luxury but Affordable Accommodation in Donegal

Accommodation	Pros	Cons	Starting Price
Lough Eske Castle Hotel	Scenic views, historic charm	Slightly out of town center	€150 per night
Harvey's Point Hotel	Lakeside location, luxury amenities	Limited parking	€140 per night
Mill Park Hotel	Central location, modern amenities	Some rooms may be small	€120 per night

Top Cheap Eats in Donegal

Restaurant	What to Try	Starting Price	Tips
Nancy's Barn	Seafood Chowder	€9	Ideal for a quick and affordable lunch
The Rusty Mackerel	Pub Grub	€10	Generous portions make it a good value meal
The Lemon Tree	Gourmet Sandwiches	€8	Opt for the lunch menu for discounted prices
The Thatch Bar & Restaurant	Traditional Irish Fare	€12	Lunch specials offer good value for money
The Corner House	Wood-Fired Pizza	€10	Lunchtime deals offer good value for money

Creative Alternatives to Experience Paid Attractions for Free in Donegal

- **Slieve League Cliffs**: While guided tours of the cliffs may require a fee, visitors can explore the nearby walking trails and viewpoints for free, taking in panoramic views of the Atlantic Ocean and the rugged coastline below.
- **Glenveagh National Park**: Enjoy a leisurely stroll through the gardens and woodlands of Glenveagh Castle, taking in the stunning scenery and tranquil atmosphere, all without spending a penny.
- **Donegal Craft Village**: Browse the artisan workshops and boutiques of the Donegal Craft Village, admiring locally crafted pottery, textiles, and jewelry, all without paying admission fees.

Best Free Audio Guides and Apps for Donegal

Guide/App	Covers	Download	Cost
Donegal Audio Guide	Historic sites, local landmarks	Website	Free
Donegal Heritage Trails	Walking routes, points of interest	App Store/Google Play Store	Free
Donegal Wild Atlantic Way	Scenic drives, attractions	App Store/Google Play Store	Free

Luxurious Yet Affordable Experiences in Donegal

- **Glenveagh Castle Tour**: Join a guided tour of Glenveagh Castle, learning about its history and architecture from knowledgeable guides, and explore the beautifully landscaped gardens and woodlands surrounding the castle, all for a nominal fee.
- **Wild Atlantic Way Drive**: Embark on a self-guided drive along the Wild Atlantic Way, exploring Donegal's rugged coastline, picturesque villages, and scenic viewpoints along the way, all at your own pace and for a modest cost.
- **Traditional Music Session**: Immerse yourself in the lively atmosphere of a traditional Irish music session at one of Donegal's cozy pubs, enjoying toe-tapping tunes and warm hospitality without breaking the bank.
- **Slieve League Cliffs**: Enjoy breathtaking views of one of the highest sea cliffs in Europe. Free to visit.
- **Glenveagh National Park**: Explore the beautiful gardens and castle grounds for free, although there's a fee to enter the castle itself.
- **Rossnowlagh Beach**: Relax on the sandy shores of this picturesque beach, which is free to access.

- **Donegal Castle**: Admire the historic architecture of this castle, which offers free entry to the grounds.
- **Easkey Castle**: Another castle to explore for free, offering panoramic views of the surrounding area.
- **Malin Head**: Visit the northernmost point of the island of Ireland, known for its rugged beauty and coastal views.
- **Glenveagh Castle Gardens**: While there's a fee to enter the castle, the gardens are free to roam and offer a serene experience.
- **Ards Forest Park**: Wander through the woodland trails and along the coastline in this scenic park, which is free to enter.
- **Dunfanaghy Workhouse**: Learn about local history and heritage at this former workhouse, which offers free admission.
- **Portsalon Beach**: Spend a day relaxing on this Blue Flag beach, enjoying the pristine sands and clear waters.
- **Horn Head**: Take a leisurely hike along the rugged cliffs of Horn Head for stunning views of the Atlantic Ocean.
- **Glenveagh Castle Viewpoint**: For a free alternative to visiting the castle, hike to viewpoints offering panoramic vistas of the castle and surrounding landscape.
- **Doagh Famine Village**: Explore this outdoor museum depicting life in Ireland during the famine years. Admission fees are reasonable.
- **Assaranca Waterfall**: Marvel at the beauty of this cascading waterfall nestled in the countryside.
- **Muckish Mountain**: Hike to the summit for panoramic views of Donegal's stunning landscape. Hiking is free, but be sure to prepare adequately.
- **Doe Castle**: Explore the ruins of this medieval stronghold overlooking Sheephaven Bay, which you can visit for free.
- **Inishowen Peninsula**: Take a scenic drive along the Inishowen 100 route, stopping at viewpoints and attractions along the way.
- **Ballymastocker Bay**: Enjoy the pristine beauty of this horseshoe-shaped beach, which was once voted the second most beautiful beach in the world by The Observer.
- **Glencomcille Folk Village**: Step back in time and explore this replica of a rural Irish village, showcasing traditional thatched cottages and exhibits. Admission prices are reasonable.
- **Letterkenny Cathedral Quarter**: Stroll through the historic streets of Letterkenny, taking in the architecture and visiting local shops and cafes.

Letterkenny

Letterkenny, located in the heart of County Donegal, is the largest town in the county and serves as a bustling hub of culture, commerce, and community. Nestled amidst the stunning landscapes of Northwest Ireland, Letterkenny offers visitors a warm welcome and a wealth of attractions to explore, from its vibrant arts scene to its rich history and picturesque surroundings.

The town's name, "Letterkenny" or "Leitir Ceanainn" in Irish, translates to "hillside of the O'Cannons," a reference to the prominent Gaelic clan that once ruled the area. Today, Letterkenny is a vibrant and cosmopolitan town, known for its friendly locals, lively atmosphere, and strong sense of community spirit.

One of Letterkenny's main attractions is its thriving arts and cultural scene, with a range of galleries, theaters, and performance spaces showcasing the best of local and international talent. Visitors can explore exhibitions at the Regional Cultural Centre, catch a show at An Grianán Theatre, or browse the artisan craft shops and boutiques scattered throughout the town.

In addition to its cultural offerings, Letterkenny boasts a rich historical heritage, with landmarks such as the Donegal County Museum and the Old Courthouse offering insights into the town's past. Visitors can also explore the nearby Glenveagh National Park, with its stunning gardens, castle, and walking trails, or take a scenic drive along the Wild Atlantic Way to discover the beauty of Donegal's rugged coastline.

Luxury but Affordable Accommodation in Letterkenny

Accommodation	Pros	Cons	Starting Price
Radisson Blu Hotel Letterkenny	Central location, modern amenities	Limited parking	€120 per night
Clanree Hotel	Leisure facilities, family-friendly	Slightly out of town center	€110 per night
Mount Errigal Hotel	Scenic views, onsite restaurant	Some rooms may be small	€100 per night

Wexford

Wexford, a charming coastal town located in the southeast of Ireland, is a hidden gem known for its rich history, vibrant arts scene, and stunning natural beauty. Situated on the shores of the Irish Sea, Wexford boasts a picturesque harbor, sandy beaches, and lush countryside, making it a popular destination for both locals and visitors alike.

With a history dating back over a thousand years, Wexford is steeped in heritage and culture. The town's medieval streets are lined with historic buildings, including the iconic Wexford Opera House, which hosts world-class performances throughout the year. Visitors can explore landmarks such as the 12th-century Selskar Abbey and the National Opera House, which offer fascinating insights into Wexford's storied past.

Wexford's vibrant arts scene is a testament to its creative spirit, with numerous galleries, studios, and cultural events showcasing the talents of local artists and performers. The town's annual Wexford Festival Opera, held in October, attracts opera enthusiasts from around the world, while its vibrant street festivals and markets offer something for everyone to enjoy.

Beyond its cultural attractions, Wexford is also a paradise for outdoor enthusiasts, with an abundance of activities to enjoy amidst its stunning natural landscapes. From scenic coastal walks and water sports along the Wexford coast to hiking trails in the nearby mountains and forests, there's no shortage of adventures to be had in this coastal haven.

Luxury but Affordable Accommodation in Wexford

Accommodation	Pros	Cons	Starting Price
Ferrycarrig Hotel	Riverside location, modern amenities	Limited dining options nearby	€120 per night
Whitford House Hotel	Spa facilities, family-friendly	Slightly out of town center	€100 per night
Talbot Hotel Wexford	Central location, leisure facilities	Some rooms may be small	€90 per night

Top Cheap Eats in Wexford

Restaurant	What to Try	Starting Price	Tips
The Yard	Traditional Irish Fare	€12	Lunch specials offer good value for money
Greenacres	Gourmet Sandwiches	€8	Opt for the lunch menu for discounted prices
The Sky & The Ground	Pub Grub	€10	Generous portions make it a good value meal
Wilds	Wood-Fired Pizza	€10	Lunchtime deals offer good value for money
The Fisherman's Bar	Seafood Chowder	€9	Ideal for a quick and affordable lunch

Creative Alternatives to Experience Paid Attractions for Free in Wexford

- **Wexford Opera House**: While ticketed performances may require a fee, visitors can explore the exterior of the iconic building and admire its modern architectural design from the outside, all without spending a penny.
- **Selskar Abbey**: Take a leisurely stroll around the historic ruins of Selskar Abbey, immersing yourself in the tranquil atmosphere and admiring the medieval architecture, for free.
- **Johnstown Castle Gardens**: Enjoy a scenic walk through the beautiful gardens surrounding Johnstown Castle, taking in the colorful floral displays and serene lakeside views, without paying admission fees.

Best Free Audio Guides and Apps for Wexford

Guide/App	Covers	Download	Cost
Wexford Audio Guide	Historic sites, local landmarks	Website	Free
Wexford Walking Tours	Guided walking routes, points of interest	App Store/Google Play Store	Free
Wexford Heritage Trail	Cultural landmarks, architectural highlights	Website	Free

Luxurious Yet Affordable Experiences in Wexford

- **Johnstown Castle Gardens**: Spend a leisurely afternoon exploring the beautiful gardens surrounding Johnstown Castle, taking in the serene lakeside views and colorful floral displays, all for free.
- **Coastal Walks**: Take a scenic coastal walk along the Wexford coast, enjoying panoramic views of the Irish Sea and rugged coastline, without breaking the bank.
- **Artisanal Tasting Tour**: Embark on a self-guided tasting tour of Wexford's artisanal producers, sampling locally crafted cheeses, chocolates, and beverages, all while soaking up the town's vibrant atmosphere, for a nominal cost.
- **Relax on Wexford's Blue Flag Beaches**: Spend a day lounging on the sandy shores of Wexford's Blue Flag beaches, such as Curracloe Beach or Rosslare Strand. Enjoy the sun, sea, and fresh sea air for a luxurious coastal experience.
- **Explore the Hook Peninsula**: Take a scenic drive along the Hook Peninsula and explore its historic lighthouses, ancient ruins, and picturesque villages. Admire the rugged coastline and panoramic views without spending a dime.
- **Visit the Irish National Heritage Park**: Immerse yourself in Ireland's past at the Irish National Heritage Park, where you can explore reconstructed ancient dwellings and learn about the country's history and heritage. While there is an admission fee, you can still enjoy the park's outdoor exhibits and walking trails for free.
- **Discover Johnstown Castle Gardens**: Wander through the beautifully landscaped gardens of Johnstown Castle and admire its ornamental lakes, woodland walks, and Victorian architecture. Entry to the gardens is free, allowing you to enjoy a taste of luxury without the cost.
- **Attend a Free Event at Wexford Arts Centre**: Keep an eye out for free exhibitions, performances, and cultural events at the Wexford Arts Centre, which showcases the best of contemporary Irish and international arts and culture.
- **Explore the Dunbrody Famine Ship**: Step back in time and explore the Dunbrody Famine Ship, a replica of a 19th-century emigrant vessel. While there is an

admission fee for guided tours, you can still admire the ship from the outside and learn about Ireland's emigration history.
- **Take a Walk along the Wexford Quays**: Stroll along the scenic Wexford Quays and enjoy views of the River Slaney and the bustling waterfront. Admire the historic buildings, colorful boats, and vibrant atmosphere of this waterfront promenade.
- **Visit the National 1798 Rebellion Centre**: Learn about one of Ireland's most significant historical events at the National 1798 Rebellion Centre in Enniscorthy. While there may be an admission fee for the museum, you can still explore the surrounding town and learn about its rebel past.
- **Explore the Wexford Wildfowl Reserve**: Discover the natural beauty of the Wexford Wildfowl Reserve, home to a variety of bird species and wildlife. Enjoy a leisurely walk along the nature trails and bird hides for a tranquil and budget-friendly outdoor experience.
- **Take a Self-Guided Walking Tour of Wexford Town**: Download a self-guided walking tour of Wexford Town and explore its historic streets, landmarks, and attractions at your own pace. Learn about the town's Viking past, medieval history, and maritime heritage as you wander through its charming streets.
-

Top Cheap Eats in Letterkenny

Restaurant	What to Try	Starting Price	Tips
The Brewery Bar	Pub Grub	€10	Generous portions make it a good value meal
The Counter Deli	Gourmet Sandwiches	€8	Opt for the lunch menu for discounted prices
The Lemon Tree	Wood-Fired Pizza	€10	Lunchtime deals offer good value for money
The Kitchen	Traditional Irish Fare	€12	Lunch specials offer good value for money
The Courtyard Bar & Grill	International Cuisine	€12	Early bird menus offer great value for money

Creative Alternatives to Experience Paid Attractions for Free in Letterkenny

- **Donegal County Museum**: While admission fees may apply for certain exhibitions, visitors can explore the exterior of the museum and learn about Donegal's history from informational plaques located nearby, all without spending a penny.
- **Letterkenny Town Park**: Take a leisurely stroll through Letterkenny Town Park, enjoying the tranquil atmosphere and scenic beauty of its gardens, lakes, and walking trails, all for free.
- **The Donegal Railway Heritage Centre**: While admission fees may apply for guided tours of the center, visitors can explore the exterior of the railway carriages and locomotives on display, learning about Donegal's railway history from informational signage, for free.

Best Free Audio Guides and Apps for Letterkenny

Guide/App	Covers	Download	Cost
Letterkenny Audio Guide	Historic sites, local landmarks	Website	Free
Letterkenny Heritage Trail App	Walking routes, points of interest	App Store/Google Play Store	Free
Donegal Wild Atlantic Way App	Scenic drives, attractions	App Store/Google Play Store	Free

Luxurious Yet Affordable Experiences in Letterkenny

- **Glenveagh Castle Tour**: Join a guided tour of Glenveagh Castle, exploring its opulent interiors, landscaped gardens, and scenic trails, all for a modest cost.
- **Glenveagh National Park**: Spend a day hiking or cycling through the stunning landscapes of Glenveagh National Park, taking in the breathtaking views of mountains, lakes, and woodlands, all for a nominal fee.
- **Traditional Music Session**: Immerse yourself in the lively atmosphere of a traditional Irish music session at one of Letterkenny's cozy pubs, enjoying toe-tapping tunes and warm hospitality without breaking the bank.

Sligo

Land of Yeats, Myth, and Majesty. Sligo, situated on the northwest coast of Ireland, is a land of rugged beauty, ancient mythology, and artistic inspiration. With its dramatic landscapes, historic sites, and vibrant cultural scene, Sligo has long captivated visitors from around the world, drawing them in with its rich heritage and natural splendor.

The county's name, "Sligo" or "Sligeach" in Irish, translates to "shelly place," a nod to its coastal location and abundance of seashells along its shores. From the majestic peaks of Benbulben and Knocknarea to the pristine beaches of Strandhill and Rosses Point, Sligo's diverse landscapes offer endless opportunities for exploration and adventure.

Sligo is perhaps best known as the birthplace of the renowned poet William Butler Yeats, whose works drew inspiration from the county's mythic past and majestic landscapes. Visitors can explore Yeats Country, tracing the poet's footsteps through sites such as Lough Gill, Dooney Rock, and the Lake Isle of Innisfree, immortalized in his poetry.

In addition to its literary connections, Sligo boasts a rich archaeological heritage, with ancient sites such as Carrowmore Megalithic Cemetery and Queen Maeve's Cairn bearing testament to its prehistoric past. The county's historic towns and villages, such as Sligo Town and Drumcliffe, are steeped in history and charm, with historic buildings, quaint streets, and welcoming locals.

Luxury but Affordable Accommodation in Sligo

Accommodation	Pros	Cons	Starting Price
Radisson Blu Hotel & Spa	Scenic views, spa facilities	Slightly out of town center	€130 per night
Sligo Park Hotel	Central location, leisure facilities	Limited parking	€120 per night
The Glasshouse Hotel	Modern design, riverside location	Some rooms may be small	€110 per night

Top Cheap Eats in Sligo

Restaurant	What to Try	Starting Price	Tips
WB's Coffee House	Gourmet Sandwiches	€8	Opt for the lunch menu for discounted prices
Coach Lane Restaurant	Traditional Irish Fare	€12	Lunch specials offer good value for money
The Draft House	Pub Grub	€10	Generous portions make it a good value meal

Sweet Beat Cafe	Vegetarian and Vegan Options	€12	Enjoy a tranquil atmosphere and delicious food
Hargadon Bros	Wood-Fired Pizza	€10	Lunchtime deals offer good value for money

Creative Alternatives to Experience Paid Attractions for Free in Sligo

- **Carrowmore Megalithic Cemetery**: While guided tours of the cemetery may require a fee, visitors can explore the surrounding landscape and admire the ancient monuments from afar, all without spending a penny.
- **Knocknarea**: Embark on a hike up Knocknarea, enjoying panoramic views of Sligo Bay and the surrounding countryside from the summit, all for free.
- **Sligo Abbey**: While admission fees may apply for guided tours of the abbey, visitors can explore the exterior of this historic landmark and admire its Gothic architecture from the outside, for free.

Best Free Audio Guides and Apps for Sligo

Guide/App	Covers	Download	Cost
Sligo Audio Guide	Historic sites, local landmarks	Website	Free
Sligo Heritage Trails App	Walking routes, points of interest	App Store/Google Play Store	Free
Yeats Trail App	Literary landmarks, scenic drives	App Store/Google Play Store	Free

Luxurious Yet Affordable Experiences in Sligo

- **Benbulben Adventure**: Join a guided hike or rock climbing excursion on Benbulben, enjoying panoramic views of Sligo's stunning landscapes and rugged coastline, all for a modest cost.
- **Seaweed Bath**: Indulge in a traditional seaweed bath at one of Sligo's spa facilities, enjoying the therapeutic benefits of local seaweed and mineral-rich waters, for a nominal fee.
- **Traditional Music Session**: Immerse yourself in the lively atmosphere of a traditional Irish music session at one of Sligo's cozy pubs, enjoying toe-tapping tunes and warm hospitality without breaking the bank.
- **Benbulben**: Hike or simply admire the majestic beauty of this iconic mountain, which dominates the Sligo skyline. Hiking is free.
- **Strandhill Beach**: Enjoy a day of relaxation or surfing on the shores of this picturesque Blue Flag beach.
- **Yeats Society and Yeats Memorial Building**: Explore the life and works of the renowned poet W.B. Yeats at this cultural center, which offers free entry.
- **Knocknarea**: Embark on a hike to the summit of this iconic hill, crowned by a massive cairn said to be the burial site of Queen Maeve. Hiking is free.
- **Lough Gill**: Take a scenic drive or boat tour around this beautiful lake, surrounded by lush greenery and dotted with islands.
- **Sligo Abbey**: Discover the history of this medieval Dominican abbey, which offers affordable entry fees.
- **Glencar Waterfall**: Marvel at the beauty of this cascading waterfall, famously mentioned in W.B. Yeats' poetry. Entrance is free.
- **Queen Maeve's Trail**: Walk or cycle along this picturesque trail, which offers stunning views of Sligo's countryside and coastline.

- **Rosses Point**: Enjoy a leisurely stroll along the scenic promenade or relax on the sandy beach at this charming seaside village.
- **Carrowmore Megalithic Cemetery**: Explore one of the largest and oldest megalithic cemeteries in Ireland, where you can wander among ancient stone monuments. Entry fees are reasonable.
- **Sligo Folk Park**: Step back in time and experience rural Irish life in the 19th century at this open-air museum. Admission prices are affordable.
- **Hazelwood Demesne**: Take a tranquil walk through the woodlands of this historic estate, which offers scenic views of Lough Gill.
- **Wild Atlantic Way Discovery Point - Mullaghmore**: Marvel at the rugged beauty of the Atlantic coastline and the picturesque village of Mullaghmore.
- **Coney Island**: Take a short ferry ride to this scenic island, known for its sandy beaches and panoramic views of Sligo Bay.
- **Sligo Town Walking Tour**: Explore the historic streets of Sligo town on a self-guided walking tour, discovering landmarks such as the Model Arts Centre and the Hawk's Well Theatre.
- **Eagles Flying**: Experience the thrill of seeing birds of prey up close at this raptor sanctuary and wildlife center. Admission prices are affordable.
- **Sligo County Museum**: Learn about the history and heritage of Sligo at this museum, which offers free entry.
- **Doorly Park**: Enjoy a peaceful stroll or a picnic in this scenic park, which boasts beautiful woodland trails and views of the Garavogue River.
- **Warrior's Run**: Participate in or watch this annual hill running race, which takes place in the scenic village of Strandhill.
- **Carrowkeel Passage Tombs**: Visit these ancient burial sites located in the Bricklieve Mountains, offering panoramic views of the surrounding countryside. Access is free.

Northern Ireland

Northern Ireland, a part of the United Kingdom, is known for its rich history, stunning landscapes, and vibrant cities. Here's a guide to exploring Northern Ireland:

Top Attractions:
- **Giant's Causeway**: A UNESCO World Heritage Site with unique hexagonal basalt columns, steeped in myth and legend.
- **Titanic Belfast**: An interactive museum located in the former shipyard where the Titanic was built, offering exhibits on the ship's construction, sinking, and legacy.
- **Carrick-a-Rede Rope Bridge**: A thrilling rope bridge spanning a 30-meter chasm between the mainland and a tiny island, offering stunning coastal views.
- **Dark Hedges**: An enchanting avenue of beech trees, featured in the TV series "Game of Thrones," known for its haunting beauty.
- **Derry/Londonderry**: A historic walled city with a rich cultural heritage, including the Guildhall, Peace Bridge, and the Tower Museum.
- **Causeway Coastal Route**: A scenic driving route along the coast, passing through quaint villages, sandy beaches, and rugged cliffs.
- **Carrickfergus Castle**: A well-preserved Norman castle dating back to the 12th century, located on the shores of Belfast Lough.
- **Mount Stewart**: A stately home with world-renowned gardens, featuring exotic plants, sculptures, and scenic walking trails.
- **Bushmills Distillery**: Ireland's oldest working distillery, offering guided tours and tastings of their award-winning Irish whiskey.
- **Mourne Mountains**: A range of granite peaks and valleys, offering hiking, climbing, and stunning views of the surrounding countryside.

Money-Saving Tips:
- **Visitor Passes**: Consider purchasing a visitor pass for attractions like Titanic Belfast or the Giant's Causeway Visitor Centre to save on admission fees.
- **Combination Tickets**: Look for combination tickets or discounted packages when visiting multiple attractions in the same area.
- **Public Transport**: Use public buses or trains to get around, which can be more affordable than renting a car.
- **Free Attractions**: Take advantage of free attractions such as parks, beaches, and historic sites to experience Northern Ireland on a budget.
- **Self-Guided Tours**: Explore cities like Belfast and Derry/Londonderry on self-guided walking tours to save on guided tour fees.

Sample Itinerary:
- Day 1: Explore Belfast, visiting Titanic Belfast, St. George's Market, and the historic Cathedral Quarter.
- Day 2: Drive the Causeway Coastal Route, stopping at Carrickfergus Castle, Carrick-a-Rede Rope Bridge, and the Dark Hedges.
- Day 3: Visit the Giant's Causeway, exploring the unique rock formations and taking a scenic walk along the coastal trails.
- Day 4: Spend the day in Derry/Londonderry, walking the city walls, visiting the Guildhall, and taking a guided tour of the Bogside murals.

- Day 5: Take a day trip to the Mourne Mountains, hiking one of the scenic trails and enjoying panoramic views of the countryside.
- Day 6: Explore the Ards Peninsula, visiting Mount Stewart House and Gardens, and relaxing on the beaches of Strangford Lough.
- Day 7: Depart from Northern Ireland, taking in any final sights or experiences before heading to your next destination.

Belfast

The capital city of Northern Ireland, is a vibrant metropolis steeped in history, culture, and a rich tapestry of stories. From its industrial heritage to its turbulent past and vibrant present, Belfast offers visitors a unique blend of old-world charm and modern innovation, making it a dynamic and captivating destination.

The city's name, "Belfast," is believed to derive from the Irish language phrase "Beal Feirste," meaning "mouth of the sandbanks," a reference to the river mouth where the city was founded. Today, Belfast is a bustling hub of activity, with a thriving arts scene, world-class attractions, and a warm and welcoming atmosphere.

One of Belfast's most iconic landmarks is the Titanic Belfast museum, located on the site of the former Harland and Wolff shipyard where the RMS Titanic was built. This award-winning visitor experience tells the story of the ill-fated ocean liner through interactive exhibits, artifacts, and multimedia displays, offering visitors a fascinating insight into Belfast's maritime heritage.

In addition to its maritime connections, Belfast is known for its political history, with landmarks such as the Peace Walls and the murals of West Belfast bearing testament to the city's troubled past. Visitors can explore these sites on guided tours, learning about the complex history of Northern Ireland and the city's journey towards peace and reconciliation.

Belfast is also a cultural hotspot, with a thriving arts scene, lively music venues, and a wealth of museums and galleries to explore. From the Ulster Museum and the MAC (Metropolitan Arts Centre) to the vibrant street art of the Cathedral Quarter, Belfast offers something for every art lover.

Luxury but Affordable Accommodation in Belfast

Accommodation	Pros	Cons	Starting Price
Europa Hotel	Central location, historic charm	Limited parking	£100 per night
Titanic Hotel Belfast	Unique setting, maritime heritage	Slightly out of city center	£120 per night
Bullitt Hotel	Modern design, vibrant atmosphere	Some rooms may be small	£90 per night

Top Cheap Eats in Belfast

Restaurant	What to Try	Starting Price	Tips
Mourne Seafood Bar	Seafood Chowder	£10	Ideal for a quick and affordable lunch
Maggie Mays	Traditional Irish Fare	£12	Lunch specials offer good value for money
Established Coffee	Gourmet Sandwiches	£8	Opt for the lunch menu for discounted prices
Boojum	Mexican Burritos	£7	Generous portions make it a good value meal
Bunsen	Classic Burgers	£10	Simple menu focuses on quality and affordability

Creative Alternatives to Experience Paid Attractions for Free in Belfast

- **Belfast City Hall**: While guided tours of City Hall may require a fee, visitors can explore the exterior of this stunning Victorian building and its surrounding grounds, all without spending a penny.
- **Ulster Museum**: Enjoy free admission to the Ulster Museum, exploring its diverse collections of art, history, and natural sciences, including the famous Egyptian mummy, Takabuti.
- **Botanic Gardens**: Take a leisurely stroll through the Botanic Gardens, admiring the exotic plants, beautiful flowerbeds, and historic Palm House, all for free.

Best Free Audio Guides and Apps for Belfast

Guide/App	Covers	Download	Cost
Belfast Audio Guide	Historic sites, local landmarks	Website	Free
Discover Belfast App	Walking routes, points of interest	App Store/Google Play Store	Free
Belfast Street Art Map	Street art, murals	Website	Free

Luxurious Yet Affordable Experiences in Belfast

- **Black Cab Tour**: Join a guided Black Cab Tour of Belfast, exploring the city's historic neighborhoods, political murals, and key landmarks, all for a modest cost.
- **Titanic Belfast Afternoon Tea**: Indulge in a luxurious afternoon tea experience at Titanic Belfast, enjoying sweet treats and savory delights inspired by the Titanic's maiden voyage, all for a nominal fee.
- **Crumlin Road Gaol Tour**: Embark on a guided tour of Crumlin Road Gaol, exploring the historic prison and learning about its fascinating history, including tales of infamous inmates and daring escapes, all for a modest cost.
- **Botanic Gardens**: Wander through these beautiful Victorian gardens, home to exotic plants, sculptures, and the iconic Palm House. Admission is free.
- **Ulster Museum**: Discover art, history, and natural science exhibitions, including the renowned Irish antiquities collection. Entry is free, though donations are appreciated.

- **Cave Hill**: Hike to the summit of this distinctive hill for panoramic views of Belfast and beyond, including the famous "Napoleon's Nose" rock formation. Hiking is free.
- **St. George's Market**: Indulge in a sensory feast at Belfast's oldest market, where you can sample local produce, gourmet foods, and artisan crafts. Entry is free.
- **Belfast Castle**: Explore the gardens and grounds of this stunning castle, perched on the slopes of Cave Hill, offering panoramic views of the city. Admission is free.
- **Crumlin Road Gaol**: Take a guided tour of this historic Victorian-era prison, which offers insight into Belfast's turbulent past. Admission fees are reasonable.
- **Black Cab Tours**: Take a guided tour of Belfast's political murals and peace walls in a traditional black cab, learning about the city's troubled history and peace process. Prices are affordable.
- **Belfast City Hall**: Admire the grandeur of this iconic civic building, both inside and out, with free guided tours available.
- **Lagan Towpath**: Enjoy a leisurely walk or cycle along this scenic riverside path, which offers views of historic landmarks and wildlife habitats.
- **Titanic Belfast Walking Tour**: Join a free walking tour of the Titanic Quarter, led by local guides who share fascinating stories about the area's maritime heritage.
- **Cathedral Quarter**: Explore Belfast's vibrant cultural district, home to art galleries, theaters, historic pubs, and street art installations.
- **Ulster Folk Museum**: Step back in time and experience rural life in Northern Ireland at this outdoor museum, which offers affordable admission prices.
- **Belfast Murals**: Take a self-guided tour of the city's political and street art murals, which reflect Belfast's complex history and cultural identity. Access is free.
- **Victoria Square Shopping Centre**: Window shop or treat yourself to some retail therapy at this modern shopping complex, which also features a dome offering panoramic views of the city.
- **Linen Hall Library**: Browse the shelves of Northern Ireland's oldest library, which houses a rich collection of books, manuscripts, and archives. Admission is free.
- **St. Anne's Cathedral**: Marvel at the stunning architecture and beautiful stained glass windows of this historic cathedral, with guided tours available at reasonable prices.
- **CS Lewis Square**: Pay homage to the beloved author of "The Chronicles of Narnia" at this public space featuring sculptures inspired by his famous works. Entry is free.
- **Belfast Hills**: Embark on a scenic drive or hike in the Belfast Hills, which offer panoramic views of the city and surrounding countryside.

Londonderry

Introduction to Londonderry: A City of History and Culture

Londonderry, also known as Derry, is a city in Northern Ireland with a rich history, vibrant culture, and stunning natural beauty. Situated on the banks of the River Foyle, Londonderry is renowned for its historic walled city, picturesque landscapes, and warm and welcoming atmosphere.

The city's name, "Londonderry," reflects its colonial past and English influence, while "Derry" is derived from the Irish word "Doire," meaning "oak grove," a nod to the ancient oak forests that once covered the area. Today, both names are used interchangeably, with "Derry" being preferred by nationalists and "Londonderry" by unionists.

One of Londonderry's most iconic landmarks is its historic city walls, which date back to the 17th century and are among the best-preserved in Europe. Walking along the walls offers visitors panoramic views of the city below, as well as insights into its turbulent history, including the Siege of Derry in 1689.

In addition to its historic walls, Londonderry is known for its vibrant cultural scene, with a range of museums, galleries, and performance spaces to explore. The Tower Museum, located within the city walls, offers exhibits on the city's history, while the Guildhall hosts concerts, exhibitions, and events throughout the year.

Londonderry is also famous for its annual Halloween celebrations, which are among the largest in Europe and attract visitors from around the world. The city comes alive with street performances, music, and fireworks, creating a festive atmosphere that captures the spirit of the season.

Luxury but Affordable Accommodation in Londonderry

Accommodation	Pros	Cons	Starting Price
City Hotel Derry	Central location, river views	Limited parking	£90 per night
Maldron Hotel Derry	Modern amenities, leisure facilities	Slightly out of city center	£80 per night
Bishop's Gate Hotel	Historic charm, boutique luxury	Some rooms may be small	£100 per night

Top Cheap Eats in Londonderry

Restaurant	What to Try	Starting Price	Tips
Hidden City Cafe	Gourmet Sandwiches	£7	Opt for the lunch menu for discounted prices
Browns In Town	Traditional Irish Fare	£10	Lunch specials offer good value for money

Pyke 'N' Pommes	Fish and Chips	£8	Generous portions make it a good value meal
Brickwork Restaurant	Wood-Fired Pizza	£9	Lunchtime deals offer good value for money
Walled City Brewery	Craft Beers, Gastropub Grub	£12	Enjoy locally brewed beers and tasty bites

Creative Alternatives to Experience Paid Attractions for Free in Londonderry

- **Free Derry Corner**: Visit Free Derry Corner, a gable wall in the Bogside neighborhood adorned with murals and political slogans, symbolizing the area's nationalist and republican heritage, all for free.
- **Peace Bridge**: Take a leisurely stroll across the Peace Bridge, spanning the River Foyle and connecting the city center with the Waterside area, offering panoramic views of the city skyline and surrounding countryside, all for free.
- **Guildhall Square**: Relax in Guildhall Square, a bustling public space in the heart of the city, surrounded by historic buildings and cultural institutions, and often hosting free events, concerts, and performances throughout the year.

Best Free Audio Guides and Apps for Londonderry

Guide/App	Covers	Download	Cost
Derry Audio Guide	Historic sites, local landmarks	Website	Free
Discover Derry App	Walking routes, points of interest	App Store/Google Play	Free
Derry Walls App	City walls, historical sites	App Store/Google Play	Free

Luxurious Yet Affordable Experiences in Londonderry

- **Foyle Cruise**: Embark on a scenic cruise along the River Foyle, enjoying panoramic views of the city skyline and surrounding countryside, all for a modest cost.
- **Craft Beer Tasting**: Indulge in a craft beer tasting experience at Walled City Brewery, sampling a selection of locally brewed beers and learning about the brewing process, all for a nominal fee.
- **Walking Tour of the City Walls**: Join a guided walking tour of the historic city walls, learning about the city's history and architecture from knowledgeable guides, all for a modest cost.
- **Guildhall**: Visit the iconic Guildhall, an architectural gem located in the heart of the city. Marvel at its stunning neo-Gothic design and explore the exhibitions inside, which often include displays on the city's history and culture. Admission is usually free.
- **Peace Bridge**: Take a leisurely stroll across the Peace Bridge, spanning the River Foyle and connecting the city center with the Ebrington Square. Enjoy the views of the river and the city skyline, especially during sunset or at night when the bridge is illuminated.
- **Tower Museum**: Discover the history of Derry at the Tower Museum, which showcases exhibitions on the city's maritime heritage, the Spanish Armada, and the Troubles. Admission fees are reasonable, and discounts may be available for students and seniors.
- **Craft Village**: Explore the Craft Village, a charming area of traditional-style buildings housing artisan shops, galleries, and cafes. Browse locally-made crafts

such as pottery, jewelry, and textiles, and perhaps treat yourself to a unique souvenir or gift.

Enniskillen

Introduction to Enniskillen: Jewel of Fermanagh's Lakelands

Enniskillen, nestled on the shores of Lough Erne in County Fermanagh, Northern Ireland, is a charming town renowned for its stunning natural beauty, rich history, and vibrant cultural scene. Surrounded by lush green countryside and dotted with picturesque lakes, Enniskillen offers visitors a tranquil escape in the heart of the Fermanagh Lakelands.

The town's name, "Enniskillen," is derived from the Irish language "Inis Ceithleann," meaning "Ceithleann's island," named after an ancient Gaelic queen. With a history dating back over 600 years, Enniskillen has played a significant role in Irish history, from its strategic location along ancient trade routes to its involvement in key historical events, such as the Battle of Maguire's Ford in 1594.

Today, Enniskillen is a vibrant and bustling town, with a wealth of attractions to explore. The town's historic center is a maze of narrow streets, lined with Georgian and Victorian buildings, charming shops, and inviting cafes. Visitors can stroll along the scenic waterfront promenade, visit the iconic Enniskillen Castle, or explore the town's vibrant arts and crafts scene.

Enniskillen is also a gateway to the natural wonders of County Fermanagh, with its tranquil lakes, meandering waterways, and rolling hills. From cruising along Lough Erne to exploring the ancient forests of Castle Archdale Country Park, there's no shortage of outdoor adventures to be had in this picturesque region.

Luxury but Affordable Accommodation in Enniskillen

Accommodation	Pros	Cons	Starting Price
Lough Erne Resort	Lakeside location, luxury amenities	Slightly out of town center	£150 per night
Killyhevlin Lakeside Hotel	Scenic views, spa facilities	Limited parking	£120 per night
Westville Hotel	Central location, modern amenities	Some rooms may be small	£100 per night

Top Cheap Eats in Enniskillen

Restaurant	What to Try	Starting Price	Tips
Dollakis	Gourmet Sandwiches	£6	Opt for the lunch menu for discounted prices
The Saddlers	Traditional Irish Fare	£10	Lunch specials offer good value for money
Franco's Restaurant	Wood-Fired Pizza	£9	Lunchtime deals offer good value for money

The Jolly Sandwich	Deli Sandwiches	£5	Generous portions make it a good value meal
Cafe Merlot	International Cuisine	£12	Early bird menus offer great value for money

Creative Alternatives to Experience Paid Attractions for Free in Enniskillen

- **Enniskillen Castle Grounds**: While admission fees may apply for entry to Enniskillen Castle, visitors can explore the beautiful grounds surrounding the castle, including the gardens, courtyards, and scenic viewpoints, all for free.
- **Crom Estate**: Enjoy a leisurely stroll through the grounds of Crom Estate, a National Trust property located near Enniskillen, admiring the stunning landscapes, historic buildings, and tranquil waterways, all for free.
- **Castle Caldwell Forest**: Take a hike or bike ride through Castle Caldwell Forest, enjoying the peaceful surroundings, diverse wildlife, and scenic views of Lower Lough Erne, all for free.

Best Free Audio Guides and Apps for Enniskillen

Guide/App	Covers	Download	Cost
Enniskillen Audio Guide	Historic sites, local landmarks	Website	Free
Fermanagh Lakelands App	Walking routes, points of interest	App Store/Google Play Store	Free
Castle Archdale Audio Guide	Nature trails, wildlife	Website	Free

Luxurious Yet Affordable Experiences in Enniskillen

- **Lough Erne Cruise**: Embark on a scenic cruise along Lough Erne, exploring its tranquil waters, lush green islands, and historic landmarks, all for a modest cost.
- **Spa Day at Killyhevlin**: Indulge in a relaxing spa day at Killyhevlin Lakeside Hotel, enjoying a range of treatments and therapies, as well as access to the hotel's leisure facilities, all for a nominal fee.
- **Enniskillen Food Tour**: Join a guided food tour of Enniskillen, sampling delicious local delicacies and learning about the town's culinary heritage from knowledgeable guides, all for a modest cost.

Unmissable things to do in Ireland

1. An Insider's Guide to Visiting Giant's Causeway

A geological marvel and a treasure trove of myth and legend nestled along the Northern Irish coast. As you embark on your journey to this extraordinary site, here's your insider's guide to ensure you make the most of your visit:

Before You Go:

- **Timing is Key:** Plan your visit during the off-peak hours or shoulder seasons to avoid crowds and fully immerse yourself in the magic of the Causeway.
- **Dress for Adventure:** Wear comfortable walking shoes and dress in layers, as the weather along the coast can be unpredictable. Don't forget your raincoat and sunscreen!
- **Book in Advance:** Secure your tickets online to skip the queues and guarantee entry, especially during peak tourist seasons.

Getting There:

- **By Car:** The Giant's Causeway is easily accessible by car, with ample parking available onsite. Take the scenic Causeway Coastal Route for breathtaking views along the way.
- **Public Transport:** Opt for the Causeway Coast and Glens bus service or join a guided tour departing from Belfast or nearby towns for a hassle-free journey.

Exploring the Causeway:

- **Visitor Centre:** Start your adventure at the Visitor Centre, where you can learn about the geological origins and mythical tales of the Causeway through interactive exhibits and audio-visual presentations.
- **Walking Trails:** Choose from a variety of walking trails, ranging from easy strolls to more challenging hikes, each offering unique perspectives of the basalt formations and coastal scenery.
- **Audio Guide:** Enhance your experience with an audio guide, available in multiple languages, providing fascinating insights into the history, folklore, and wildlife of the area.

Must-See Highlights:

- **The Grand Causeway:** Marvel at the iconic hexagonal basalt columns that stretch into the sea, formed by ancient volcanic activity and erosion over millions of years.
- **Giant's Boot:** Discover the legendary Giant's Boot, a massive basalt formation resembling a giant's discarded shoe, nestled amidst the rugged landscape.

- **The Wishing Chair:** Seek out the Wishing Chair, a natural stone throne said to grant wishes to those who sit upon it. Don't forget to make a wish!

Insider Tips:
- **Early Bird Gets the View:** Beat the crowds by arriving early in the morning or late in the afternoon for uninterrupted views and photo opportunities.
- **Explore Beyond the Causeway:** Venture off the beaten path to explore nearby attractions such as the Carrick-a-Rede Rope Bridge, Dunluce Castle, and the Dark Hedges for a truly immersive experience.
- **Pack a Picnic:** Bring along a picnic and enjoy a scenic lunch overlooking the Causeway, surrounded by the breathtaking beauty of the Northern Irish coastline.

Respecting the Environment:
- **Leave No Trace:** Help preserve the natural beauty of the Causeway by following the principles of Leave No Trace, disposing of waste responsibly, and staying on designated paths.
- **Respect Wildlife:** Keep a respectful distance from wildlife and refrain from feeding or disturbing them, allowing them to thrive in their natural habitat.
- **Support Sustainable Practices:** Choose eco-friendly tour operators and businesses that prioritize sustainability and conservation efforts in the area.

The Legend of Fionn mac Cumhaill:

Central to the folklore surrounding The Giant's Causeway is the legend of Fionn mac Cumhaill, a legendary Irish giant said to have created the causeway in a fit of rage and rivalry. According to the myth, Fionn, also known as Finn McCool, resided in the Antrim coast, where he lived with his wife, Oonagh. Across the sea in Scotland lived another giant, Benandonner, who was renowned for his immense size and strength.

One day, Benandonner challenged Fionn to a duel, taunting him with insults across the water. Determined to defend his honor, Fionn accepted the challenge and set to work constructing a causeway across the sea to confront his adversary. With each mighty blow of his hammer, Fionn shaped the basalt columns, creating a path that stretched from Ireland to Scotland.

As the day of reckoning drew near, Oonagh devised a cunning plan to protect her husband. Knowing that Benandonner dwarfed Fionn in size, she disguised Fionn as a baby and placed him in a cradle. When Benandonner arrived at their doorstep, he was greeted by Oonagh, who informed him that Fionn was out, but that he could wait and meet the baby, their son.

Upon seeing the size of the "baby," Benandonner grew fearful, imagining the size of the father. He hastily retreated, tearing up the causeway behind him to prevent Fionn from pursuing him. Thus, the legend explains the geological phenomenon of the Giant's Causeway and the similar basalt formations on the Scottish Isle of Staffa, known as Fingal's Cave, as remnants of this epic rivalry between two giants.

Local Folklore and Superstitions:

Beyond the tale of Fionn mac Cumhaill, The Giant's Causeway is steeped in local folklore and superstitions, passed down through generations. Some believe that the columns were crafted by the hands of an ancient giantess, while others attribute their formation to the legendary hero, Finn McCool. Still, others tell of mermaids and sea creatures who inhabit the coastal waters, lending an air of mystery to the already otherworldly landscape.

One of the most enduring superstitions surrounding The Giant's Causeway is the belief in its mystical powers. It is said that walking barefoot on the basalt columns can bring good luck and healing, while others claim that touching the stones can grant wishes or provide protection from harm. Visitors often leave offerings of coins or small tokens, hoping to invoke the blessings of the ancient spirits that dwell within the rocks.

The Mythic Landscape:

As visitors traverse the rugged terrain of The Giant's Causeway, they are enveloped in a sense of awe and wonder, surrounded by towering columns that seem to defy the laws of nature. Each step unveils a new vista, a new perspective on the ancient landscape and the stories it holds. From the imposing cliffs that guard the coast to the hidden sea caves that dot the shoreline, every feature of the Causeway is imbued with a sense of magic and mystery.

For centuries, poets, artists, and storytellers have been drawn to the haunting beauty of this place, seeking inspiration in its rugged shores and dramatic vistas. The Giant's Causeway has inspired countless works of art and literature, from epic poems to folk songs, each one capturing a glimpse of the mythic landscape and the tales that echo through its ancient stones.

2. **The Burren Perfumery** - Visit this small, independent perfumery in County Clare, where natural scents are crafted using locally sourced ingredients and traditional methods.

- **Starting Price:** Free admission; prices for products vary.
  - **How to Get There:**
  - By Public Transport: Take Bus Eireann Route 350 from Galway to Lisdoonvarna, then transfer to a local taxi or shuttle service to reach the Burren Perfumery in County Clare.

The Irish National Leprechaun Museum

- **Starting Price:** €16 for adults; discounts available for students and seniors.
  - **How to Get There:**
  - By Public Transport: From Dublin city center, take the Luas tram to the Jervis stop, which is a short walk from the museum.

The Seaweed Baths of Strandhill - Relax and rejuvenate in a traditional seaweed bath on the shores of County Sligo, believed to have health benefits for the skin and body.

- **Starting Price:** Approximately €30 for a seaweed bath.
  - **How to Get There:**
  - By Public Transport: Take Bus Eireann Route 64 from Sligo to Strandhill.

The Waterford Walls Street Art Festival

- **Starting Price:** Free admission to view street art; ticket prices may apply for related events.
  - **How to Get There:**
  - By Public Transport: Waterford is well-connected by train and bus services from major cities like Dublin and Cork.

The Irish Potato Famine Exhibition

- **Starting Price:** Admission fees vary; check the museum's website for current prices.
  - **How to Get There:**
  - By Public Transport: Take Bus Eireann or Irish Rail services to Castlebar, County Mayo, then transfer to a local bus or taxi to reach the exhibition.

The National Leprechaun Museum

- **Starting Price:** €16 for adults; discounts available for students and seniors.
  - **How to Get There:**
  - By Public Transport: The museum is centrally located in Dublin, within walking distance from major attractions and public transportation hubs.

The Butter Museum

- **Starting Price:** €6 for adults; discounts available for students and seniors.
  - **How to Get There:**
  - By Public Transport: The museum is situated in Cork city center, easily accessible by bus or on foot.

The Kilmainham Gaol Museum

- **Starting Price:** €8 for adults; discounts available for students and seniors.
  - **How to Get There:**
    - By Public Transport: Take the Luas tram to the Museum stop, or use Dublin Bus routes 69 or 79 from the city center.

The Hellfire Club

- **Starting Price:** Free admission to the site.
  - **How to Get There:**
    - By Public Transport: From Dublin city center, take the Dublin Bus Route 15 to the Montpelier Hill stop, then follow signs for the Hellfire Club.

The Antrim Hedge Maze

- **Starting Price:** Admission fees vary; check the park's website for current prices.
  - **How to Get There:**
    - By Public Transport: Take a train or bus to Belfast, then transfer to a local bus or taxi to Castlewellan Forest Park.

The Irish Sky Garden

- **Starting Price:** Free admission; donations appreciated.
  - **How to Get There:**
    - By Public Transport: The garden is located near Skibbereen in County Cork, accessible by car or taxi from nearby towns.

The Magic Road

- **Starting Price:** Free to experience the phenomenon.
  - **How to Get There:**
    - By Public Transport: From Dundalk, take Bus Eireann Route 161 to Carlingford, then follow signs to the Magic Road.

The Puck Fair

- **Starting Price:** Free admission to the fair; fees may apply for certain events and activities.
  - **How to Get There:**
    - By Public Transport: Killorglin is accessible by Bus Eireann from major cities like Cork, Limerick, and Galway.

The Blarney Stone

- **Starting Price:** Admission to Blarney Castle: €18 for adults.
  - **How to Get There:**
    - By Public Transport: Take a train or bus to Cork city, then transfer to a local bus or taxi to Blarney Castle.

Shopping

- **Irish Wool Products:** From sweaters to blankets, Ireland is renowned for its high-quality wool products. Look for bargains at local markets or outlets for authentic Irish knitwear at discounted prices.
- **Claddagh Rings:** A traditional Irish symbol of love, loyalty, and friendship, Claddagh rings make for meaningful and affordable souvenirs. You can find them at various jewelry shops and souvenir stores across the country. The Claddagh ring originated in the Irish fishing village of Claddagh, near Galway City, in the 17th century. Legend has it that a local goldsmith named Richard Joyce, who was captured and enslaved by Algerian pirates, crafted the first Claddagh ring during his captivity. Upon his release and return to Ireland, Joyce presented the ring to his sweetheart, symbolizing his enduring love and devotion despite their separation.
- **Irish Whiskey:** Ireland is famous for its whiskey, and you can often find great bargains on bottles of Irish whiskey at distilleries, duty-free shops, and supermarkets.
- **Irish Pottery:** Handcrafted pottery is a popular souvenir in Ireland, and you can find unique pieces at local pottery studios and craft markets for reasonable prices.
- **Tweed Clothing:** Tweed jackets, hats, and scarves are classic Irish garments known for their durability and style. Look for bargains at local tweed shops or outlets.
- **Irish Linen:** Linen products such as tablecloths, napkins, and towels are another traditional Irish souvenir. Look for bargains at linen outlets or souvenir shops.
- **Irish Music CDs:** Bring a piece of Irish culture home with you by purchasing CDs of traditional Irish music. You can often find bargains on CDs at music stores and tourist shops.
- **Irish Art Prints:** Ireland's stunning landscapes have inspired countless artists. Look for bargains on prints of Irish artwork at local galleries, art markets, and souvenir shops.
- **Irish Crystal:** Waterford Crystal is world-famous for its craftsmanship and elegance. While it can be pricey, you can often find discounted pieces at outlet stores or during sales events.
- **Irish Food Products:** Stock up on delicious Irish treats such as chocolate, biscuits, and jams at supermarkets or specialty food shops for affordable prices.
- **Secondhand Books:** Ireland has a rich literary tradition, and you can find bargains on secondhand books at charity shops, flea markets, and book fairs.
- **Irish Fairy Tales:** Pick up a book of Irish fairy tales or folklore for a unique souvenir that captures the magic of Ireland's storytelling tradition.
- **Irish Souvenir Tea Towels:** Quirky and practical, souvenir tea towels featuring Irish motifs and designs make for inexpensive and lightweight gifts.
- **Irish-themed Trinkets:** Look for small Irish-themed trinkets such as keychains, fridge magnets, and bookmarks at souvenir shops for affordable souvenirs to bring home.
- **Irish-themed Apparel:** T-shirts, hats, and accessories featuring Irish symbols or humorous slogans are fun and affordable souvenirs to remember your trip by.
- **Irish Seaweed Products:** Seaweed-based skincare products, such as soaps, lotions, and bath salts, are unique souvenirs that harness the natural benefits of Ireland's coastal waters.

- **Irish Handmade Candles:** Handcrafted candles made from beeswax or soy wax are unique and eco-friendly souvenirs that capture the essence of Ireland's natural beauty.
- **Irish-made Crafts:** Support local artisans by purchasing handmade crafts such as pottery, jewelry, textiles, and woodwork at craft markets or artisan fairs.
- **Irish Herbal Products:** Herbal teas, tinctures, and skincare products made from native Irish plants and herbs are unique souvenirs with natural benefits.
- **Irish Language Books:** Learn a bit of the Irish language with books or phrasebooks featuring Irish Gaelic (Gaeilge) for a unique and educational souvenir.

Best Thrift Stores and Thrift by the Kilo:

- **Thrift Stores:**
- Dublin: Siopaella, Dublin Vintage Factory, and Oxfam Vintage
- Cork: Miss Daisy Blue and Cork Penny Dinners Charity Shop
- **Thrift by the Kilo:**
- Dublin: Tola Vintage and The Blue Room Kilos
- Galway: Siopaella Galway

Best Flea Markets:

- Dublin: Dublin Flea Market
- Cork: Mother Jones Flea Market
- Galway: Galway Market
- Belfast: St. George's Market

Outlet Shopping:

- Kildare Village: Offers designer outlet shopping near Dublin.
- Blanchardstown Centre: Houses various outlet stores including Nike, Adidas, and more.

Rent Designer Clothes:

- Designer Room: Based in Dublin, offers rental services for designer clothing and accessories.

What to Do at Night for Free in Ireland:

- **Stargazing**: Head to a remote area away from city lights for a free night of stargazing.
- **Live Music Sessions**: Many pubs offer free traditional music sessions, especially in towns and cities with a vibrant music scene.
- **Night Walks**: Explore historic areas or scenic viewpoints at night for a different perspective.
- **Beach Bonfire**: Gather friends for a beach bonfire, where you can enjoy the sound of crashing waves under the starry sky.
- **Outdoor Film Screenings**: Keep an eye out for free outdoor film screenings in parks or public spaces during the summer months.
- **Art Galleries**: Some art galleries offer free admission during evening hours or on specific nights of the week.
- **Local Events**: Check local event listings for free festivals, performances, or cultural events happening in your area.
- **Night Markets**: Some cities host night markets with food stalls, artisanal crafts, and live entertainment.
- **Volunteer Opportunities**: Consider volunteering for evening events or activities, such as community clean-ups or charity fundraisers.
- **Self-Guided Tours**: Take a self-guided walking tour of your city's landmarks or historical sites at night, when they are often illuminated.

Cheapest Onward Flights and Airlines Flying Cheap from Ireland

From Dublin to Cork, Shannon to Knock, Ireland boasts several airports serving as gateways to both domestic and international destinations.

- **Ryanair**: Known for its budget flights across Europe, Ryanair offers cheap onward flights from Ireland to various destinations from $2!
- **Aer Lingus**: Ireland's national carrier often has promotional fares and discounts on onward flights to Europe and the United States.

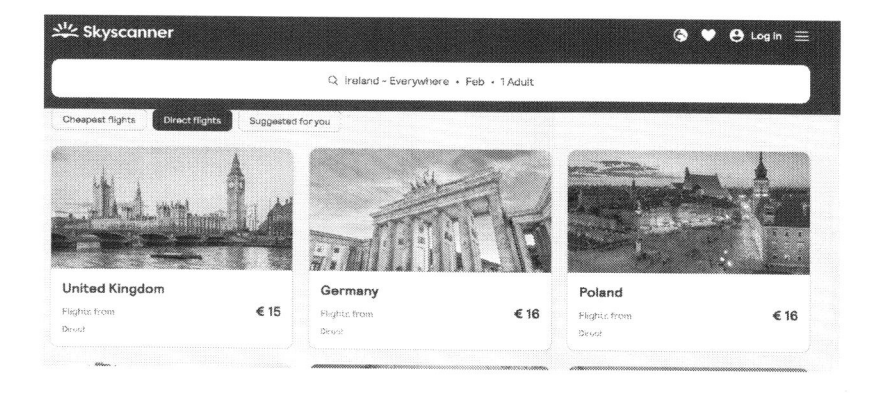

Cheapest Airport Lounges in Ireland

Airport Lounge	Location	Starting Price	Amenities
Aspire Lounge	Cork Airport	€25 per person	Comfortable seating, Complimentary snacks and beverages, Free Wi-Fi, Newspapers and magazines
Executive Lounge	Dublin Airport	€25 per person	Quiet environment, Complimentary food and drinks, Alcoholic beverages available for purchase, Shower facilities available
Jack Doyle's Bar & Lounge	Shannon Airport	€20 per person	Casual atmosphere, Complimentary snacks and soft drinks, Alcoholic beverages available for purchase, TV screens with live sports coverage
Causeway Lounge	Belfast Airport	£20 per person	Relaxing ambiance, Complimentary snacks and beverages, Free Wi-Fi, Newspapers and magazines

Irish Language

Today, Irish is recognized as the first official language of Ireland alongside English, and efforts continue to promote its use and preservation. While the number of fluent speakers remains relatively small compared to English speakers, there is a growing appreciation for the cultural and linguistic heritage of the Irish language, ensuring that it remains an important part of Ireland's identity.

The history of the Irish language, also known as Gaeilge or Irish Gaelic, is deeply intertwined with the history of Ireland itself. Irish is a Celtic language and is one of the oldest written languages in Europe. Its origins can be traced back to the arrival of Celtic tribes in Ireland around 500 BCE. These early Celtic settlers brought with them their own language, which evolved over time to become what is now known as Irish.

Throughout Ireland's history, the Irish language played a central role in the country's culture, identity, and literature. It was the language of the ancient Irish sagas, myths, and poetry, preserving the rich oral tradition of the Celtic people. Irish monks were instrumental in the preservation and spread of knowledge during the Dark Ages, with many important manuscripts being written in Irish.

However, the language faced numerous challenges over the centuries, particularly during periods of English colonization and British rule. English became the dominant language of administration, education, and commerce, leading to a decline in the use of Irish. Penal laws enacted by the British government further suppressed the language, contributing to its marginalization and decline.

The 19th century saw a revival of interest in the Irish language and culture, known as the Gaelic Revival. Organizations such as the Gaelic League (Conradh na Gaeilge) were established to promote the use of Irish and to preserve Ireland's linguistic heritage. Efforts were made to reintroduce Irish into schools, and there was a renewed interest in Irish literature, folklore, and music.

Despite these efforts, the Irish language continued to face challenges in the 20th century, particularly with the urbanization and modernization of Ireland. English remained the dominant language in most areas, and Irish-speaking communities became increasingly isolated. However, there has been a resurgence of interest in the language in recent decades, with initiatives to promote Irish language education, bilingual signage, and media content.

- **Dia dhuit** (dee-uh gwitch) - Hello
- **Conas atá tú?** (kun-us uh-taw too) - How are you?
- **Go raibh maith agat** (guh rah mah uh-gut) - Thank you
- **Slán go fóill** (slawn guh foy-ill) - Goodbye for now
- **An bhfuil cead agam dul go dtí an leithreas?** (un will k-yad ah-gum dull guh dee un leh-russ) - May I go to the restroom?
- **Cén t-am é?** (kayn tawm ay) - What time is it?
- **Tá mé tinn** (taw may chin) - I am sick

- **Is maith liom é** (iss my lum ay) - I like it
- **An bhfuil tú saor in aisce?** (un will too sare in ash-keh) - Are you free?
- **Sláinte!** (slawn-che) - Cheers!

Common Complaints of Tourists Visiting Ireland with Solutions

- **Unpredictable Weather**: Solution - Pack layers and waterproof clothing, and plan indoor activities for rainy days.
- **Overcrowded Tourist Attractions**: Solution - Visit popular attractions early in the morning or during off-peak seasons to avoid crowds.
- **Expensive Accommodation**: Solution - Look for budget accommodations such as hostels, guesthouses, or self-catering options, and book in advance for better deals.
- **Language Barrier**: Solution - Learn some basic Irish phrases or use translation apps to communicate with locals.
- **High Cost of Food and Dining**: Solution - Explore local markets for affordable food options, and look for lunch specials or early bird menus at restaurants.
- **Difficulty Finding Parking**: Solution - Use public transportation or park-and-ride services when visiting cities, and research parking options in advance for rural areas.
- **Limited Public Transport Options**: Solution - Plan your itinerary around available bus and train schedules, and consider renting a car for more flexibility in rural areas.
- **Lack of Accessibility for People with Disabilities**: Solution - Research accessibility options at tourist attractions and accommodations, and communicate any specific needs in advance.

Money Mistakes to Avoid

Mistake	Solution	Notes
Not Researching Exchange Rates	Check exchange rates before exchanging money	Exchange rates can fluctuate, impacting the amount of local currency you receive. Consider using credit cards wisely.
Overlooking ATM Fees	Use ATMs affiliated with your bank	ATM fees can add up quickly, especially if you're using non-partner ATMs. Look for fee-free options or plan ahead.
Excessive Dining Out	Cook some meals or opt for budget eateries	Dining out every meal can be expensive. Consider cooking meals in accommodation or dining at budget-friendly places.
Ignoring Public Transportation Options	Utilize buses, trains, and discounted passes	Public transportation is often cheaper than taxis or rental cars. Look for multi-day passes or tourist discounts.
Paying Full Price for Attractions	Look for discounts, combo tickets, or passes	Many attractions offer discounts for students, seniors, or group bookings. Bundle tickets for savings where possible.
Not Budgeting for Unexpected Expenses	Set aside funds for emergencies	Unexpected expenses can arise, such as medical costs or lost items. Have a contingency fund for peace of mind.
Overspending on Souvenirs	Stick to a budget or opt for meaningful items	Souvenirs can be pricey. Set a budget beforehand or focus on purchasing meaningful items rather than impulse buys.
Ignoring Free Activities and Attractions	Take advantage of free museums, parks, etc.	Ireland offers many free attractions and activities. Research options to maximize your experiences without spending.

VAT REFUND

Yes, tourists visiting Ireland may be eligible for a Value Added Tax (VAT) refund on certain purchases made during their stay. Here's how the VAT refund process generally works in Ireland:

- **Eligibility Criteria:** To qualify for a VAT refund, you typically need to be a non-EU resident and make purchases from participating retailers who offer tax-free shopping.
- **Minimum Purchase Amount:** There is usually a minimum purchase amount required to be eligible for a VAT refund. This threshold varies depending on the country, but in Ireland, it is typically around €30 to €50 per transaction.
- **Request a VAT Refund Form:** When making a purchase, inform the retailer that you are a tourist and request a VAT refund form (also known as a Tax-Free Shopping Cheque).
- **Complete the Form:** Fill out the VAT refund form with your personal details, passport number, and purchase information. Make sure to keep your receipts as proof of purchase.
- **Get the Form Stamped:** Before departing Ireland, you must get the VAT refund form stamped by customs at the point of exit (usually at the airport or seaport). This validates the form and verifies that you are taking the goods out of the country.

- **Submit the Form:** After receiving the customs stamp, submit the stamped VAT refund form to the tax refund company or service provider. This can usually be done at designated refund counters at the airport or by mail.
- **Receive Refund:** Once the refund company processes your claim, you will receive a refund of the VAT amount (minus any handling fees) either in cash, to your credit card, or via bank transfer, depending on the refund service provider.

It's important to note that not all purchases are eligible for a VAT refund, and some items, such as food, drink, and services, are generally excluded. Additionally, there may be administrative fees or minimum purchase requirements associated with the VAT refund process. Therefore, it's advisable to inquire about the specific terms and conditions with the retailer before making your purchase.

Irish History

Understanding Irish history is essential for grasping the complexities of Ireland's past, present, and future. Spanning thousands of years, from ancient Celtic tribes to modern-day political struggles, Ireland's history is marked by triumphs, tragedies, and enduring resilience.

The Celts

The earliest inhabitants of Ireland were the Celtic peoples, who arrived on the island around 500 BCE. These early Celts brought with them a distinct culture characterized by intricate art, mythology, and a reverence for nature. Celtic society was organized into clans or tuatha, each governed by a chieftain or king. The Celts practiced animistic religions, worshipping a pantheon of gods and goddesses associated with natural phenomena such as the sun, moon, and earth.

One of the most striking aspects of Celtic culture is its intricate artwork, which is characterized by intricate knotwork, spirals, and other geometric patterns. These motifs can be seen adorning ancient artifacts such as the Ardagh Chalice and the Book of Kells, showcasing the Celts' mastery of metalwork and craftsmanship. Today, Celtic art continues to inspire contemporary artists and designers, with Celtic motifs appearing in everything from jewelry and tattoos to clothing and home decor.

The Celts also had a profound reverence for nature, worshipping a pantheon of gods and goddesses associated with natural phenomena such as the sun, moon, and earth. Sites such as the Hill of Tara and Newgrange served as sacred centers of ritual and ceremony, where offerings were made to the gods and ceremonies were held to mark the changing seasons. Even today, the landscape of Ireland is dotted with ancient stone circles, burial mounds, and other sacred sites that bear witness to the Celts' deep spiritual connection to the land.

In addition to their artistic and spiritual contributions, the Celts also played a crucial role in shaping Ireland's social and political organization. Celtic society was organized into clans or tuatha, each governed by a chieftain or king who wielded both political and religious authority. The concept of kingship was central to Celtic culture, with kings and queens serving as both secular rulers and spiritual leaders who were believed to have divine authority.

The legacy of the Celts can be seen and felt throughout modern Ireland, from the Gaelic language and traditional music to the enduring popularity of Celtic mythology and folklore. The Irish language, known as Gaeilge, is descended from the Celtic languages spoken by the ancient Celts and is still spoken by a minority of Irish people today. Similarly, traditional Irish music, with its haunting melodies and lively rhythms, is deeply rooted in Celtic musical traditions and continues to be celebrated and performed at festivals and gatherings throughout the country. Celtic mythology and folklore also continue to captivate the imaginations of people around the world, with stories of heroic warriors, mystical creatures, and ancient gods and goddesses forming an integral part of Irish cultural identity. The legends of Cu Chulainn, the Morrigan, and the Tuatha de Danann are just a few examples of the rich tapestry of myths and legends that have been passed down through generations of Irish storytellers.

Celtic mythology features a diverse pantheon of gods and goddesses, each associated with different aspects of nature, society, and the human experience. Some of the most prominent Celtic deities include:

- **Dagda:** The chief god in Irish mythology, often depicted as a wise and powerful figure associated with fertility, abundance, and the earth.
- **Morrigan:** A goddess of war, fate, and sovereignty, often depicted as a shape-shifter and associated with crows and ravens.
- **Brigid:** A triple goddess associated with healing, poetry, and smithcraft, revered as a patroness of both fire and water.
- **Lugh:** A multi-talented god associated with skills, craftsmanship, and leadership, often depicted as a warrior and a master of all trades.
- **Cernunnos:** A horned god associated with nature, fertility, and the wilderness, often depicted with antlers and associated with animals and the forest.

Myths and Legends:

Celtic mythology is replete with tales of heroic warriors, magical creatures, and epic battles between gods and monsters. Some of the most famous myths and legends include:

- **The Táin Bó Cúailnge:** An epic saga recounting the exploits of the hero Cu Chulainn and the cattle raid of Cooley, one of the greatest feats of Irish mythology.
- **The Children of Lir:** A tragic tale of enchantment and transformation, in which four siblings are turned into swans by their jealous stepmother and must wander the waters of Ireland for centuries.
- **The Voyage of Bran:** A mythical journey to the Otherworld, in which the hero Bran embarks on a voyage to a magical island and encounters otherworldly beings and wonders.
- **The Wooing of Étaín:** A tale of love, jealousy, and transformation, in which the fairy princess Étaín is pursued by both the mortal hero Midir and the jealous fairy king Fuamnach.

Irish pagan traditions

Irish pagan traditions and beliefs are deeply rooted in the island's ancient past, dating back thousands of years to the time of the Celtic peoples who inhabited the land. These ancient traditions were shaped by a reverence for nature, a belief in the power of the elements, and a rich tapestry of myths, legends, and rituals that sought to explain the mysteries of the world.

Central to Irish pagan beliefs was the concept of animism, the belief that all living and non-living things possess a spirit or soul. This animistic worldview led the ancient Celts to worship a pantheon of gods and goddesses associated with natural phenomena such as the sun, moon, earth, and sea. These deities were seen as embodying the forces of nature and were often invoked through prayers, offerings, and rituals to ensure fertility, protection, and prosperity.

One of the most important aspects of Irish pagan traditions was the celebration of seasonal festivals known as the Wheel of the Year. These festivals marked key points in the agricultural calendar and were observed with feasting, music, dancing, and ceremonies that honored the changing seasons and the cycles of nature. The four major festivals of the Wheel of the Year were:

- Imbolc: Celebrated in early February, Imbolc marked the beginning of spring and was dedicated to the goddess Brigid, the patroness of poetry, healing, and smithcraft. Imbolc was a time for purification, cleansing, and the lighting of fires to symbolize the return of light and warmth after the darkness of winter.
- Beltane: Held on May 1st, Beltane was a celebration of fertility, growth, and the abundance of summer. Bonfires were lit to honor the sun god Bel, and rituals were performed to encourage the fertility of crops, livestock, and people. Beltane was also a time for courtship and matchmaking, with couples leaping over bonfires for luck and fertility.
- Lughnasadh: Occurring in early August, Lughnasadh was the first harvest festival of the year, dedicated to the god Lugh, the skilled craftsman and warrior. It was a time for feasting, games, and competitions, as well as rituals to give thanks for the bounty of the land and to ensure a successful harvest.
- Samhain: Celebrated on October 31st, Samhain marked the end of the harvest season and the beginning of winter. It was a liminal time when the boundaries between the physical and spiritual worlds were believed to be thin, allowing for communication with the ancestors and spirits. Samhain was also a time for divination, feasting, and honoring the dead.

In addition to seasonal festivals, Irish pagan traditions also included rituals and practices aimed at protecting against malevolent forces and ensuring the well-being of the community. Talismans, charms, and amulets were commonly used for protection, while rituals such as the lighting of torches, the ringing of bells, and the chanting of incantations were performed to ward off evil spirits and curses.

Despite the influence of Christianity and the passage of time, elements of Irish pagan traditions and beliefs continue to endure in modern Irish culture. From the celebration of St. Brigid's Day on February 1st to the customs surrounding Halloween, or Samhain, on October 31st, these ancient traditions are woven into the fabric of Irish identity, connecting the people of Ireland to their rich spiritual heritage and the rhythms of the natural world.

Saint Patrick and The Irish Patron Saints

One of the most significant events in ancient Irish history was the arrival of Saint Patrick in the 5th century CE. Patrick, a Christian missionary, is credited with converting Ireland to Christianity and establishing the Catholic Church as the dominant religious institution. The spread of Christianity had a profound impact on Irish society, leading to the construction of monasteries, the development of written language, and the preservation of knowledge through illuminated manuscripts.

The arrival of Saint Patrick in 5th century CE marked a transformative moment in ancient Irish history, forever altering the spiritual and cultural landscape of the island. Born in Roman Britain, Patrick was initially captured by Irish pirates and sold into slavery in Ireland. During his captivity, Patrick found solace in his faith and cultivated a deep connection to Christianity. After escaping captivity, Patrick returned to Britain, where he underwent religious training and eventually became ordained as a bishop.

Driven by a divine calling, Patrick returned to Ireland as a missionary, intent on spreading the teachings of Christianity to the pagan inhabitants of the island. Armed with a fervent belief in the power of faith and a profound love for the Irish people, Patrick embarked on a mission to convert the island to Christianity and establish the Catholic Church as the dominant religious institution.

Patrick's efforts were met with both resistance and acceptance, as he traversed the length and breadth of Ireland, preaching the gospel and baptizing converts. Through his tireless dedication and unwavering conviction, Patrick succeeded in converting kings, chieftains, and common folk alike, gradually eroding the influence of pagan beliefs and rituals.

The spread of Christianity brought about profound changes in Irish society, as the teachings of Christ supplanted the ancient pagan religions that had long held sway over the hearts and minds of the Celtic peoples. Monasteries emerged as centers of learning and spirituality, providing refuge for scholars, monks, and seekers of knowledge. These monastic communities became bastions of faith and scholarship, where manuscripts were painstakingly copied, illuminated, and preserved for future generations. The development of Irish patron saints is intertwined with the spread of Christianity in Ireland and the establishment of monastic communities. Here are more famous Irish Patron Saints:

- **Saint Brigid**: Often referred to as "Mary of the Gaels," Saint Brigid is one of Ireland's patron saints alongside Patrick and Columba. She is associated with fertility, healing, and springtime. Brigid's feast day, February 1st, marks the beginning of spring in the Celtic calendar and is celebrated with rituals such as the weaving of Brigid's crosses, symbolizing protection and blessings.
- **Saint Columba**: Also known as Columcille, Saint Columba is regarded as one of the 'Twelve Apostles of Ireland' and is considered one of the three patron saints of Ireland, alongside Patrick and Brigid. Columba is associated with learning, poetry, and spirituality. He founded monasteries, including the famous monastery at Iona, which became a center of learning and missionary work.

- **Saint Brendan the Navigator**: Saint Brendan is celebrated for his legendary voyages, particularly his journey to the "Isle of the Blessed" or "Saint Brendan's Island." He is often invoked by sailors and travelers for protection during their journeys. Brendan symbolizes courage, exploration, and spiritual quest.
- **Saint Kevin of Glendalough**: Saint Kevin is associated with solitude, contemplation, and harmony with nature. He founded the monastic settlement of Glendalough, nestled in the Wicklow Mountains, where he lived a life of prayer and asceticism. Kevin's story inspires a reverence for the beauty of creation and the importance of inner reflection.
- **Saint Brónach**: Saint Brónach is less widely known but is venerated locally in County Down. She is associated with maternal protection and is said to have comforted Saint Patrick during his trials. Brónach represents the nurturing and caring aspects of Irish spirituality.
- **Saint Declan of Ardmore**: Saint Declan is revered in the south of Ireland, particularly in County Waterford. He is associated with miracles, particularly in relation to healing and the protection of animals. Declan embodies the compassion and kindness deeply rooted in Irish tradition.
- **Saint Ita of Killeedy**: Known as the "Foster Mother of the Irish Saints," Saint Ita is associated with hospitality, generosity, and the education of young people. She founded a school and monastery at Killeedy in County Limerick, where she nurtured the spiritual and intellectual growth of her community.

The development of written language, particularly the Irish script known as Ogham, flourished under the influence of Christianity, enabling the recording of Irish myths, legends, and religious texts. The art of illumination, with its intricate designs and vibrant colors, became synonymous with the Irish monastic tradition, producing masterpieces such as the Book of Kells and the Book of Durrow.

The preservation of knowledge through illuminated manuscripts ensured the survival of Ireland's cultural heritage, even in the face of external threats and upheavals. These manuscripts served as repositories of wisdom, scholarship, and artistic expression, enriching the spiritual and intellectual life of the Irish people for centuries to come.

There are some major FREE festivals celebrating Irish patron saints:

Festival	Date	Key Features
St. Patrick's Day	March 17th	Parades, wearing of green, traditional music, feasting
St. Brigid's Day	February 1st	Weaving of Brigid's crosses, spring rituals, prayers for healing
St. Columba's Day	June 9th	Commemoration of his life and missionary work, pilgrimage to Iona
St. Brendan's Day	May 16th	Celebrations of exploration, maritime heritage, prayers for safe travels
St. Kevin's Day	June 3rd	Reflection on solitude and nature, pilgrimage to Glendalough
St. Declan's Day	July 24th	Pilgrimage to Ardmore, prayers for healing and protection
St. Ita's Day	January 15th	Reflection on hospitality and education, prayers for teachers and students

These festivals are typically free to attend and offer opportunities for communal celebration, reflection, and cultural exchange centered around the lives and legacies of Irish patron saints.

The Viking Age: Raiders and Settlers

The Viking Age, which began in the late 8th century, brought further upheaval to Ireland. Norse raiders from Scandinavia, known as Vikings, pillaged coastal settlements and established trading ports along the Irish coast. Despite their reputation as fierce warriors, the Vikings also contributed to Irish society, introducing new technologies, trade networks, and political institutions. The Viking presence in Ireland lasted for several centuries and left a lasting imprint on Irish culture and heritage.

Dublin, founded by the Vikings in the 9th century, stands as a testament to their enduring influence in Ireland. Originally a small settlement known as Dyflin, Dublin quickly grew into a bustling trading hub under Viking rule. The city's strategic location on the east coast made it an ideal center for maritime trade, attracting merchants from across Europe and beyond. Today, tourists flock to Dublin to explore its rich Viking heritage, with attractions such as Dublinia offering immersive experiences that recreate Viking Dublin through interactive exhibits and historical reenactments.

In addition to Dublin, the Viking presence in Ireland is evident in other cities and towns along the coast. Waterford, for example, boasts Ireland's largest Viking settlement, known as the Viking Triangle. This historic district is home to a wealth of archaeological sites and museums dedicated to preserving and showcasing Ireland's Viking heritage. Visitors can wander through ancient streets, explore Viking artifacts, and learn about the daily lives of Norse settlers who once called this area home.

The Viking Age brought significant upheaval to Ireland, as Norse raiders launched plundering expeditions along the coast, targeting monasteries, villages, and wealthy estates. These raids, while devastating to local communities, also brought about cultural exchange and interaction between the Norse and Gaelic populations. Over time, many Vikings chose to settle in Ireland permanently, intermarrying with the local population and contributing to the island's rich tapestry of culture and identity.

Despite their reputation as fierce warriors, the Vikings were also skilled craftsmen, traders, and diplomats. They introduced new technologies, such as shipbuilding techniques and metalworking methods, which revolutionized Irish industry and commerce. Viking trade networks connected Ireland to distant lands, facilitating the exchange of goods, ideas, and cultural practices across Europe. Moreover, the Vikings established political institutions and governance structures that laid the groundwork for Ireland's later feudal system.

The Viking Age was a transformative period in Ireland's history, marked by both conflict and cooperation between Norse invaders and the indigenous population. While the Vikings left a legacy of warfare and conquest, they also made significant contributions to Irish society, economy, and culture. Today, Ireland's Viking heritage continues to captivate the imagination of visitors, offering a glimpse into a fascinating chapter of the island's past.

Medieval Ireland: Castles, Monasteries, and Norman Conquests

Medieval Ireland witnessed the construction of magnificent castles, the rise of powerful monastic institutions, and the arrival of the Normans in the 12th century. Tourists are intrigued by iconic landmarks such as the Rock of Cashel, a medieval fortress and ecclesiastical complex, and Trim Castle, one of the largest Norman castles in Ireland. The Book of Kells, an illuminated manuscript housed at Trinity College Dublin, also provides insights into medieval Ireland's artistic and literary heritage.

One of the most striking features of medieval Ireland is its magnificent castles, which served as symbols of power, prestige, and defense. Among these iconic landmarks is the Rock of Cashel, a towering fortress and ecclesiastical complex perched atop a limestone hill in County Tipperary. With its imposing walls and ancient ruins, the Rock of Cashel offers visitors a glimpse into Ireland's medieval past, blending elements of both secular and religious authority.

Another notable example is Trim Castle, located in County Meath and renowned as one of the largest Norman castles in Ireland. Built by Hugh de Lacy in the late 12th century, Trim Castle is a testament to Norman military engineering and strategic planning. Its formidable walls, moat, and towers evoke a sense of medieval grandeur, inviting visitors to explore its storied halls and courtyards.

In addition to castles, medieval Ireland was also home to vibrant monastic communities, which played a central role in the island's religious and cultural life. Monasteries such as Clonmacnoise, Glendalough, and Mellifont Abbey served as centers of learning, prayer, and artistic expression, attracting pilgrims and scholars from far and wide. Today, these ancient monastic sites offer visitors a glimpse into Ireland's spiritual heritage, with their weathered ruins and intricate carvings bearing witness to centuries of devotion and devotion.

The Book of Kells, an illuminated manuscript housed at Trinity College Dublin, serves as a testament to medieval Ireland's artistic and literary heritage. Created by monks in the 9th century, the Book of Kells is renowned for its intricate illustrations and elaborate calligraphy, providing invaluable insights into the island's cultural and intellectual achievements during the Middle Ages.

Medieval Ireland is a fascinating tapestry of castles, monasteries, and Norman conquests, each contributing to the rich tapestry of Ireland's history and heritage. From the towering fortresses of Trim Castle to the serene beauty of Glendalough's monastic ruins, these landmarks offer visitors a glimpse into a bygone era of chivalry, piety, and political intrigue.

The Tudor Conquest and Plantations

The Tudor Conquest began in earnest with the arrival of King Henry VII to the English throne in 1485. Seeking to strengthen England's grip on its neighboring island, Henry initiated a series of military campaigns aimed at subduing the independent Gaelic lords of Ireland and asserting English authority. The Tudor monarchs viewed Ireland as a strategic asset, both in terms of territorial expansion and as a potential source of revenue and resources.

One of the most notable figures of the Tudor Conquest was King Henry VIII, whose reign saw the implementation of ambitious plantation schemes aimed at colonizing and "civilizing" Ireland. The plantation policy involved the confiscation of land from Gaelic chieftains and its redistribution to English settlers, often under the guise of promoting agricultural development and fostering loyalty to the crown. These plantations laid the groundwork for the colonization of Ireland by English and Scottish settlers, leading to the displacement of native Irish landholders and the imposition of English law and governance.

The most infamous of these plantations was the Plantation of Ulster, initiated by King James I in the early 17th century. Under this scheme, large tracts of land in Ulster were confiscated from Gaelic lords and granted to English and Scottish settlers, known as "planters." The Plantation of Ulster had profound and lasting effects on the demographic, cultural, and political makeup of the region, shaping the identity of Northern Ireland to this day.

The Tudor Conquest and Plantations also had significant cultural and religious implications for Ireland. The English crown sought to impose Protestantism as the dominant faith, leading to religious conflict and persecution of Catholicism. The Tudor monarchs, particularly Queen Elizabeth I, viewed Catholicism as a threat to their authority and sought to suppress its influence through measures such as the imposition of the English Book of Common Prayer and the suppression of Catholic religious practices.

Despite the efforts of the Tudor monarchs to assert English control over Ireland, resistance to English rule persisted among the native Irish population. The Tudor Conquest was marked by sporadic uprisings and rebellions, as Gaelic lords and Irish clans sought to resist the encroachment of foreign rule and preserve their traditional way of life. These conflicts, such as the Nine Years' War and the Desmond Rebellions, underscored the deep-seated divisions and tensions that characterized Anglo-Irish relations during this period.

The Great Famine: Tragedy and Emigration

The Great Famine of the mid-19th century remains one of the most tragic chapters in Irish history, leaving a profound and lasting impact on the country. The failure of the potato crop, exacerbated by British policies and economic inequalities, led to mass starvation, disease, and emigration. Tourists pay homage to the victims of the Famine at poignant memorials such as the Famine Museum at Strokestown Park and the Great Famine Exhibition at the National Museum of Ireland.

At the heart of the Great Famine lies the catastrophic failure of the potato crop, upon which a significant portion of the Irish population depended for sustenance. The introduction of the potato in the 16th century had transformed Irish agriculture, offering high yields and nutritional value, particularly for the impoverished rural populace. However, the dependence on this single crop rendered Ireland vulnerable to disaster, as evidenced by the devastation wrought by the potato blight, a fungal disease that ravaged potato fields across the country from 1845 onwards.

The impact of the famine was not solely a result of natural forces but was exacerbated by British policies and socio-economic structures that perpetuated Irish vulnerability and exploitation. Landownership patterns, characterized by absentee English landlords and the concentration of land in the hands of a privileged few, marginalized Irish tenant farmers and exacerbated rural poverty. British laissez-faire economic ideology further compounded the crisis, as relief efforts were limited, and exports of food continued unabated from Ireland to Britain, exacerbating the scarcity of food for the Irish population.

The consequences of the Great Famine were devastating and far-reaching. As the blight decimated potato crops year after year, millions faced starvation and disease, with mortality rates soaring and families torn apart by death and emigration. Rural communities were particularly hard hit, with the loss of livelihoods and homes driving many into destitution and despair. The suffering of the famine years is commemorated at poignant sites such as the Famine Museum at Strokestown Park and the Great Famine Exhibition at the National Museum of Ireland, where visitors can gain insight into the harrowing experiences of those who lived through this period of profound hardship.

Moreover, the Great Famine catalyzed significant shifts in Irish society and politics, igniting a burgeoning nationalist movement and fueling demands for self-determination and social justice. The failure of British authorities to adequately respond to the crisis exposed the injustices of colonial rule and deepened resentment towards British domination. Irish nationalism, which had been simmering for centuries, gained momentum as calls for land reform, political autonomy, and cultural revival reverberated throughout the country.

Emigration emerged as a defining feature of the post-famine landscape, as millions of desperate Irish men, women, and children sought refuge abroad in search of a better life. The Irish diaspora expanded rapidly, with waves of emigrants settling in the United States, Canada, Australia, and beyond, where they would leave an enduring imprint on their adopted homelands. The phenomenon of mass emigration not only depleted Ireland of its population but also fueled transnational networks of solidarity and support, as Irish communities abroad rallied to assist their compatriots and preserve their cultural heritage.

The legacy of the Great Famine endures in the collective memory of the Irish people, shaping their identity and sense of resilience in the face of adversity. The famine represents a pivotal moment in Irish history, marking the culmination of centuries of oppression and exploitation, yet also inspiring acts of solidarity, resilience, and defiance. Today, as Ireland grapples with new challenges and opportunities in a rapidly changing world, the lessons of the famine years remain relevant, serving as a reminder of the importance of social justice, solidarity, and the enduring human spirit in times of crisis.

The 19th century saw the emergence of Irish nationalism and the struggle for independence from British rule. The Great Famine of the 1840s, caused by a devastating potato blight, resulted in mass starvation, disease, and emigration. The famine highlighted the injustices of British colonial rule and fueled calls for Irish self-determination.

The Easter Rising and Irish Independence

The Easter Rising of 1916 marked a turning point in Ireland's struggle for independence from British rule. Tourists are drawn to sites such as the General Post Office (GPO) in Dublin, where the rebels made their stand, and Kilmainham Gaol, where the leaders of the Rising were executed. The subsequent War of Independence and the establishment of the Irish Free State in 1922 further shape Ireland's modern identity.

The late 19th and early 20th centuries witnessed the rise of various nationalist movements, culminating in the Easter Rising of 1916. This armed rebellion against British rule marked a watershed moment in Irish history and paved the way for the eventual establishment of the Irish Free State in 1922. The partition of Ireland, however, resulted in the creation of Northern Ireland, leading to decades of sectarian conflict known as the Troubles.

The Easter Rising of 1916 stands as a defining moment in the annals of Irish history, a bold assertion of national identity against the backdrop of British colonial rule. It was more than just a rebellion; it was a cultural and political awakening that reverberated through the soul of Ireland, igniting the flames of independence that had smoldered for centuries.

At the turn of the 20th century, Ireland found itself in the grip of fervent nationalism. The Irish people were increasingly disillusioned with British rule, which they viewed as oppressive and unjust. The rise of various nationalist movements, such as the Irish Republican Brotherhood and Sinn Féin, reflected this growing discontent and laid the groundwork for the events that would unfold in 1916.

On Easter Monday, April 24th, 1916, a group of rebels seized key locations in Dublin, including the iconic General Post Office (GPO), and proclaimed the establishment of an Irish Republic. Led by figures like Patrick Pearse, James Connolly, and Thomas Clarke, these brave men and women dared to challenge the might of the British Empire, despite facing overwhelming odds.

The Easter Rising was not only a military struggle but also a cultural uprising. The rebels sought to assert Ireland's cultural heritage and revive its Gaelic traditions in the face of British cultural hegemony. Symbols such as the Irish language, music, and literature played a crucial role in galvanizing support for the cause and inspiring future generations of Irish nationalists.

The aftermath of the Easter Rising was swift and brutal. The British authorities swiftly moved to suppress the rebellion, rounding up the leaders and participants and subjecting them to courts-martial and harsh sentences. Fourteen leaders, including Pearse, Connolly, and Clarke, were executed by firing squad, their deaths immortalized in the collective memory of the Irish people.

Yet, far from extinguishing the flames of rebellion, the executions served to ignite them further. The martyrdom of the Easter Rising leaders galvanized support for the cause of Irish independence, turning public opinion against British rule and fueling a surge in nationalist sentiment across the country.

The years that followed the Easter Rising were marked by turmoil and upheaval as Ireland embarked on a path towards independence. The subsequent War of Independence, fought between Irish republican forces and British Crown forces, saw guerrilla warfare, reprisals, and acts of sabotage unfold across the island.

The signing of the Anglo-Irish Treaty in 1921 paved the way for the establishment of the Irish Free State the following year, effectively partitioning the island and granting limited independence to 26 of its counties. While hailed as a victory by some, the treaty proved divisive, leading to a bitter civil war between pro- and anti-treaty forces.

The legacy of the Easter Rising and the struggle for independence continues to shape Ireland's modern identity. Sites such as the GPO and Kilmainham Gaol serve as poignant reminders of the sacrifices made by those who fought for Irish freedom. The Rising remains a touchstone of Irish nationalism, celebrated annually on Easter Sunday with ceremonies and commemorations across the country.

However, the partition of Ireland and the creation of Northern Ireland in 1921 cast a long shadow over the island's history, leading to decades of sectarian conflict known as the Troubles. The scars of this troubled past still linger, reminding Ireland of the challenges that come with the pursuit of freedom and self-determination.

The Troubles: Conflict and Reconciliation

The Troubles, a period of sectarian violence and political conflict in Northern Ireland from the late 1960s to the late 1990s, loom large in Ireland's recent history. Tourists interested in this complex and sensitive topic may visit the Peace Walls in Belfast, which still divide communities, or take guided tours of areas affected by the conflict, gaining insights into efforts towards reconciliation and peace-building.

The Troubles, which lasted from the late 1960s to the late 1990s, saw violence, terrorism, and political deadlock in Northern Ireland. The conflict, rooted in sectarian divisions between Catholic nationalists and Protestant unionists, resulted in thousands of deaths and left deep scars on Irish society. The Good Friday Agreement of 1998 brought an end to the violence and established a framework for peace and reconciliation in Northern Ireland.

Ireland Today

One of the most striking aspects of Ireland today is its booming economy, which has transformed the country into a global hub for technology and innovation. Over the past few decades, Ireland has attracted some of the world's leading tech companies, earning it the nickname "the Silicon Valley of Europe." Major players such as Google, Facebook, Apple, and Microsoft have established significant operations in Ireland, drawn by the country's skilled workforce, favorable business environment, and strategic location within the European Union. The presence of these tech giants has not only bolstered Ireland's economy but has also helped to cement its reputation as a leading center for research, development, and entrepreneurship.

Socially, Ireland has undergone significant changes in recent decades, with strides made in areas such as LGBTQ+ rights, gender equality, and multiculturalism. The legalization of same-sex marriage in 2015 and the repeal of the Eighth Amendment, which restricted access to abortion, in 2018 are notable examples of Ireland's progressive social policies. The country has also welcomed immigrants from around the world, contributing to its cultural diversity and enriching its social fabric.

Many Irish people have a penchant for self-deprecating humor, poking fun at themselves and their cultural quirks. Wit and banter are highly valued in Irish society, and self-deprecating humor is often used as a way to disarm and connect with others. The ability to laugh at oneself is seen as a sign of humility and good-naturedness, and no topic is off-limits when it comes to making a joke. Whether poking fun at politicians, the weather, or their own misfortunes, the Irish have a knack for finding humor in everyday life.

The "Sure It'll Be Grand" Mentality

You'll find that the aaverage Irish person often adopts a laid-back attitude, commonly expressing optimism and resilience in the face of challenges.

Key Figures in Irish History

Irish history is rich with key figures who have left a lasting impact on the nation's trajectory. One such figure is Daniel O'Connell, known as "The Liberator." O'Connell was a 19th-century political leader who campaigned tirelessly for Catholic emancipation and the repeal of discriminatory laws against Catholics in Ireland. His use of peaceful, constitutional methods, such as mass mobilization and the power of oratory, set a precedent for future leaders seeking social change through non-violent means.

Another prominent figure is Michael Collins, a revolutionary leader during the Irish War of Independence. Collins played a pivotal role in organizing the Irish Republican Army (IRA) and negotiating the Anglo-Irish Treaty of 1921, which led to the establishment of the Irish Free State. His strategic brilliance and charisma earned him respect both as a military leader and a statesman, though his life was tragically cut short in the Irish Civil War.

Eamon de Valera is another significant figure in Irish history, often considered the architect of modern Ireland. A leader in the Easter Rising of 1916 and subsequent events, de Valera served multiple terms as Taoiseach (Prime Minister) and later as President of Ireland. His political career spanned several decades, during which he shaped Ireland's economic policies, constitutional framework, and foreign relations, leaving a profound mark on the country's development.

In more recent times, Mary Robinson stands out as an influential figure in Irish history. She became the first female President of Ireland in 1990, breaking gender barriers and championing human rights and equality throughout her tenure. Robinson's presidency was marked by her advocacy for marginalized communities, both domestically and internationally, and her efforts to promote peace and reconciliation in Northern Ireland.

Irish Superstitions

Irish culture is steeped in mythology, folklore, and superstition, with beliefs and practices passed down through generations. These superstitions, ranging from the mundane to the extraordinary, offer a fascinating glimpse into the psyche of the Irish people and their deep connection to the mystical and supernatural. In this detailed guide, we'll explore a myriad of Irish superstitions, uncovering their origins, significance, and enduring presence in modern-day Ireland.

- The Celtic Influence: Many Irish superstitions can be traced back to the ancient Celts, who revered nature and held a deep respect for the unseen forces of the world.
- Christian Adaptations: With the arrival of Christianity in Ireland, pagan beliefs were often assimilated into Christian practices, resulting in a blending of old and new superstitions.
- Cultural Traditions: Ireland's tumultuous history, including periods of invasion, famine, and oppression, has contributed to the development of superstitions as a means of coping with uncertainty and adversity.

Everyday Superstitions

- Knocking on Wood: One of the most well-known superstitions, knocking on wood is believed to ward off bad luck or prevent jinxing oneself.
- Spilling Salt: Spilling salt is said to bring bad luck, but tossing a pinch of salt over your left shoulder is believed to counteract the negativity.
- Black Cats: In Irish folklore, black cats are often associated with witchcraft and considered harbingers of misfortune if they cross your path.

Superstitions for Good Luck

- Four-Leaf Clovers: Finding a four-leaf clover is considered extremely lucky in Irish tradition, as each leaf is believed to represent faith, hope, love, and luck.
- Lucky Horseshoes: Hanging a horseshoe above the door is thought to bring good luck and ward off evil spirits. The horseshoe should always be hung with the open end facing upward to catch and hold good fortune.
- Wedding Superstitions: Irish weddings are steeped in superstition, from wearing something blue to carrying a horseshoe for luck. Tying the knot on a weekday is also considered auspicious, while marrying in May is believed to bring bad luck.

Superstitions for Bad Luck

- Walking Under Ladders: It's considered unlucky to walk under a ladder, as it's believed to invite misfortune or even death. This superstition likely originated from the shape of the ladder resembling a triangle, which was associated with the Holy Trinity.

- Breaking Mirrors: Breaking a mirror is said to bring seven years of bad luck, a superstition rooted in ancient beliefs that mirrors were portals to the soul and breaking one could shatter the soul's reflection.

Superstitions Surrounding Death and the Afterlife

- Banshees: In Irish folklore, banshees are female spirits believed to wail and keen as a warning of impending death. Hearing the cry of a banshee is considered a harbinger of doom.
- Wake Superstitions: Traditionally, wakes were held for the deceased, and various superstitions surrounded the rituals, including covering mirrors to prevent the deceased's spirit from becoming trapped.

Superstitions in Nature

- Fairy Folklore: Ireland is renowned for its fairy folklore, with numerous superstitions surrounding the mischievous and sometimes malevolent fairy folk. It's believed that offending the fairies could result in their wrath and bring bad luck.
- Sacred Trees and Holy Wells: Certain trees and wells throughout Ireland are believed to possess healing powers or spiritual significance, and offerings are often left to appease the spirits that dwell within them.

While some may dismiss them as mere superstition, for many, they serve as a source of comfort, guidance, and connection to the mystical world that lies just beyond the realm of the everyday. As you traverse the verdant landscapes of Ireland, keep an eye out for signs and symbols that hint at the enduring presence of these age-old beliefs, for in the land of saints and scholars, the veil between the seen and the unseen is often tantalizingly thin.

Top 20 Luxury experiences to have in Ireland on a Budget

- **Cooking Class at Ballymaloe Cookery School:** Learn to cook traditional Irish dishes using fresh, locally sourced ingredients at one of Ireland's most renowned cooking schools.
- **Seaweed Bath at Voya Seaweed Baths:** Relax and rejuvenate in a traditional seaweed bath along the coast of County Sligo, known for its therapeutic properties and stunning ocean views.
- **Stay in an Ocean View Apartment in Lahinch:** Book a stay in a cozy oceanfront apartment in Lahinch, County Clare, and wake up to breathtaking views of the Atlantic Ocean.
- **Guided Tour of Kylemore Abbey:** Explore the picturesque grounds and historic interiors of Kylemore Abbey in Connemara, County Galway, with a guided tour of this iconic Irish estate.
- **Cruise on Lough Corrib:** Embark on a scenic cruise along Lough Corrib in County Galway, admiring the tranquil waters and stunning landscapes of Ireland's second-largest lake.
- **Traditional Irish Music Session at Matt Molloy's Pub:** Immerse yourself in the lively atmosphere of a traditional Irish music session at Matt Molloy's Pub in Westport, County Mayo, featuring talented local musicians.
- **Visit the Cliffs of Moher Visitor Experience:** Take a stroll along the dramatic cliffs and marvel at the panoramic views of the Atlantic Ocean from one of Ireland's most iconic natural landmarks.
- **Whiskey Tasting at the Irish Whiskey Museum:** Discover the history and heritage of Irish whiskey with a guided tasting session at the Irish Whiskey Museum in Dublin's city center.
- **Guided Tour of Kilkenny Castle:** Step back in time with a guided tour of Kilkenny Castle, one of Ireland's most majestic medieval castles, located in the heart of Kilkenny City.
- **Horseback Riding on the Beach in County Donegal:** Experience the thrill of horseback riding on the sandy shores of Donegal's beautiful beaches, surrounded by stunning coastal scenery.
- **Explore the Botanic Gardens in Dublin:** Wander through the tranquil oasis of the National Botanic Gardens in Dublin, home to a stunning collection of plant species from around the world.
- **Cultural Walking Tour of Galway City:** Join a guided walking tour of Galway City's historic streets and landmarks, including the Spanish Arch, Galway Cathedral, and Eyre Square.
- **Visit the Giant's Causeway in Northern Ireland:** Marvel at the otherworldly landscape of hexagonal basalt columns along the Northern Irish coast, a UNESCO World Heritage Site and one of Ireland's most iconic natural wonders.
- **Picnic at Powerscourt Gardens:** Pack a gourmet picnic and spend a leisurely day exploring the manicured gardens and cascading waterfalls of Powerscourt Estate in County Wicklow.
- **Boat Trip to Skellig Michael:** Embark on a boat trip to Skellig Michael, an ancient monastic site and filming location for Star Wars, located off the coast of County Kerry.

- **Guided Tour of the Old Jameson Distillery in Dublin:** Learn about the craftsmanship and heritage of Jameson Irish whiskey with a guided tour of the Old Jameson Distillery in Dublin's Smithfield.
- **Cycling the Great Western Greenway:** Rent a bike and cycle along the Great Western Greenway, a scenic trail that follows the route of the old Westport to Achill railway line in County Mayo.
- **Visit the National Museum of Ireland - Archaeology:** Explore the fascinating exhibits and archaeological treasures of the National Museum of Ireland in Dublin, including the famous Ardagh Chalice and Tara Brooch.
- **Day Trip to the Aran Islands:** Take a ferry to the rugged Aran Islands off the coast of County Galway and discover ancient stone forts, dramatic cliffs, and traditional Irish culture.
- **Gourmet Dining Experience at a Michelin-starred Restaurant:** Treat yourself to a gourmet dining experience at one of Ireland's Michelin-starred restaurants, offering exquisite cuisine and impeccable service at surprisingly affordable prices.

Checklist of Top 20 Things to Do

- [x] Visit the Cliffs of Moher
- [x] Explore Dublin's Temple Bar district
- [x] Take a tour of the Guinness Storehouse
- [x] Kiss the Blarney Stone at Blarney Castle
- [x] Drive the Ring of Kerry
- [x] Visit Trinity College and the Book of Kells
- [x] Experience traditional music in a local pub
- [x] Explore the Wild Atlantic Way
- [x] Discover the history of Belfast with a black taxi tour
- [x] Take a ferry to the Aran Islands
- [x] Hike in Connemara National Park
- [x] Explore the Giant's Causeway
- [x] Visit Kylemore Abbey
- [x] Tour the Kilmainham Gaol in Dublin
- [x] Enjoy a traditional Irish breakfast
- [x] Take a boat tour of the Skellig Islands
- [x] Explore the Dingle Peninsula
- [x] Visit the Rock of Cashel
- [x] Take a walk along the Cliffs of Moher Coastal Trail
- [x] Attend a Gaelic football or hurling match

Recap: how to have a $10,000 trip to Ireland for $1,000

Aspect	Cost	Details
Flights	$200	Look for budget airlines or low-cost carriers, book well in advance, consider flexible dates for cheaper options.
Accommodation	$100	Stay in unique Bed and Breakfast (B&B) accommodations, which are often more affordable than hotels and offer a more authentic Irish experience.
Transportation	$100	Purchase a Leap Card for discounted fares on public transportation in major cities like Dublin, Cork, and Galway.
Attractions	$100	Invest in a Dublin Pass or Heritage Card for discounted or free entry to major attractions and heritage sites.
Food & Drink	$200	Opt for self-catering options such as grocery shopping, too good to go, and cooking your meals occasionally, and indulge in local pub grub for affordable dining experiences.
Tours & Activities	$100	Look for free walking tours, hiking trails, and cultural events offered by local communities or tourism boards.
Souvenirs & Gifts	$100	Shop at local markets and artisan shops for unique, budget-friendly souvenirs and gifts.
Miscellaneous	$200	Allocate a buffer for unexpected expenses or emergencies.

Total Cost: $1,000

By carefully planning and making use of discount passes, transportation options, and unique accommodation choices, you can experience the beauty and charm of Ireland on a budget without sacrificing the quality of your trip. Remember to research thoroughly, book in advance whenever possible, and embrace the spirit of adventure as you explore the Emerald Isle.

The secret to saving HUGE amounts of money when travelling to Ireland is…

Your mindset. Money is an emotional topic, if you associate words like cheapskate, Miser (and its £9.50 to go into Charles Dickens London house, oh the Irony) with being thrifty when traveling you are likely to say 'F-it' and spend your money needlessly because you associate pain with saving money. You pay now for an immediate reward. Our brains are prehistoric; they focus on surviving day to day. Travel companies and hotels know this and put trillions into making you believe you will be happier when you spend on their products or services. Our poor brains are up against outdated programming and an onslaught of advertisements bombarding us with the message: spending money on travel equals PLEASURE. To correct this carefully lodged propaganda in your frontal cortex, you need to imagine your future self.

Saving money does not make you a cheapskate. It makes you smart. How do people get rich? They invest their money. They don't go out and earn it; they let their money earn more money. So every time you want to spend money, imagine this: while you travel, your money is working for you, not you for money. While you sleep, the money, you've invested is going up and up. That's a pleasure a pricey entrance fee can't give you. Thinking about putting your money to work for you tricks your brain into believing you are not withholding pleasure from yourself, you are saving your money to invest so you can go to even more amazing places. You are thus turning thrifty travel into a pleasure fueled sport.

When you've got money invested - If you want to splash your cash on a first-class airplane seat - you can. I can't tell you how to invest your money, only that you should. Saving $20 on taxis doesn't seem like much, but over time you could save upwards of $15,000 a year, which is a deposit for a house which you can rent on Airbnb to finance more travel. Your brain making money looks like your brain on cocaine, so tell yourself saving money is making money.

Scientists have proved that imagining your future self is the easiest way to associate pleasure with saving money. You can download FaceApp — which will give you a picture of what you will look like older and grayer, or you can take a deep breath just before spending money and ask yourself if you will regret the purchase later.

The easiest ways to waste money traveling are:

Getting a taxi. The solution to this is to always download the google map before you go. Many taxi drivers will drive you around for 15 minutes when the place you were trying to get to is a 5-minute walk… remember while not getting an overpriced taxi to tell yourself, 'I am saving money to free myself for more travel.'
Spending money on overpriced food when hungry. The solution: carry snacks. A banana and an apple will cost you, in most places, less than a dollar.

Spending on entrance fees to top-rated attractions. If you really want to do it, spend the money happily. If you're conflicted, sleep on it. I don't regret spending $200 on a sky dive over the Great Barrier Reef; I regret going to the top of the shard on a cloudy day in Ireland for $60. Only you can know, but make sure it's your decision and not the marketing directors at said top-rated attraction.

Telling yourself 'you only have the chance to see/eat/experience it now'. While this might be true, make sure YOU WANT to spend the money. Money spent is money you can't invest, and often you can have the same experience for much less.

You can experience luxurious travel on a small budget, which will trick your brain into thinking you're already a high-roller, which will mean you'll be more likely to act like one and invest your money. Stay in five-star hotels for $5 by booking on the day of your stay on booking.com to enjoy last-minute deals. You can go to fancy restaurants using daily deal sites. Ask your airline about last-minute upgrades to first-class or business. I paid $100 extra on a $179 ticket to Cuba from Germany to be bumped to Business Class. When you ask, it will surprise you what you can get both at hotels and airlines.

Travel, as the saying goes, is the only thing you spend money on that makes you richer. You can easily waste money, making it difficult to enjoy that metaphysical wealth. The biggest money saving secret is to turn bargain hunting into a pleasurable activity, not an annoyance. Budgeting consciously can be fun, don't feel disappointed because you don't spend the $60 to go into an attraction. Feel good because soon that $60 will soon earn money for you. Meaning, you'll have the time and money to enjoy more metaphysical wealth while your bank balance increases.

So there it is. You can save a small fortune by being strategic with your trip planning. We've arranged everything in the guide to offer the best bang for your buck. Which means we took the view that if it's not an excellent investment for your money, we wouldn't include it. Why would a guide called 'Super Cheap' include lots of overpriced attractions? That said, if you think we've missed something or have unanswered questions, ping me an email: philgtang@gmail.com I'm on central Europe time and usually reply within 8 hours of getting your mail. We like to think of our guide books as evolving organisms helping our readers travel better cheaper. We use reader questions via email to update this book year round so you'll be helping other readers and yourself.

Don't put your dreams off!

Time is a currency you never get back and travel is its greatest return on investment. Plus, now you know you can visit Ireland for a fraction of the price most would have you believe.

"May you always have a clean shirt, a clear conscience, and enough coins in your pocket to buy a pint!"

Thank you for reading

Dear **Lovely Reader**,

If you have found this book useful, please consider writing a quick review on Online Retailers.

One person from every 1000 readers leaves a review on Online Retailers. It would mean more than you could ever know if you were one of our 1 in 1000 people to take the time to write a brief review.

Thank you so much for reading again and for spending your time and investing your trips future in Super Cheap Insider Guides.

One last note, please don't listen to anyone who says 'Oh no, you can't visit Ireland on a budget'. Unlike you, they didn't have this book. You can do ANYWHERE on a budget with the right insider advice and planning. Sure, learning to travel to Ireland on a budget that doesn't compromise on anything or drastically compromise on safety or comfort levels is a skill, but this guide has done the detective work for you. Now it is time for you to put the advice into action.

Phil and the Super Cheap Insider Guides Team

P.S If you need any more super cheap tips we'd love to hear from you e-mail me at philgtang@gmail.com, we have a lot of contacts in every region, so if there's a specific bargain you're hunting we can help you find it.

> "May the road rise up to meet you.
> May the wind be always at your back.
> May the sun shine warm upon your face;
> the rains fall soft upon your fields
> and until we meet again,
> may God hold you in the palm of His hand."

DISCOVER YOUR NEXT VACATION

✅ LUXURY ON A BUDGET APPROACH

✅ CHOOSE FROM 107 DESTINATIONS

✅ EACH BOOK PACKED WITH REAL-TIME LOCAL TIPS

All are available in Paperback and e-book on Online Retailers:
https://www.Online Retailers.com/dp/B09C2DHQG5

Several are available as audiobooks. You can watch excerpts of ALL for FREE on YouTube: https://youtube.com/channel/UCxo9YV8-M9P1cFosU-Gjnqg

COUNTRY GUIDES

Super Cheap AUSTRALIA
Super Cheap CANADA
Super Cheap DENMARK
Super Cheap FINLAND
Super Cheap FRANCE
Super Cheap GERMANY
Super Cheap ICELAND
Super Cheap ITALY
Super Cheap JAPAN
Super Cheap LUXEMBOURG
Super Cheap MALDIVES 2024
Super Cheap NEW ZEALAND
Super Cheap NORWAY
Super Cheap SPAIN
Super Cheap SWITZERLAND

MORE GUIDES

Super Cheap ADELAIDE 2024
Super Cheap ALASKA 2024
Super Cheap AUSTIN 2024
Super Cheap BANGKOK 2024
Super Cheap BARCELONA 2024
Super Cheap BELFAST 2024
Super Cheap BERMUDA 2024
Super Cheap BORA BORA 2024

Super Cheap Great Barrier Reef 2024
Super Cheap CAMBRIDGE 2024
Super Cheap CANCUN 2024
Super Cheap CHIANG MAI 2024
Super Cheap CHICAGO 2024
Super Cheap DOHA 2024
Super Cheap DUBAI 2024
Super Cheap DUBLIN 2024
Super Cheap EDINBURGH 2024
Super Cheap GALWAY 2024
Super Cheap LAS VEGAS 2024
Super Cheap LIMA 2024
Super Cheap LISBON 2024
Super Cheap MALAGA 2024
Super Cheap Machu Pichu 2024
Super Cheap MIAMI 2024
Super Cheap Milan 2024
Super Cheap NASHVILLE 2024
Super Cheap NEW ORLEANS 2024
Super Cheap NEW YORK 2024
Super Cheap PARIS 2024
Super Cheap SEYCHELLES 2024
Super Cheap SINGAPORE 2024
Super Cheap ST LUCIA 2024
Super Cheap TORONTO 2024
Super Cheap TURKS AND CAICOS 2024
Super Cheap VENICE 2024
Super Cheap VIENNA 2024
Super Cheap YOSEMITE 2024
Super Cheap ZURICH 2024
Super Cheap ZANZIBAR 2024

Bonus Travel Hacks

I've included these bonus travel hacks to help you plan and enjoy your trip to Ireland cheaply, joyfully, and smoothly. Perhaps they will even inspire you to start or renew a passion for long-term travel.

Common pitfalls when it comes to allocating money to <u>your desires</u> while traveling

Beware of Malleable mental accounting

Let's say you budgeted spending only $30 per day in Ireland but then you say well if I was at home I'd be spending $30 on food as an everyday purchase so you add another $30 to your budget. Don't fall into that trap as the likelihood is you still have expenses at home even if its just the cost of keeping your freezer going.

Beware of impulse purchases in Ireland

Restaurants that you haven't researched and just idle into can sometimes turn out to be great, but more often, they turn out to suck, especially if they are near tourist attractions. Make yourself a travel itinerary including where you'll eat breakfast and lunch. Dinner is always more expensive, so the meal best to enjoy at home or as a takeaway. This book is full of incredible cheap eats. All you have to do is plan to go to them.

Social media and FOMO (Fear of Missing Out)

'The pull of seeing acquaintances spend money on travel can often be a more powerful motivator to spend more while traveling than seeing an advertisement.' Beware of what you allow to influence you and go back to the question, what's the best money I can spend today?

Now-or-never sales strategies

One reason tourists are targeted by salespeople is the success of the now-or-never strategy. If you don't spend the money now… your never get the opportunity again. Rarely is this true.

Instead of spending your money on something you might not actually desire, take five minutes. Ask yourself, do I really want this? And return to the answer in five minutes. Your body will either say an absolute yes with a warm, excited feeling or a no with a weak, obscure feeling.

Unexpected costs

> "Holding on to anger is like grasping a hot coal with the intent of throwing it at someone else; you only hurt yourself." The Buddha.

One downside to traveling is unexpected costs. When these spring up from airlines, accommodation providers, tours and on and on, they feel like a punch in the gut. During the pandemic my earnings fell to 20% of what they are normally. No one was traveling, no one was buying travel guides. My accountant out of nowhere significantly raised his fee for the year despite the fact there was a lot less money to count. I was so angry I consulted a lawyer who told me you will spend more taking him to court than you will paying his bill. I had to get myself into a good feeling place before I paid his bill, so I googled how to feel good paying someone who has scammed you.

The answer: Write down that you will receive 10 times the amount you are paying from an unexpected source. I did that. Four months later, the accountant wrote to me. He had applied for a COVID subsidy for me and I would receive... you guessed it almost exactly 10 times his fee.

Make of that what you want. I don't wish to get embroiled in a conversation about what many term 'woo-woo', but the result of my writing that I would receive 10 times the amount made me feel much, much better when paying him. And ultimately, that was a gift in itself. So next time some airline or train operator or hotel/ Airbnb sticks you with an unexpected fee, immediately write that you will receive 10 times the amount you are paying from an unexpected source. Rise your vibe and skip the added price of feeling angry.

Hack your allocations for your Ireland Trip

"The best trick for saving is to eliminate the decision to save." Perry Wright of Duke University.

Put the money you plan to spend in Ireland on a pre-paid card in the local currency. This cuts out two problems - not knowing how much you've spent and totally avoiding expensive currency conversion fees.

You could even create separate spaces. This much for transportation, this for tours/entertainment, accommodation and food. We are reluctant to spend money that is pre-assigned to categories or uses.

Write that you want to enjoy a $3,000 trip for $500 to your Ireland trip. Countless research shows when you put goals in writing, you have a higher chance of following through.

Spend all the money you want to on buying experiences in Ireland

"Experiences are like good relatives that stay for a while and then leave. Objects are like relatives who move in and stay past their welcome." Daniel Gilbert, psychologist from Harvard University.

Economic and psychological research shows we are happier buying brief experiences on vacation rather than buying stuff to wear so give yourself freedom to spend on experiences knowing that the value you get back is many many times over.

Make saving money a game

There's one day a year where all the thrift shops where me and my family live sell everything there for a $1. My wife and I hold a contest where we take $5 and buy an entire outfit for each other. Whoever's outfit is liked more wins. We also look online to see whose outfit would have cost more to buy new. This year, my wife even snagged me an Armani coat for $1. I liked the coat when she showed it to me, but when I found out it was $500 new; I liked it and wore it a lot more.

Quadruple your money

Every-time you want to spend money, imagine it quadrupled. So the $10 you want to spend is actually $40. Now imagine that what you want to buy is four times the price. Do you still want it? If yes, go enjoy. If not, you've just saved yourself money, know you can choose to invest it in a way that quadruples or allocate it to something you really want to give you a greater return.

Understand what having unlimited amounts of money to spend in Ireland actually looks like

Let's look at what it would be like to have unlimited amounts of money to spend on your trip to Ireland.

Isolation

You take a private jet to your private Ireland hotel. There you are lavished with the best food, drink, and entertainment. Spending vast amounts of money on vacation equals being isolated.

If you're on your honeymoon and you want to be alone with your Amore, this is wonderful, but it can be equally wonderful to make new friends. Know this a study 'carried out by Brigham Young University, Utah found that while obesity increased risk of death by 30%, loneliness increased it by half.'

Comfort

Money can buy you late check outs of five-star hotels and priority boarding on airlines, all of which add up to comfort. But as this book has shown you, saving money in Ireland doesn't minimize comfort, that's just a lie travel agencies littered with glossy brochures want you to believe.

You can do late-check outs for free with the right credit cards and priority boarding can be purchased with a lot of airlines from $4. If you want to go big with first-class or business, flights offset your own travel costs by renting your own home or you can upgrade at the airport often for a fraction of what you would have paid booking a business flight online.

MORE TIPS TO FIND CHEAP FLIGHTS

"The use of travelling is to regulate imagination by reality, and instead of thinking how things may be, to see them as they are." Samuel Jackson

If you're working full-time, you can save yourself a lot of money by requesting your time off from work starting in the middle of the week. Tuesdays and Wednesdays are the cheapest days to fly. You can save thousands just by adjusting your time off.

The simplest secret to booking cheap flights is open parameters. Let's say you want to fly from Chicago to Paris. You enter the USA in from and select Ireland under to. You may find flights from New York City to Paris for $70. Then you just need to find a cheap flight to NYC. Make sure you calculate full costs, including if you need airport accommodation and of course getting to and from airports, **but in nearly every instance open parameters will save you at least half the cost of the flight.**

 If you're not sure about where you want to go, use open parameters to show you the cheapest destinations from your city. Start with skyscanner.net they include the low-cost airlines that others like Kayak leave out. Google Flights can also show you cheap destinations. To see these leave the WHERE TO section blank. Open parameters can also show you the cheapest dates to fly. If you're flexible, you can save up to 80% of the flight cost. Always check the weather at your destination before you book. Sometimes a $400 flight will be $20, because it's monsoon season. But hey, if you like the rain, why not?

ALWAYS USE A PRIVATE BROWSER TO BOOK FLIGHTS

Skyscanner and other sites track your IP address and put prices up and down based on what they determine your strength of conviction to buy. e.g. if you've booked one-way and are looking for the return, these sites will jack the prices up by in most cases 50%. Incognito browsing pays.

Use a VPN such as Hola to book your flight from your destination

Install Hola, change your destination to the country you are flying to. The location from which a ticket is booked can affect the price significantly as algorithms consider local buying power.

Choose the right time to buy your ticket.

Choose the right time to buy your ticket, as purchasing tickets on a Sunday has been proven to be cheaper. If you can only book during the week, try to do it on a Tuesday.

Mistake fares

Email alerts from individual carriers are where you can find the best 'mistake fares". This is where a computer error has resulted in an airline offering the wrong fare. In my experience, it's best to sign up to individual carriers email lists, but if you ARE lazy Secret Flying puts together a daily roster of mistake fares. Visit https://www.secretflying.com/errorfare/ to see if there're any errors that can benefit you.

Fly late for cheaper prices

Red-eye flights, the ones that leave later in the day, are typically cheaper and less crowded, so aim to book that flight if possible. You will also get through the airport much quicker at the end of the day. Just make sure there's ground transport available for when you land. You don't want to save $50 on the airfare and spend it on a taxi to your accommodation.

Use this APP for same day flights

If your plans are flexible, use 'Get The Flight Out' (http://www.gtfoflights.com/) a fare tracker Hopper that shows you same-day deeply discounted flights. This is best for long-haul flights with major carriers. You can often find a British Airways round-trip from JFK Airport to Heathrow for $300. If you booked this in advance, you'd pay at least double.

Take an empty water bottle with you

Airport prices on food and drinks are sky high. It disgusts me to see some airports charging $10 for a bottle of water. ALWAYS take an empty water bottle with you. It's relatively unknown, but most airports have drinking water fountains past the security check. Just type in your airport name to wateratairports.com to locate the fountain. Then once you've passed security (because they don't allow you to take 100ml or more of liquids) you can freely refill your bottle with water.

Round-the-World (RTW) Tickets

It is always cheaper to book your flights using a DIY approach. First, you may decide you want to stay longer in one country, and a RTW will charge you a hefty fee for changing your flight. Secondly, it all depends on where and when you travel and as we have discussed, there are many ways to ensure you pay way less than $1,500 for a year of flights. If you're travelling long-haul, the best strategy is to buy a return ticket, say New York, to Bangkok and then take cheap flights or transport around Asia and even to Australia and beyond.

Cut your costs to and from airports

Don't you hate it when getting to and from the airport is more expensive than your flight! And this is true in so many cities, especially European ones. For some reason, Google often shows the most expensive options. Use Omio to compare the cheapest transport options and save on airport transfer costs.

Car sharing instead of taxis

Check if Ireland has car sharing at the airport. Often they'll be tons of cars parked at the airport that are half the price of taking a taxi into the city. In most instances, you register your driving licence on an app and scan the code on the car to get going.

Checking Bags

Sometimes you need to check bags. If you do, put an AirTag inside. That way, you'll be about to see when you land where your bag is. This saves you the nail biting wait at baggage claim. And if worse comes to worst, and you see your bag is actually in another city, you can calmly stroll over to customer services and show them where your bag is.

Is it cheaper and more convenient to send your bags ahead?

Before you check your bags, check if it's cheaper to send them ahead of you with sendmybag.com obviously if you're staying in an Airbnb, you'll need to ask the hosts permission or you can time them to arrive the day after you. Hotels are normally very amenable.

What Credit Card Gives The Best Air Miles?

You can slash the cost of flights just for spending on a piece of plastic.

LET'S TALK ABOUT DEBT

Before we go into the best cards for each country, let's first talk about debt. The US system offers the best and biggest rewards. Why? Because they rely on the fact that many people living in the US will not pay their cards in full and the card will earn the bank significant interest payments. Other countries have a very different attitude towards money, debt, and saving than Americans. Thus in Germany and Austria the offerings aren't as favourable as the UK, Ireland and Australia, where debt culture is more widely embraced. The takeaway here is this: **Only spend on one of these cards when you have set-up an automatic total monthly balance repayment. Don't let banks profit from your lizard brain!**

The best air-mile credit cards for those living in the UK

Amex Preferred Rewards Gold comes out top for those living in the UK for 2024.

Here are the benefits:

- 20,000-point bonus on £3,000 spend in first three months. These can be used towards flights with British Airways, Virgin Atlantic, Emirates and Etihad, and often other rewards, such as hotel stays and car hire.
- 1 point per £1 spent
- 1 point = 1 airline point
- Two free visits a year to airport lounges
- No fee in year one, then £140/yr

The downside:

- Fail to repay fully and it's 59.9% rep APR interest, incl fee

You'll need to cancel before the £140/yr fee kicks in year two if you want to avoid it.

The best air-mile credit cards for those living in Canada

Aeroplan is the superior rewards program in Canada. The card has a high earn rate for Aeroplan Points, generating 1.5 points per $1 spent on eligible purchases. Look at the specifics of the eligible purchases https://www.aircanada.com/ca/en/aco/home/aeroplan/earn.html. If you're not spending on these things AMEX's Membership Rewards program offers you the best returns in Canada.

The best air-mile credit cards for those living in Germany

If you have a German bank account, you can apply for a Lufthansa credit card.

Earn 50,000 award miles if you spend $3,000 in purchases and paying the annual fee, both within the first 90 days.

Earn 2 award miles per $1 spent on ticket purchases directly from Miles & More integrated airline partners.

Earn 1 award mile per $1 spent on all other purchases.

The downsides

the €89 annual fee

Limited to fly with Lufthansa and its partners but you can capitalise on perks like the companion pass and airport lounge vouchers.

You need excellent credit to get this card.

The best air-mile credit cards for those living in Austria

"In Austria, Miles & More offers you a special credit card. You get miles for each purchase with the credit card. The Miles & More program calculates miles earned based on the distance flown and booking class. For European flights, the booking class is a flat rate. For intercontinental flights, mileage is calculated by multiplying the booking class by the distance flown." They offer a calculator so you can see how many points you could earn: https://www.miles-and-more.com/at/en/earn/airlines/mileage-calculator.html

The best air-mile credit cards for those living in Spain:

"The American Express card is the best known and oldest to earn miles, thanks to its membership Rewards program. When making payments with this card, points are added, which can then be exchanged for miles from airlines such as Iberia, Air Europa, Emirates or Alitalia." More information is available here: https://www.americanexpress.com/es-es/

The best air-mile credit cards for those living in Australia

ANZ Rewards Black comes out top for 2024.

180,000 bonus ANZ Reward Points (can get an $800 gift card) and $0 annual fee for the first year with the ANZ Rewards Black
Points Per Spend: 1 Velocity point on purchases of up to $5,000 per statement period and 0.5 Velocity points thereafter.
Annual Fee: $0 in the first year, then $375 after.
Ns no set minimum income required, however, there is a minimum credit limit of $15,000 on this card.

Here are some ways you can hack points onto this card: https://www.pointhacks.com.au/credit-cards/anz-rewards-black-guide/

The best air-mile credit card solution for those living in the USA with a POOR credit score

The downside to Airline Mile cards is that they require good or excellent credit scores, meaning 690 or higher.

If you have bad credit and want to use credit card air lines you will need to rebuild your credit poor. The Credit One Bank® Platinum Visa® for Rebuilding Credit is a good credit card for people with bad credit who don't want to place a deposit on a secured card. The Credit One Platinum Visa offers a $300 credit limit, rewards, and the potential for credit-limit increases, which in time will help rebuild your score.

PLEASE don't sign-up for any of these cards if you can't trust yourself to repay it in full monthly. This will only lead to stress for you.

Country	Credit Card	Pros	Cons	Requires Good Credit Score?
USA	Chase Sapphire Preferred	- 60,000 bonus points after spending $4,000 in the first 3 months. - Points transfer 1:1 to leading airline and hotel loyalty programs. - $95 annual fee. - Additional benefits like trip cancellation/interruption insurance and rental car coverage.	- $95 annual fee after the first year. - Higher minimum spend requirement for bonus points. - Limited travel redemption options compared to premium cards.	Yes
UK	Amex Preferred Rewards Gold	- 20,000-point bonus on £3,000 spend in the first 3 months. - 1 point per £1 spent. - Two free visits per year to airport lounges. - No fee in the first year, then £140/year.	- High 59.9% representative APR interest rate if balance isn't repaid in full. - £140 annual fee after the first year. - Limited acceptance compared to Visa/Mastercard.	Yes
Australia	ANZ Rewards Black	- 180,000 bonus ANZ Reward Points and $0 annual fee for the first year. - 1 Velocity point on purchases up to $5,000 per statement period. - No set minimum income required.	- $375 annual fee after the first year. - Limited rewards on purchases over $5,000 per statement period. - Limited airline partnerships compared to other cards.	Yes
Canada	American Express Gold Rewards Card	- 25,000 Membership Rewards points after spending $1,500 in the first 3 months. - $100 annual travel credit. - Flexible redemption options including travel, merchandise, and gift cards.	- $150 annual fee. - Limited acceptance compared to Visa/Mastercard. - Higher minimum spend requirement compared to some other cards.	Yes

Country	Credit Card	Pros	Cons	Requires Good Credit Score?
Germany	Lufthansa Miles & More Credit Card	- Earn 50,000 award miles upon spending $3,000 within the first 90 days. - 2 award miles per $1 spent on ticket purchases from Miles & More integrated partners.	- €89 annual fee. - Limited to flights with Lufthansa and its partners. - Requires excellent credit.	Yes
Austria	Miles & More Credit Card	- Earn miles for each purchase. - Redeem miles for flights based on distance flown and booking class. - Offers a mileage calculator for estimating points.	- Limited to the Miles & More program. - Annual fee and other charges may apply. - May have limited acceptance compared to other cards.	Yes
Switzerland	SWISS Miles & More Credit Card	- Earn miles for every purchase. - Priority boarding and check-in with SWISS. - No foreign transaction fees.	- Limited to the Miles & More program. - Annual fee and other charges may apply. - May have limited acceptance compared to other cards.	Yes

Frequent Flyer Memberships

"Points" and "miles" are often used interchangeably, but they're usually two very different things. Maximise and diversify your rewards by utilising both.

A frequent-flyer program (FFP) is a loyalty program offered by an airline. They are designed to encourage airline customers to fly more to accumulate points (also called miles, kilometres, or segments) which can be redeemed for air travel or other rewards.

You can sign up with any FFP program for free. There are three major airline alliances in the world: Oneworld, SkyTeam and Star Alliance. I am with One World https://www.oneworld.com/members because the points can be accrued and used for most flights.

The best return on your points is to use them for international business or first class flights with lie-flat seats. You would need 3 times more miles compared to an economy flight, but if you paid cash, you'd pay 5 - 10 times more than the cost of the economy flight, so it really pays to use your points only for upgrades. The worst value for your miles is to buy an economy seat or worse, a gift from the airlines gift-shop.

Sign up for a family/household account to pool miles together. If you share a common address, you can claim the miles with most airlines. You can use AwardWallet to keep track of your miles. Remember that they only last for 2 years, so use them before they expire.

Airline	Frequent Flyer Membership	Pros	Cons
Delta Air Lines	SkyMiles	- No blackout dates for award flights. - Ability to earn miles through flights, credit card spending, and partners.	- Variable award pricing. - Limited availability of saver-level award seats. - Miles expiration policy.
American Airlines	AAdvantage	- Extensive network of routes and partners. - Elite status perks include complimentary upgrades, priority boarding, and waived fees.	- Dynamic award pricing. - Limited availability of saver-level award seats. - Some benefits restricted to elite members.
United Airlines	MileagePlus	- Wide range of redemption options including flights, upgrades, and merchandise. - Star Alliance membership offers access to global network.	- Variable award pricing. - Limited availability of saver-level award seats. - Some elite benefits restricted to higher-tier members.
Southwest Airlines	Rapid Rewards	- No blackout dates or seat restrictions on award flights. - Companion Pass program allows a designated companion to fly for free (excluding taxes and fees).	- Points value can vary depending on fare class. - Limited international routes compared to other carriers.

British Airways	Executive Club	- Avios points can be redeemed for flights, upgrades, and partner awards. - Tiered membership offers benefits like lounge access and priority check-in.	- High fuel surcharges on some award flights. - Distance-based award chart may not offer good value for short-haul flights. - Limited partner availability.
Emirates	Skywards	- Access to luxury experiences like first-class flights and premium lounges. - Family membership allows pooling of miles for faster rewards.	- High fuel surcharges on some award flights. - Limited availability of premium cabin award seats. - Tier-based earning and benefits.

How to get 70% off a Cruise

An average cruise can set you back $4,000. If you dream of cruising the oceans, but find the pricing too high, look at repositioning cruises. You can save as much as 70% by taking a cruise which takes the boat back to its home port.

These one-way itineraries take place during low cruise seasons when ships have to reposition themselves to locations where there's warmer weather.

To find a repositioning cruise, go to vacationstogo.com/repositioning_cruises.cfm. This simple and often overlooked booking trick is great for avoiding long flights with children and can save you so much money!

It's worth noting we don't have any affiliations with any travel service or provider. The links we suggest are chosen based on our experience of finding the best deals.

Cruise Line	Repositioning Cruise Offerings	Pros	Cons
Royal Caribbean	- Offers repositioning cruises between continents, such as transatlantic or transpacific voyages.	- Opportunity to explore multiple destinations during one cruise. - Typically longer itineraries with more sea days. - Potential for lower fares compared to traditional cruises due to one-way routes.	- Limited availability as repositioning cruises are seasonal and occur during specific times of the year. - Some passengers may prefer shorter, port-intensive itineraries. - May involve one-way airfare or additional travel arrangements.
Princess Cruises	- Repositioning cruises span various regions, including Asia, Europe, and the Americas.	- Offers diverse itineraries with stops in different countries and regions. - Longer duration allows for more onboard activities and relaxation. - Potential for lower fares compared to regular sailings.	- Limited departure dates and availability as repositioning cruises typically occur during shoulder seasons. - One-way itinerary may require additional travel arrangements.
Celebrity Cruises	- Transatlantic and transpacific repositioning cruises between Europe, the Caribbean, and Alaska.	- Modern luxury experience with upscale amenities and dining options. - Opportunity to visit multiple destinations in one trip. - Possibility of special onboard events or enrichment programs during longer voyages.	- Limited availability as repositioning cruises are seasonal and occur during specific times of the year. - Higher fares for premium amenities and services may not fit all budgets. - Potential for additional costs associated with one-way travel.

Holland America	- Offers transatlantic and transpacific repositioning cruises, including itineraries between Europe, the Caribbean, and Alaska.	- Classic cruising experience with traditional elegance and attentive service. - Enrichment programs and onboard activities tailored for longer voyages. - Chance to explore diverse ports of call across continents.	- Limited departure dates and availability as repositioning cruises typically occur during shoulder seasons. - One-way itinerary may require additional travel arrangements.
Norwegian Cruise Line	- Repositioning cruises between the Caribbean, Europe, and Alaska, offering diverse itineraries with multiple sea days.	- Freestyle cruising concept allows for flexibility in dining and entertainment options. - Wide range of onboard activities and entertainment to suit various interests. - Possibility of lower fares compared to standard sailings.	- Limited availability as repositioning cruises are seasonal and occur during specific times of the year. - May involve one-way airfare or additional travel arrangements. - Some passengers may prefer shorter, port-intensive itineraries.

Relaxing at the Airport

The best way to relax at the airport is in a lounge where they provide free food, drinks, comfortable chairs, luxurious amenities (many have showers) and, if you're lucky, a peaceful ambience. If you're there for a longer time, look for Airport Cubicles, sleep pods which charge by the hour.

You can use your FFP Card (Frequent Flyer Memberships) to get into select lounges for free. Check your eligibility before you pay.

If you're travelling a lot, I'd recommend investing in a Priority Pass for the airport.

It includes 850-plus airport lounges around the world. The cost is $99 for the year and $27 per lounge visit or you can pay $399 for the year all inclusive.

If you need a lounge for a one-off day, you can get a Day Pass. Buy it online for a discount, it always works out cheaper than buying at the airport. Use www.LoungePass.com.

Lounges are also great if you're travelling with kids, as they're normally free for kids and will definitely cost you less than snacks for your little ones. The rule is that kids should be seen and not heard, so consider this before taking an overly excited child who wants to run around, or you might be asked to leave even after you've paid.

Method	Pros	Cons
Priority Pass	- Access to a large network of airport lounges worldwide- Various membership levels available- Some plans include free visits	- Annual membership fee- Additional fee for guest visits- Limited to participating lounges
Credit Card	- Complimentary lounge access as a card benefit- Additional travel perks- No need for separate membership	- High annual fee for premium cards- Limited to specific lounges- May require minimum spending or qualifications
Airline Status	- Lounge access based on frequent flyer status- Available to elite members of airline loyalty programs	- Requires achieving and maintaining elite status- Limited to specific airlines and alliances
Day Passes	- Flexibility to purchase access only when needed- No annual commitment	- Can be expensive for frequent travelers- Availability may be limited depending on lounge capacity and policies
Membership Programs	- Annual membership provides consistent lounge access- Loyalty benefits with the airline- Access to additional perks depending on program	- Annual membership fee- Limited to lounges operated by the airline or its partners
Subscription Services	- Pay-per-visit access- No annual commitment- Access to a variety of lounges	- Per-visit fee may add up for frequent travelers- Limited availability in some airports- Additional fees for certain features or lounges

How to spend money

Bank ATM fees vary from $2.50 per transaction to as high as $5 or more, depending on the ATM and the country. You can completely skip those fees by paying with card and using a card which can hold multiple currencies.

Budget travel hacking begins with a strategy to spend without fees. Your individual strategy depends on the country you legally reside in as to what cards are available. Happily there are some fin-tech solutions which can save you thousands on those pesky ATM withdrawal fees and are widely available globally. Here are a selection of cards you can pre-charge with currency for Ireland:

N26

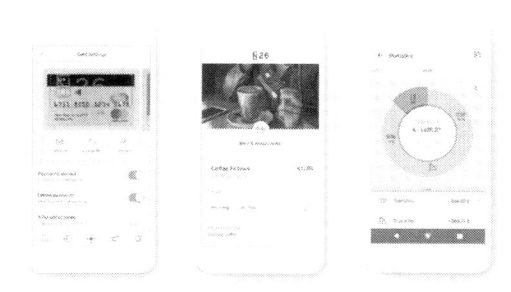

N26 is a 12-year-old digital bank. I have been using them for over 6 years. The key advantage is fee-free card transactions abroad. They have a very elegant app, where you can check your timeline for all transactions listed in real time or manage your in-app security anywhere. The card you receive is a Mastercard so you can use it everywhere. If you lose the card, you don't have to call anyone, just open the app and swipe 'lock card'. It puts your purchases into a graph automatically so you can see what you spend on. You can open an account from abroad entirely online, all you need is your passport and a camera n26.com

Revolut

Revolut is a multi-currency account that allows you to hold and exchange 29 currencies and spend fee-free abroad. It's a UK based neobank, but accepts customers from all over the world.

Wise debit card

If you're going to be in one place for a long time, the Wise debit card is like having your travel money on a card – it lets you spend money at the real exchange rate.

Monzo

Monzo is good if your UK based. They offer a fee-free UK account. Fee-free international money transfers and fee-free spending abroad.

The downside

The cards above are debit cards, meaning you need to have money in those accounts to spend it. This comes with one big downside: safety. Credit card issuers' have "zero liability" meaning you're not liable for unauthorised charges. All the cards listed above do provide cover for unauthorised charges but times vary greatly in how quickly you'd get your money back if it were stolen.

The best option is to check in your country to see which credit cards are the best for travelling and set up monthly payments to repay the whole amount so you don't pay unnecessary interest. In the USA, Schwab regularly ranks at the top for travel credit cards. Credit cards are always the safer option when abroad simply because you get your money back faster if its stolen and if you're renting cars, most will give you free insurance when you book the car rental using the card, saving you money.

Always withdraw money; never exchange.

Money exchanges, whether they be on the streets or in the airports will NEVER give you a good exchange rate. Do not bring bundles of cash. Instead, withdraw local currency from the ATM as needed and try to use only free ATMs. Many in airports charge you a fee to withdraw cash. Look for bigger ATMs attached to banks to avoid this.

Recap

- Take cash from local, non-charging ATMs for the best rates.
- Never change at airport exchange desks unless you absolutely have to, then just change just enough to be able get to a bank ATM.
- Bring a spare credit card for emergencies.
- Split cash in various places on your person (pockets, shoes) and in your luggage. It's never sensible to keep your cash or cards all in one place.
- In higher risk areas, use a money belt under your clothes or put $50 in your shoe or bra.

Revolut
Revolut is a multi-currency account that allows you to hold and exchange 29 currencies and spend fee-free abroad. It's a UK based neobank, but accepts customers from all over the world.

Wise debit card
If you're going to be in one place for a long time the Wise debit card is like having your travel money on a card – it lets you spend money at the real exchange rate.

Monzo
Monzo is good if your UK based. They offer a fee-free UK account. Fee-free international money transfers and fee-free spending abroad.

The downside

The cards above are debit cards, meaning you need to have money in those accounts to spend it. This comes with one big downside: safety. Credit card issuers' have "zero liability" meaning you're not liable for unauthorised charges. All of the cards listed above do provide cover for unauthorised charges but times vary greatly in how quickly you'd get your money back if it were stolen.

The best option is to check in your country to see which credit cards are the best for travelling and set up monthly payments to repay the whole amount so you don't pay unnecessary interest. In the USA, Schwab[4] regularly ranks at the top for travel credit cards. Credit cards are always the safer option when abroad simply because you get your money back faster if its stolen and if you're renting cars, most will give you free insurance when you book the car rental using the card, saving you money.

Always withdraw money; never exchange.

Money exchanges whether they be on the streets or in the airports will NEVER give you a good exchange rate. Do not bring bundles of cash. Instead withdraw local currency from the ATM as needed and try to use only free ATM's. Many in airports charge you a fee to withdraw cash. Look for bigger ATM's attached to banks to avoid this.

Recap

- Take cash from local, non-charging ATMs for the best rates.
- Never change at airport exchange desks unless you absolutely have to, then just change just enough to be able get to a bank ATM.
- Bring a spare credit card for emergencies.
- Split cash in various places on your person (pockets, shoes) and in your luggage. Its never sensible to keep your cash or cards all in one place.
- In higher risk areas, use a money belt under your clothes or put $50 in your shoe or bra.

---

[4] Charles Schwab High Yield Checking accounts refund every single ATM fee worldwide, require no minimum balance and have no monthly fee.

Card Provider	Pre-Charge Currency Feature	Pros	Cons
Revolut	Ability to pre-charge multiple currencies onto the card	- Convenient for international travel and spending in different countries.	- Limited physical presence (mostly app-based). - Some fees may apply for certain transactions or currency conversions.
TransferWise	Multi-currency account with prepaid card	- Low-cost international transfers and currency conversion.	- Limited availability of physical card in some regions. - Some fees may apply for certain transactions or currency conversions.
N26	N26 You and N26 Metal offer multi-currency functionality	- No foreign transaction fees for card usage abroad.	- Limited availability of N26 Metal and its features in some regions. - Some fees may apply for certain transactions.
Wise (formerly known as TransferWise)	Borderless account with debit card	- Ability to hold and convert multiple currencies with real exchange rates.	- Limited ATM withdrawal allowance before fees apply. - Some fees may apply for certain transactions or currency conversions.
Monzo	Monzo Plus offers multi-currency functionality	- Easy management of money in different currencies.	- Limited availability of Monzo Plus and its features in some regions. - Some fees may apply for certain transactions.
Bunq	Bunq Travel Card with multi-currency feature	- No foreign transaction fees and competitive exchange rates.	- Limited availability of Bunq Travel Card and its features in some regions. - Some fees may apply for certain transactions.
Payoneer	Payoneer Prepaid Mastercard with multi-currency support	- Ability to receive funds from international clients and hold multiple currencies.	- Relatively high fees for currency conversion and ATM withdrawals. - Limited use for retail purchases in some regions.

How NOT to be ripped off

"One of the great things about travel is that you find out how many good, kind people there are."
— Edith Wharton

The quote above may seem ill placed in a chapter entitled how not to be ripped off, but I included it to remind you that the vast majority of people do not want to rip you off. In fact, scammers are normally limited to three situations:

1. Around heavily visited attractions - these places are targeted purposively due to sheer footfall. Many criminals believe ripping people off is simply a numbers game.
2. In cities or countries with low-salaries or communist ideologies. If they can't make money in the country, they seek to scam foreigners. If you have travelled to India, Morocco or Cuba you will have observed this phenomenon.
3. When you are stuck and the person helping you know you have limited options.

Scammers know that most people will avoid confrontation. Don't feel bad about utterly ignoring someone and saying no. Here are six strategies to avoid being ripped off:

1. **Never ever agree to pay as much as you want. Always decide on a price before.**

Whoever you're dealing with is trained to tell you, they are uninterested in money. This is a trap. If you let people do this they will ask for MUCH MORE money at the end, and because you have used there service, you will feel obliged to pay. This is a conman's trick and nothing more.

2. Pack light

You can move faster and easier. If you take heavy luggage, you will end up taking taxis which are comparatively very costly over time.

3. NEVER use the airport taxi service. Plan to use public transport before you reach the airport.

4. Don't buy a sim card from the airport. Buy from the local supermarkets it will cost 50% less.

5. Eat at local restaurants serving regional food

Food defines culture. Exploring all delights available to the palate doesn't need to cost enormous sums.

6. **Ask the locals what something should cost,** and try not to pay over that.

7. **If you find yourself with limited options.** e.g. your taxi dumps you on the side of the road because you refuse to pay more (common in India and parts of South America) don't act desperate and negotiate as if you have other options or you will be extorted.

8. Don't blindly rely on social media[5]

Let's say you post in a Facebook group that you want tips for travelling to The Maldives. A lot of the comments you will receive come from guides, hosts and restaurants doing their own promotion. It's estimated that 50% or more of Facebook's current monthly active users are fake. And what's worse, a recent study found Social media platforms leave 95% of reported fake accounts up. These accounts are the digital versions of the men who hang around the Grand Palace in Bangkok telling tourists its closed, to divert you to shops where they will receive a commission for bringing you.

It can also be the case that genuine comments come from people who have totally different interests, beliefs and yes, budgets to yours. Make your experience your own and don't believe every comment you read.

Bottom line: use caution when accepting recommendations on social media and always fact-check with your own research.

Small tweaks on the road add up to big differences in your bank balance

Take advantage of other hotel amenities

If you fancy a swim but you're nowhere near the ocean, try the nearest hotel with a pool. As long as you buy a drink, the hotel staff will probably grant you access.

Fill up your mini bar for free.

Fill up your mini bar for free by storing things from the breakfast bar or grocery shop in your mini bar to give you a greater selection of drinks and food without the hefty price tag.

Save yourself some ironing

Use the steam from the shower to get rid of wrinkles in clothing. If something is creased, leave it trapped with the steam in the bathroom overnight for even better results.

See somewhere else for free

Opt for long stopovers, allowing you to experience another city without spending much money.

Wear your heaviest clothes

On the plane to save weight in your pack, allowing you to bring more with you. Big coats can then be used as pillows to make your flight more comfortable.

Don't get lost while you're away.

Find where you want to go using Google Maps, then type 'OK Maps' into the search bar to store this information for offline viewing.

---

[5] https://arstechnica.com/tech-policy/2019/12/social-media-platforms-leave-95-of-reported-fake-accounts-up-study-finds/

Use car renting services

Share Now or Car2Go allow you to hire a car for 2 hours for $25 in a lot of European countries.

Share Rides

Use sites like blablacar.com to find others who are driving in your direction. It can be 80% cheaper than normal transport. Just check the drivers reviews.

Use free gym passes

Get a free gym day pass by googling the name of a local gym and free day pass.

When asked by people providing you a service where you are from..

If there's no price list for the service you are asking for, when asked where you are from, Say you are from a lesser-known poorer country. I normally say Macedonia, and if they don't know where it is, add it's a poor country. If you say UK, USA, the majority of Europe bar the well-known poorer countries taxi drivers, tour operators etc will match the price to what they think you pay at home.

Set-up a New Uber/ other car hailing app account for discounts

By googling you can find offers with $50 free for new users in most cities for Uber/ Lyft/ Bolt and alike. Just set up a new gmail.com email account to take advantage.

Where and How to Make Friends

"People don't take trips, trips take people." – John Steinbeck

Become popular at the airport

Want to become popular at the airport? Pack a power bar with multiple outlets and just see how many friends you can make. It's amazing how many people forget their chargers, or who packed them in the luggage that they checked in.

Stay in Hostels

First of all, Hostels don't have to be shared dorms, and they cater to a much wider demographic than is assumed. Hostels are a better environment for meeting people than hotels, and more importantly, they tended to open up excursion opportunities that further opened up that opportunity.

Or take up a hobby

If hostels are a definite no-no for you; find an interest. Take up a hobby where you will meet people. I've dived for years and the nature of diving is you're always paired up with a dive buddy. I met a lot of interesting people that way.

Small tweaks on the road add up to big differences in your bank balance

Take advantage of other hotel's amenities

If you fancy a swim but you're nowhere near the ocean, try the nearest hotel with a pool. As long as you buy a drink, the hotel staff will likely grant you access.

Fill up your mini bar for free.

Fill up your mini bar for free by storing things from the breakfast bar or grocery shop in your mini bar to give you a greater selection of drinks and food without the hefty price tag.

Save yourself some ironing

Use the steam from the shower to get rid of wrinkles in clothing. If something is creased, leave it trapped with the steam in the bathroom overnight for even better results.

See somewhere else for free

Opt for long stopovers, allowing you to experience another city without spending much money.

Wear your heaviest clothes

on the plane to save weight in your pack, allowing you to bring more with you. Big coats can then be used as pillows to make your flight more comfortable.

Don't get lost while you're away.

Find where you want to go using Google Maps, then type 'OK Maps' into the search bar to store this information for offline viewing.

Use car renting services

Share Now or Car2Go allow you to hire a car for 2 hours for $25 in a lot of Europe.

Share Rides

Use sites like blablacar.com to find others who are driving in your direction. It can be 80% cheaper than normal transport. Just check the drivers reviews.

Use free gym passes

Get a free gym day pass by googling the name of a local gym and free day pass.

When asked by people providing you a service where you are from..

If there's no price list for the service you are asking for, when asked where you are from, Say you are from a lesser-known poorer country. I normally say Macedonia, and if they don't know where it is, add it's a poor country. If you say UK, USA, the majority of Europe bar the well-known poorer countries taxi drivers, tour operators etc will match the price to what they think you pay at home.

Set-up a New Uber/ other car hailing app account for discounts

By googling you can find offers with $50 free for new users in most cities for Uber/ Lyft/ Bolt and alike. Just set up a new gmail.com email account to take advantage.

Where and How to Make Friends

"People don't take trips, trips take people." – John Steinbeck

Become popular at the airport

Want to become popular at the airport? Pack a power bar with multiple outlets and just see how many friends you can make. It's amazing how many people forget their chargers, or who packed them in the luggage that they checked in.

Stay in Hostels

First of all, Hostels don't have to be shared dorms, and they cater to a much wider demographic than is assumed. Hostels are a better environment for meeting people than hotels, and more importantly they tended to open up excursion opportunities that further opened up that opportunity.

Or take up a hobby

If hostels are a definite no-no for you; find an interest. Take up a hobby where you will meet people. I've dived for years and the nature of diving is you're always paired up with a dive buddy. I met a lot of interesting people that way.

When unpleasantries come your way...

We all have our good and bad days travelling, and on a bad day you can feel like just taking a flight home. Here are some ways to overcome common travel problems:

Anxiety when flying

It has been over 40 years since a plane has been brought down by turbulence. Repeat that number to yourself: 40 years! Planes are built to withstand lighting strikes, extreme storms and ultimately can adjust course to get out of their way. Landing and take-off are when the most accidents happen, but you have statistically three times the chance of winning a huge jackpot lottery, then you do of dying in a plane crash.

If you feel afraid on the flight, focus on your breathing saying the word 'smooth' over and over until the flight is smooth. Always check the airline safety record on airlinerating.com I was surprised to learn Ryanair and Easyjet as much less safe than Wizz Air according to those ratings because they sell similarly priced flights. If there is extreme turbulence, I feel much better knowing I'm in a 7 star safety plane.

Supplements can really help relieve the symptoms of anxiety. Here are the best. I've taken all of these and never have problems, but please consult a medical doctor if you are on any other medications.

Supplement	Benefits	Cons
Magnesium Glycinate	- Tons of clinical data say it helps relax muscles and promote calmness.	- May cause gastrointestinal discomfort in some individuals.
CBD oil (Cannabidiol)	- May help reduce anxiety and promote relaxation	- Legality and regulations may vary by region.
Valerian Root	- Herbal remedy for anxiety and sleep	- May cause drowsiness and dizziness.
Chamomile	- Herbal tea with calming properties.	- May cause allergic reactions in some individuals.

Wanting to sleep instead of seeing new places

This is a common problem. Just relax, there's little point doing fun things when you feel tired. Factor in jet-lag to your travel plans. When you're rested and alert you'll enjoy your new temporary home much more. Many people hate the first week of a long-trip because of jet-lag and often blame this on their first destination, but its rarely true. Ask travellers who 'hate' a particular place and you will see that very often they either had jet-lag or an unpleasant journey there.

Going over budget

Come back from a trip to a monster credit card bill? Hopefully, this guide has prevented you from returning to an unwanted bill. Of course, there are costs that can creep up and this is a reminder about how to prevent them making their way on to your credit card bill:

- To and from the airport. Solution: leave adequate time and take the cheapest method - book before.
- Baggage. Solution: take hand luggage and post things you might need to yourself.
- Eating out. Solution: go to cheap eats places and suggest those to friends.
- Parking. Solution: use apps to find free parking
- Tipping. Solution Leave a modest tip and tell the server you will write them a nice review.
- Souvenirs. Solution: fridge magnets only.
- Giving to the poor. (This one still gets me, but if you're giving away $10 a day - it adds up) Solution: volunteer your time instead and recognise that in tourist destinations many beggars are run by organised crime gangs.

Price v Comfort

I love traveling. I don't love struggling. I like decent accommodation, being able to eat properly and see places and enjoy. I am never in the mood for low-cost airlines or crappy transfers, so here's what I do to save money.

- Avoid organised tours unless you are going to a place where safety is a real issue. They are expensive and constrain your wanderlust to typical things. I only recommend them in Algeria, Iran and Papua New Guinea - where language and gender views pose serious problems all cured by a reputable tour organiser.
- Eat what the locals do.
- Cook in your Airbnb/ hostel where restaurants are expensive.
- Shop at local markets.
- Spend time choosing your flight, and check the operator on arilineratings.com
- Mix up hostels and Airbnbs. Hostels for meeting people, Airbnb for relaxing and feeling 'at home'.

Eat Hot Meals While You're Exploring

This is one hack that saves my family thousands a year. Using a thermos allows you to eat hot food while enjoying the sights. Here's a guide on how to do it effectively along with some recipes:

- **Choose the Right Thermos**: Look for thermoses with double-wall insulation and a wide mouth for easy filling and cleaning.

- **Preheat the Thermos**: Fill the thermos with boiling water and let it sit for a few minutes before pouring out the water and adding your hot food. This will help to maintain the temperature of your meal for longer.
- **Choose the right food**: soups, stews, pasta dishes, or even oatmeal for breakfast. Anything crispy will go soggy in the thermos.

Now, here are some food ideas that work well for packing in a thermos:

- **Hotdogs:** Just cook the dogs, pack buns and ketchup etc and you have a meal for four or more. This is great at outdoor markets with kids and can save you $20 + a day.
- **Chicken Congee**: A chicken porridge.
- **Vegetable Soup**: A hearty vegetable soup with beans or lentils is a satisfying and nutritious option. Make a big batch at home and portion it into the thermos for a warm and comforting meal on the go.
- **Chili**: Cook up a batch of your favorite chili recipe and pack it in the thermos. It's flavorful, filling, and perfect for chilly days.
- **Pasta with Tomato Sauce**: Cook your favorite pasta and toss it with a rich tomato sauce. This dish reheats well and tastes delicious straight from the thermos.
- **Curry**: Prepare a flavorful curry with vegetables, tofu, chicken, or meat of your choice. Serve it with rice or naan bread for a complete meal.
- **Oatmeal**: For breakfast on the go, make a batch of oatmeal with your favorite toppings such as nuts, fruits, and honey. It will stay warm and keep you full until lunchtime.

Not knowing where free toilets are

Use Toilet Finder - https://play.google.com/store/apps/details?id=com.bto.toilet&hl=en

Your Airbnb is awful

Airbnb customer service is notoriously bad. Help yourself out. Try to sort things out with the host, but if you can't, take photos of everything e.g bed, bathroom, mess, doors, contact them within 24 hours. Tell them you had to leave and pay for new accommodation. Ask politely for a full refund including booking fees. With photographic evidence and your new accommodation receipt, they can't refuse.

The airline loses your bag

Go to the Luggage desk before leaving the airport and report the bag missing. Hopefully you've headed the advice to put an AirTag in your checked bag and you can show them where to find your bag. Most airlines will give you an overnight bag, ask where you're staying and return the bag to you within three days. It's extremely rare for Airlines to lose your bag due to technological innovation, but if that happens you should submit an insurance claim after the three days is up, including receipts for everything you had to buy in the interim.

Your travel companion lets you down

Whether it's a breakup or a friend cancelling, it sucks and can ramp up costs. The easiest solution to finding a new travel companion is to go to a well-reviewed hostel and find someone you want to travel with. You should spend at least three days getting to know this person before you suggest travelling together. Finding someone in person is always better than finding someone online, because you can get a better idea of whether you will have a smooth journey together. Travel can make or break friendships.

Culture shock

I had one of the strongest culture shocks while spending 6 months in Japan. It was overwhelming how much I had to prepare when I went outside of the door (googling words and sentences what to use, where to go, which station and train line to use, what is this food called in Japanese and how does its look etc.). I was so tired constantly but in the end I just let go and went with my extremely bad Japanese. If you feel culture shocked its because your brain is referencing your surroundings to what you know. Stop comparing, have Google translate downloaded and relax.

Your Car rental insurance is crazy expensive

I always use carrentals.com and book with a credit card. Most credit cards will give you free insurance for the car, so you don't need to pay the extra. Some unsavoury companies will bump the price up when you arrive. Ask to speak to a manager. If this doesn't resolve, it google "consumer ombudsman for NAME OF COUNTRY." and seek an immediate full refund on the balance difference you paid. It is illegal in most countries to alter the price of a rental car when the person arrives to pickup a pre-arranged car.

A note on Car Rental Insurance

Always always always rent a car with a credit card that has rental vehicle coverage built into the card and is automatically applied when you rent a car. Then there's no need to buy additional rental insurance (check with your card on the coverage they protect some exclude collision coverage). Do yourself a favour when you step up to the desk to rent the car tell the agent you're already covered and won't be buying anything today. They work on commission and you'll save time and your patience avoiding the upselling.

You're sick

First off ALWAYS, purchase travel insurance. Including emergency transport up to $500k even to back home, which is usually less than $10 additional. I use https://www.comparethemarket.com/travel-insurance/ to find the best days. If I am sick I normally check into a hotel with room service and ride it out.

Make a Medication Travel Kit

Take travel sized medications with you:

- Antidiarrheal medication (for example, bismuth subsalicylate, loperamide)
- Medicine for pain or fever (such as acetaminophen, aspirin, or ibuprofen)
- Throat Lozenges

Save yourself from most travel related hassles

- Do not make jokes with immigration and customs staff. A misunderstanding can lead to HUGE fines.

- Book the most direct flight you can find nonstop if possible.

- Carry a US$50 bill for emergency cash. I have entered a country and all ATM and credit card systems were down. US$ can be exchanged nearly anywhere in the world and is useful in extreme situations, but where possible don't exchange, as you will lose money.

- Check, and recheck, required visas and such BEFORE the day of your trip. Some countries, for instance, require a ticket out of the country in order to enter. Others, like the US and Australia, require electronic authorisation in advance.

- Airport security is asinine and inconsistent around the world. Keep this in mind when connecting flights. Always leave at least 2 hours for international connections or international to domestic. In Stansted for example, they force you to buy one of their plastic bags, and remove your liquids from your own plastic bag.... just to make money from you. And this adds to the time it will take to get through security, so lines are long.

- Wiki travel is perfect to use for a lay of the land.

- Expensive luggage rarely lasts longer than cheap luggage, in my experience. Fancy leather bags are toast with air travel.

Food

- When it comes to food, eat in local restaurants, not tourist-geared joints. Any place with the menu in three or more languages is going to be overpriced.

- Take a spork - a knife, spoon and fork all in one.

Water Bottle

Take a water bottle with a filter. We love these ones from Water to Go.

Empty it before airport security and separate the bottle and filter as some airport people will try and claim it has liquids...

Bug Sprays

If you're heading somewhere tropical spray your clothes with Permethrin before you travel. It lasts 40 washes and saves space in your bag. A 'Bite Away' zapper can be used after the bite to totally erase it. It cuts down on the itching and erases the bite from your skin.

Order free mini's

Don't buy those expensive travel sized toiletries, order travel sized freebies online. This gives you the opportunity to try brands you've never used before, and who knows, you might even find your new favourite soap.

Take a waterproof bag

If you're travelling alone you can swim without worrying about your phone, wallet and passport laying on the beach.

You can also use it as a source of entertainment on those ultra budget flights.

Make a private entertainment centre anywhere

Always take an eye-mask, earplugs, a scarf and a kindle reader - so you can sleep and entertain yourself anywhere!

The best Travel Gadgets

The door alarm

If you're nervous and staying in private rooms or airbnbs take a door alarm. For those times when you just don't feel safe, it can help you fall asleep. You can get tiny ones for less than $10 from Online Retailers: https://www.Online Retailers.com/Travel-door-alarm/s?k=Travel+door+alarm

Smart Blanket

Online Retailers sells a 6 in 1 heating blanket that is very useful for cold plane or bus trips. Its great if you have poor circulation as it becomes a detachable Foot Warmer: Online Retailers http://amzn.to/2hTYIOP I paid $49.00.

The coat that becomes a tent

https://www.adiff.com/products/tent-jacket. This is great if you're going to be doing a lot of camping.

Clever Tank Top with Secret Pockets

Keep your valuables safe in this top. Perfect for all climates. https://www.Online Retailers.com/Clever-Travel-Companion-Unisex-secret/dp/B00O94PXLE on Online Retailers for $39.90

Optical Camera Lens for Smartphones and Tablets

Leave your bulky camera at home. Turn your device into a high-performance camera. Buy on Online Retailers for $9.95

Travel-sized Wireless Router with USB Media Storage

Convert any wired network to a wireless network. Buy on Online Retailers for $17.99

Buy a Scrubba Bag to wash your clothes on the go

Or a cheaper imitable. You can wash your clothes on the go.

Hacks for Families

Rent an Airbnb apartment so you can cook

Apartments are much better for families, as you have all the amenities you'd have at home. They are normally cheaper per person too. We are the first travel guide publisher to include Airbnb's in our recommendations if you think any of these need updating you can email me at philgtang@gmail.com

Shop at local markets

Eat seasonal products and local products. Get closer to the local market and observe the prices and the offer. What you can find more easily, will be the cheapest.

Take Free Tours

Download free podcast tours of the destination you are visiting. The podcast will tell you where to start, where to go, and what to look for. Often you can find multiple podcast tours of the same place. Listen to all of them if you like, each one will tell you a little something new.

Pack Extra Ear Phones

If you go on a museum tour, they often have audio guides. Instead of having to rent one for each person, take some extra earphones. Most audio tour devices have a place to plug in a second set.

Buy Souvenirs Ahead of Time

If you are buying souvenirs somewhere touristy, you are paying a premium price. By ordering the same exact products online, you can save a lot of money.

Use Cheap Transportation

Do as the locals do, including weekly passes.

Carry Reusable Water Bottles

Spending money on water and other beverages can quickly add up. Instead of paying for drinks, take some refillable water bottles.

Combine Attractions

Many major cities offer ticket bundles where one price gets you into 5 or 6 popular attractions. You will need to plan ahead of time to decide what things you plan to do on vacation and see if they are selling these activities together.

Pack Snacks

Granola bars, apples, baby carrots, bananas, cheese crackers, juice boxes, pretzels, fruit snacks, apple sauce, grapes, and veggie chips.

Stick to Carry-On Bags

Do not pay to check a large bag. Even a small child can pull a carry-on.

Visit free art galleries and museums

Just google the name + free days.

Eat Street Food

There's a lot of unnecessary fear around this. You can watch the food prepared. Go for the stands that have a steady queue.

Travel Gadgets for Families

Dropcam

Are what-if scenarios playing out in your head? Then you need Dropcam.

'Dropcam HD Internet Wi-Fi Video Monitoring Cameras help you watch what you love from anywhere. In less than a minute, you'll have it setup and securely streaming video to you over your home Wi-Fi. Watch what you love while away with Dropcam HD.'

Approximate Price: $139

Kelty-Child-Carrier

Voted as one of the best hiking essentials if you're traveling with kids and can carry a child up to 18kg.

Jetkids Bedbox

No more giving up your own personal space on the plane with this suitcase that becomes a bed.

How to Believe Something You Don't Believe

"Our deepest fear is not that we are inadequate. Our deepest fear is that we are powerful beyond measure." Marianne Williamson.

To embark on a luxurious trip to Ireland on a budget requires more than just the tips in this book and financial planning; it demands a shift in mindset. It require you believing in abundance, in your ability to have anything you really want. While it may seem daunting, especially when faced with harsh realities of the cost of living crisis, etc, **fostering a belief in abundance is truly life-changing.**

The common advice is to "act as if" or "feel as if." I wholeheartedly concur, yet the challenge arises when one's circumstances appear far from prosperous. You're juggling multiple jobs, drowning in debt, and attempting to conjure the feeling of opulence? How is this even possible?

I understand this struggle intimately. I grew up poor in London. I was a kid from a run-down council estate where gang violence sent nine of my closest friends to prison. I went to an average state school. At 19 I went to one of England's elite universities to study Law. Out of 2,000 students, it was just me who didn't come from a background of privilege. Talk about a fish out of water?

I didn't just feel poor; I was. My clothes had holes, I couldn't afford a laptop or even books (even on a scholarship) and don't even get me started on culture and etiquette. It felt like I was playing a game without knowing the rules. I was about to quit and then my dad said this : "You are better than everyone here because you earned you spot. You've weathered losses that would break others." It was a lie, a big fat one, that would hurt me later, but boy, did it get me through law school.

I graduated top of my class, secured a prestigious job, and even launched my own successful business. Yet, despite my newfound wealth and the errant belief that I was "better", I still felt like the kid from the council estate with holes in my shoes.

Life gives you what you believe. I lost most of my money investing in a start-up, and of course, I found a strange comfort in my familiar poverty. **This sparked an introspective journey: How could I believe in abundance and success when my own mind seemed to be comfortable in poverty? How could I believe something I didn't believe?**

First, I recognized that abundance comes in many forms. I replaced 'money' with 'abundance.' Somehow, this just felt way less stressful than the word 'money.' I don't know how it feels for you, but try it out.

I was pretty horrified to release my core belief was I was somehow better off poor but when I finally did, I embarked on the journey to transform my relationship with abundance. Since undertaking this journey in 2016. I've accomplished significant milestones: purchasing a home in Vienna, pursuing my passion for writing travel guides, getting married, having two children, and embracing abundance. **These are the exact steps I took to believe…**

Affirmations

Affirmations are positive statements that challenge self-sabotaging and negative thoughts. Repeating these affirmations make most people feel like "this is a load of bull". That's why you have to find a belief that is believable and specific to the desired outcome you are going for. Was it true that I was better than everyone at the University because I came from poverty? No. It most definitely wasn't, but believing it gave me the confidence I needed to succeed (and fuelled my ego).

- **Find your believable affirmation**: You could start with "I'm in the process of taking lots of luxury vacations every year". If you add "I'm in the process" it makes it way more believable. In the beginning, I just repeated to myself: 'I can have everything and anything I desire.'
- **Consistency in Writing:** It's crucial to write down affirmations daily, preferably in the morning and before bed, to strengthen the new belief. Merely placing them somewhere isn't enough; research suggests that when we're constantly exposed to something, we tune it out. By physically writing out the affirmations, you engage muscle memory, imprinting them more deeply.

Visualization

Used widely in sports psychology and personal development for its effectiveness in enhancing performance and fostering belief in one's abilities. "If you go there in the mind, you're go there in the body."

- **Detailed Imagery:** The more detailed your visualization, the more effective it will be. Imagine the sights, sounds, and feelings associated with your desired belief or outcome. You might imagine, the hot sun on your back, the air skirting over your skin in that aircon'ed bar.
- **Know it works**: A study published in Psychosomatic Medicine investigated the effects of pre-surgery visualization on surgical outcomes. Patients who practiced guided imagery and visualization before undergoing surgery experienced shorter hospital stays, fewer postoperative complications, and faster recovery times compared to those who didn't engage in visualization exercises. This research shows that mental rehearsal can positively impact surgical outcomes and recovery processes. If it can affect surgery outcomes, it can affect your vacation!
- **Visualise your rich person problems**: My first job out of university was risk assessment. I was promoted again and again because I could identify the risks of any endeavor within 15 seconds. My brain still works like that. I take my 3-year-old swimming, and before we've even gotten in the pool, I've identified 14 threats and a flat surface to deliver CPR to her… It's a human trait to worry so why not use your ability to worry to your advantage? Imagine all the "problems" you'll have when you're abundant. Your cocktail on a tropical beach might be too cold. You might forget to tax-deduct all the donations you made to charities. You might tip someone really well and find them hugging you desperately. Don't take this too far; you don't want to manifest actual problems, but it definitely redirects your mind to believe you are rich.

Mo' Money Mo' Problems isn't true

Contrary to the popular notion that "more money, more problems," recent studies suggest otherwise. Achieving a certain level of financial comfort alleviates many concerns. Research indicates that individuals who feel financially secure tend to experience higher levels of overall life satisfaction and lower levels of stress. This comfort allows for greater flexibility in decision-making, reduces anxiety about meeting basic needs, and provides a sense of stability for the future. While excessive wealth does not necessarily equate to happiness, having enough resources to cover necessities and pursue meaningful experiences significantly enhance your quality of life.

Behavioral Experiments

Behavioral experiments involve acting as if you already hold the new belief. This "fake it till you make it" approach can gradually shift your internal beliefs to align with your actions.

- **Dress the Part:** In London we say "If you look good, you feel good." Consider upgrading your look. This doesn't mean splurging on designer brands; it's about being smart and feeling good in what you wear. Think of it as costume design for the movie of your life where you're the wealthy protagonist. Clean, well-fitted, and confident clothes can change your self-perception and how others perceive you.
- **Focus on Abundance:** Redirect your attention towards abundance rather than scarcity. Instead of dwelling on what you lack, consciously focus on the abundance that surrounds you, such as the beauty of nature, the support of loved ones, or the opportunities to travel. When you see a beautiful car, say to yourself, someone else has that beautiful car, I can have one too, thanks for showing me, it's possible.
- **Create an Abundance Journal:** Keep a journal dedicated to recording moments of abundance, gratitude, and success in your life. Regularly write down your achievements, blessings, and things you're thankful for.
- **Steal beliefs**: Once my friend who is never sick said, "No bacteria could ever conquer me," I decided to adopt the same mindset and my stomach issues, especially while traveling in India, disappeared. If you hear someone say "money always comes so easy to me" don't be jealous, just start affirming that for yourself.
- **Help people:** When we give to others of compliments, time, praise, money, it is always returned to us and can let our minds know, we have enough to share.
- **Spend a day being aware of your thoughts:** Identify and challenge any limiting beliefs you have about money, such as "money is hard to come by" or "I'll never be wealthy." Replace these beliefs with thoughts, such as "I am capable of creating wealth" or "I attract abundance into my life effortlessly." The prefrontal cortex produces our thoughts. It is 40% of our entire brain. This region, located at the front of the brain is not producing stone cold facts. It's pulling information from life experience and things around us to generate thoughts.

Trying to believe something you don't yet believe is about making a genuine effort to adopt a new belief, and it feels very challenging at first. Dismissing the importance of financial abundance overlooks the practical realities of navigating the world we live in and the opportunities it presents. Set your intention to believe it is right for you to be abundant and keep looking for evidence that it is true - and gradually you will believe you are entitled to all the abundance life has to offer. You do!

How I got hooked on luxury on a budget travelling

"We're on holiday" is what my dad used to say, justifying our accumulation of debt that eventually led to losing our home and possessions when I was 11. We transitioned from the suburban tranquility of Hemel Hempstead to a dilapidated council estate in inner-city London, near my dad's new job as a refuge collector, a euphemism for a dustbin man. I watched my dad go through a nervous breakdown while losing touch with all my school friends.

My dad reveled in striding up to hotel lobby desks without a care, repeatedly booking overpriced holidays on credit cards. The reality hit hard—we couldn't afford any of them. Eventually, my dad had no option but to declare bankruptcy. When my mum discovered the extent of our debt, our family unit disintegrated—a succinct, albeit painful, summary of events that steered me towards my life's passion: budget travel without compromising on enjoyment, safety, or comfort.

At 22, I embarked on full-time travel, writing the inaugural Super Cheap Insider guide for friends visiting Norway, a venture I accomplished on less than $250 over a month.. I understand firsthand the suffocating burden of debt and how the flippant notion of "we're on vacation" fails to absolve financial responsibility; in fact, it contradicts the essence of travel—freedom.

Many skeptics deemed my dream of LUXURY budget travel unattainable. I hope this guide proves otherwise, showcasing insider hacks that render budget travel luxurious.

And if my tale of hardship brought you down, I apologize. My dad has since remarried and happily works as a chef at a prestigious hotel in London—the kind he used to take us to!

A final word...

There's a simple system you can use to think about budget travel. In life, we can choose two of the following: cheap, fast, or quality. So if you want it cheap and fast, you will get lower quality service. Fast-food is the perfect example. The system holds true for purchasing anything while traveling. I always choose cheap and quality, except at times when I am really limited on time. Normally, you can make small tweaks to make this work for you. Ultimately, you must make choices about what's most important to you and heed your heart's desires.

'Your heart is the most powerful muscle in your body. Do what it says.' Jen Sincero

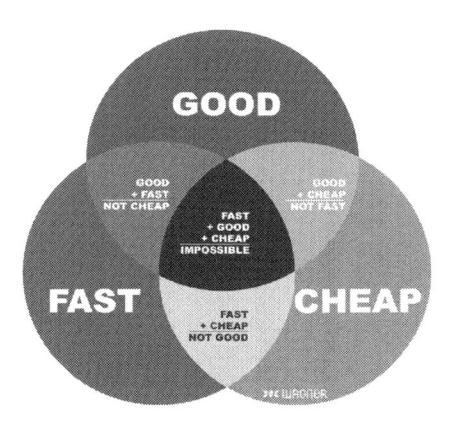

If you've found this book useful, please select five stars, it would mean genuinely make my day to see I've helped you.

If you've found this book useful, please select some stars, it would mean genuinely make my day to see I've helped you.

Copyright

Published in Great Britain in 2024 by Super Cheap Insider Guides LTD.

Copyright © 2024 Super Cheap Insider Guides LTD.

The right of Phil G A Tang to be identified as the Author of the Work has been asserted in accordance with the Copyright, Designs and Patents Act 1988.

All rights reserved.

No part of this publication may be reproduced, stored in a retrieval system, or transmitted, in any form or by any means without the prior written permission of the publisher, nor be otherwise circulated in any form of binding or cover other than that in which it is published and without a similar condition being imposed on the subsequent purchaser.

All rights reserved. No part of this publication may be reproduced, distributed, or transmitted in any form or by any means, including photocopying, recording, or other electronic or mechanical methods, without the prior written permission of the publisher, except in the case of brief quotations embodied in critical reviews and certain other noncommercial uses permitted by copyright law.

Made in the USA
Columbia, SC
30 April 2024